GOOD CAPITALISM, BAD CAPITALISM

PREVIOUS BOOKS AUTHORED OR EDITED BY
RAYMOND PARSONS

The Mbeki Inheritance: South Africa's Economy 1990–2004

Parsons' Perspective: Focus on the Economy

Manuel, Markets and Money: Essays in Appraisal

Zumanomics: Which Way to Shared Prosperity in South Africa?

Zumanomics Revisited: The Road from Mangaung to 2030

GOOD CAPITALISM, BAD CAPITALISM

The Role of Business in South Africa

RAYMOND PARSONS
WITH ALI PARRY

First published by Jacana Media (Pty) Ltd in 2018

10 Orange Street
Sunnyside
Auckland Park 2092
South Africa
+2711 628 3200
www.jacana.co.za

© Raymond Parsons and Ali Parry, 2018

All rights reserved.

This book has been subject to an academic peer-review process.

ISBN 978-1-4314-2618-8

Edited by Russell Martin
Proofread by Lara Jacob
Cover design by Shawn Paikin & Maggie Davey
Set in Stempel Garamond 10/14.5pt
Printed and bound by ABC Press, Cape Town
Job no. 003240

Every effort has been made to trace copyright holders and to obtain permission for the use of copyrighted material. The authors and publisher apologise for any errors or omissions, and would be grateful if notified of any corrections that should be incorporated in future reprints or editions of this book.

See a complete list of Jacana titles at www.jacana.co.za

Dedicated to all past, present and future business people committed to building a prosperous and inclusive South Africa

Contents

Abbreviations and acronyms ix
About the authors xiii
Preface xv

1   Genesis 1
2   Apartheid and capitalism in South Africa: Good or bad business? 16
3   The Economic Advisory Council: Doing good by stealth? 44
4   Business and social dialogue in South Africa 57
5   From organised to disorganised business: What has gone wrong? 86
6   The case for a strong organised business movement in South Africa 110
7   Is a more unified voice for business possible? 140
8   Business in South Africa: The answer or the enemy? 155
9   Lessons and choices for South Africa 175

Annexures 198
Endnotes 204
Bibliography 209
Index 215

Abbreviations and acronyms

AgriSA	Agri South Africa
AHI	Afrikaanse Handelsinstituut
ANC	African National Congress
AsgiSA	Accelerated and Shared Growth Initiative for South Africa
ASSOCOM	Association of Chambers of Commerce of South Africa
BASA	Banking Association South Africa
BBC	Black Business Council
BCEA	Basic Conditions of Employment Act
BEE	Black Economic Empowerment
BIC	Bantu Investment Corporation
BLSA	Business Leadership South Africa
BMF	Black Management Forum
BSA	Business South Africa
BUSA	Business Unity South Africa
CBM	Consultative Business Movement
CCCI	Cape Chamber of Commerce and Industry
CDE	Centre for Development and Enterprise
CODESA	Convention for a Democratic South Africa
COSATU	Congress of South African Trade Unions
CSIR	Council for Scientific and Industrial Research
DA	Democratic Alliance
DSM	Decision Support Model
DTI	Department of Trade and Industry
EAC	Economic Advisory Council

EDP	Economic Development Programme
EFF	Economic Freedom Fighters
FABCOS	Foundation for African Business and Consumer Services
FCI	Federated Chamber of Industries
FEDUSA	Federation of Unions of South Africa
GDP	Gross Domestic Product
GEAR	Growth, Employment and Redistribution strategy
GNU	Government of National Unity
ICC	International Chamber of Commerce
ICT	Information and communication technology
IDI	Inclusive Development Index
ILO	International Labour Organization
IPAP	Industrial Policy Action Plan
IPPs	Independent Power Producers
IRP	Integrated Resource Plan
JCCI	Johannesburg Chamber of Commerce and Industry
LRA	Labour Relations Act
MISTRA	Mapungubwe Institute for Strategic Reflection
MLC	Millennium Labour Council
MTBPS	Medium-Term Budget Policy Statement
MTSP	Medium-Term Strategic Plan
NAAMSA	National Association of Automobile Manufacturers of South Africa
NAFCOC	National African Federated Chamber of Commerce
NBI	National Business Initiative
NDP	National Development Plan
NEDLAC	National Economic Development and Labour Council
NEF	National Economic Forum
NEPAD	New Partnership for Africa's Development
NGP	New Growth Path
NMC	National Manpower Commission

ABBREVIATIONS AND ACRONYMS

NPC	National Planning Commission
NRDC	National Regional Development Council
OECD	Organisation for Economic Cooperation and Development
RAU	Rand Afrikaans University
RDP	Reconstruction and Development Programme
SABS	South African Bureau of Standards
SACCI	South African Chamber of Commerce and Industry
SACCOLA	South African Employers' Consultative Committee on Labour Affairs
SACOB	South African Chamber of Business
SACP	South African Communist Party
SARB	South African Reserve Bank
SAREC	South African Renewable Energy Council
SBI	Small Business Institute
SEIFSA	Steel and Engineering Industries Federation of Southern Africa
SETA	Sector Education and Training Authority
SMME	Small, medium and micro enterprise
SOE	State-owned enterprise
SONA	State of the Nation Address
S&P	Standard & Poor's
TRC	Truth and Reconciliation Commission
UN	United Nations
WEF	World Economic Forum
WTO	World Trade Organization

About the authors

RAYMOND PARSONS is a prominent South African economist who has divided his working life between organised business and academia and over the years has been a leading figure in the complex interactions between organised business and public policy-makers. He is currently a professor at the North-West University Business School. Professor Parsons studied economics at the universities of Cape Town, Oxford and Copenhagen before joining organised commerce and industry as an economist, eventually becoming the first Director-General of the then newly formed South African Chamber of Business (SACOB) in 1990. He was subsequently Deputy CEO of Business Unity South Africa (BUSA), a position he held until 2013. He has served on various official bodies over the years, including the Board of Directors of the South African Reserve Bank (SARB) and the National Economic Development and Labour Council (NEDLAC), and the Council of Nelson Mandela University. He also holds an honorary doctorate from Nelson Mandela University and has lectured at the universities of the Witwatersrand and Pretoria. In 2017 Professor Parsons was bestowed the rare honour of honorary life membership by the Economic Society of South Africa (of which he is a past President) in recognition of his distinguished contribution to economic thinking in South Africa. This is his sixth book.

ALI PARRY has more than thirty years of experience as a researcher, educator and consultant in the fields of economic development and international trade. She is an Extraordinary Research Scientist in the North-West University's TRADE (Trade and Development) research entity and Director of Trade Matters (Pty) Ltd. After completing her postgraduate studies, Ali joined the South African Foreign Trade Organisation (SAFTO) where she was involved in establishing and subsequently managing the SA

Institute of Export as SAFTO's professional export education arm. In the 1990s she went on to co-found the International Trade Institute of Southern Africa (ITRISA) and for many years was head of academic operations and programme development. Ali has written extensively on a wide range of economic and business topics, and regularly participates in local and international projects aimed at building knowledge and capacity in the trade and development spheres. A member of the Professional Editors' Guild, she also coaches academics and researchers in the techniques of writing high-impact articles, reports and opinion pieces.

Preface

THIS BOOK HAS BEEN WRITTEN IN times of great upheavals in South Africa and inevitably bears the marks of the times. I hope that I have not unduly steeped myself in the flood of the present but have succeeded in examining what wider economic and business perspectives can be brought to bear in understanding the South African situation and in proposing some solutions. It also bridges the end of the Zuma era and the beginning of the Ramaphosa one. Every credible analyst has now had to look deeply into his or her crystal ball again, reinterpreting both light and shadow, as events have unfolded in South Africa. It is always tempting to rush to conclusions, but experience suggests that pausing and analysing fundamentals is usually preferable.

'South Africa is the man', said political analyst Gareth van Onselen, 'with no long-term memory, trapped in the permanent nightmare that is his short-term recollection.' And so it often seems to be the case when we come to the big economic debate in South Africa and when we discuss key 'isms' like capitalism, socialism or communism. The existing books on the subject could fill a library and so it may be argued that all that needs to be said about South Africa on these issues has, at least for the time being, already been well said. Yet as Francis Bacon once remarked, 'Some books are to be tasted, others to be swallowed, and some few to be chewed and digested.'

I therefore feel compelled to make a further modest contribution. I hope this additional narrative on South Africa's economic and business history will offer a few new perspectives, reignite useful debate and, with the assistance of some additional history, move us closer to a more useful 'ism', namely, pragmatism. In all of this, the role of business has inevitably again been put under the microscope and the landscape of capitalism in South Africa reassessed. The lessons of the past need to be examined in arriving at present-day solutions.

I therefore thought it helpful in this (my sixth) book to retrace and interpret the mainstream of business opinion over several decades – good, bad and indifferent – and to highlight where under both apartheid and democracy it succeeded or failed in influencing the course of events. This covers both business in general and organised business in particular. An effective, overall 'voice' for business still eludes South Africa. Given changed political and economic circumstances, the book therefore revisits how business in South Africa has come to where and what it is now – and why ultimately the nurturing and expansion of entrepreneurship also remain vitally important.

In this process I have attempted to see the pattern and design of the wood rather than the singularity of each tree. This goal admittedly allows for greater focus but may offer less coverage. Much of the debate about the role of business in South Africa is, however, still with us as the Jacob Zuma years recede and the mandates of President Cyril Ramaphosa take hold. There is still a great deal of 'unfinished business' (in every sense of this term) on South Africa's national agenda and events continue to overtake us.

The writing of this book turned out to be a more complex task, requiring far deeper research, than I originally envisaged. Complicating the process was the rapid unfolding of political events, which necessitated regular tweaking of the conclusions drawn and key messages conveyed. I was only able to cope by drawing heavily on the advice and input of others – academic colleagues, researchers, business people, trade unionists, politicians, civil servants, economists, business journalists and other witnesses to the history I was seeking to assess and reinterpret. The North-West University Business School and other departments in the Faculty of Economic and Management Sciences provided encouragement and support. I gratefully acknowledge my obligation to all those who contributed with suggestions, criticisms and information; there are too many to list them by name.

That said, I was able to access many business people and officials involved (or previously involved) in business associations like BUSA, BLSA, SACCI, BBC, NAFCOC, SEIFSA, the Chamber of Mines, the Johannesburg Chamber of Commerce and Industry, and the Cape Chamber of Commerce and Industry, who willingly made time available to be consulted. Some leading business figures involved in former organisations and structures like ASSOCOM, the FCI, SACOB, the AHI, the CBM and the South Africa Foundation who could still be traced also offered their insights. Where they could not be personally contacted, their articles and statements were perused.

In addition, access to representatives of the NEDLAC constituencies was invaluable in discerning the dynamics of social dialogue in South Africa. Then there were people previously connected with the Economic Advisory Council, or who had done some research on it, who generously shared their impressions of the EAC – a rather forgotten but important structure which existed from 1960 to 1994. The EAC eventually came to enjoy a chapter on its own as a result of these people's inputs.

I would also like to express my deep appreciation to Ali Parry, who so ably assisted in the drafting and editing of various chapters. It would not have been possible to do justice to what was required without her help. Her excellent professional skills gave crucial support to the completion of the task. My thanks also go to Jacob van Rensburg for his role as a reliable research assistant who helped to fill certain gaps in the compilation of the book.

I originally formed a small group to use at the outset as a sounding board for the shaping of the book and I convey my grateful thanks to Brian Angus, Gavin Keeton, Keith Lockwood and Ben van Rensburg for constituting that group. To Madelene Loubser, whose home in Arniston was, from time to time, the location for lengthy spells of strenuous drafting, I express my gratitude for her hospitality and support.

Finally, my thanks to the team at Jacana Media who, under the enthusiastic and expert guidance of Bridget Impey, ensured that the manuscript successfully passed through all the stages of its metamorphosis into the final book you now have in your hands.

The usual caveat applies that I alone remain ultimately responsible for what now finally appears in print.

– RAYMOND PARSONS
APRIL 2018

Formation of the first Chamber of Commerce in Marseille, 1599

1
Genesis

> The fact of progress is written plain and large on the page of history; but progress is not a law of nature. The ground gained by one generation may be lost by the next.
> – HAL FISHER, HISTORIAN

Setting the scene

THE WOUNDS OF APARTHEID AND colonialism in South Africa remain open and raw. The often heated and polarised public debate in South Africa testifies to the post-apartheid trauma in this country and the strong passions it still arouses. In the UK at the end of the First World War, a famous poster with an accusatory pointing finger asked those who were thought to have shirked their duty: 'What did you do in the War?' And so the question here might be: 'What did you do under apartheid?' And more importantly: 'What have you done in its aftermath?' Much has already been written and said about who did what – both under apartheid and in the transition to democracy in 1994 – and especially what a number of critical stakeholders did, or did not do, about apartheid in its heyday.

There have been competing versions of the business history of this period – ranging from the radical to the liberal – and the literature is extensive. The debate has not receded. And inevitably over the years, the role of the business community in South Africa has remained under the microscope and the battle lines have frequently been drawn, as they often were under apartheid. Black Economic Empowerment (BEE) policies and other supporting legislation have been fine-tuned to redress historical imbalances. But these have often drawn the ire of key segments of business as being utopian or impractical, or only favouring a few. Nevertheless, measures to entrench employment equity practices have been stepped up over the years, as have other redress-type policies across a broad front.

Yet the glaring reality remains that, while the black majority has political power, it still does not enjoy sufficient economic power. It is out of this disparity that the growing pressure for 'radical economic transformation' has emerged. There is a widespread need to deal more effectively with the challenges of unemployment, poverty and inequality and to correct historical imbalances, but we must accept that these overarching goals will remain a distant pipe dream unless economic opportunities for all are enhanced. There is at present immense preoccupation with the extent to which South Africa's economic performance and prospects are sub-optimal. In this process the business community is also expected to redefine its role and to focus in particular on the ways in which it can deliver more value-added and inclusive growth.

So what has been the role of business in South Africa in the past and what new perspectives can be provided to help business tackle the country's socio-economic challenges in a more direct manner? It may have become a cliché to claim, as the philosopher Santayana once did, that 'those who cannot remember the past are condemned to repeat it'. But like many clichés, it embodies much truth and acts as both a yardstick for gauging what was potentially attainable in terms of rolling back apartheid at its peak and a partial record of what was actually achieved – or not achieved – given the realities of the situation. It is important to provide a textured analysis of the economic and social environment in which business has had to operate, both before and since South Africa's transition to democracy, but also not to be shy to reveal where business (and organised business) failed to make a difference because it was either unable or unwilling to do so.

If at this stage the attitude of any reader is, for ideological or other reasons, that business played no useful role in the apartheid era – or was totally complicit in it – then they should read no further. Nothing in the subsequent chapters will change that view. But if there is at least a willingness to look anew at the evidence, while not necessarily accepting all the conclusions, then read on.

We need to recognise that for many intellectuals there is an inner contradiction about the economic process. On the one hand, they take pleasure in technological developments that can make people better off and raise standards of living. On the other hand, they feel that the pervasive influence of business destroys values and that market discipline is an unnecessarily harsh one. These two approaches are usually reconciled by attributing to the 'force' of 'progress' everything they like about the process, and to the 'force' of 'capitalism' everything they dislike. And the term 'socialism' suffers from ambiguity in part because some conservatives often stigmatise as 'socialist' any action by the state that they do not happen to like.

To some degree, the difference is also one between those who cry 'let justice be done, if the skies fall' and those who would regard the falling of the skies as a consequence that must be taken into account before one can decide whether a particular action is, or is not, just. We need to weigh the evidence and strike a balance.

Furthermore, a personal perspective will contribute to a fuller understanding of developments in South Africa's recent business history. The inspiration for this book came to a large extent from the many years that I spent in the organised business sector in South Africa, which gave me a close-up view of the evolving dynamics between the business sector and government and how this has played out economically and socially. It was a unique opportunity to see how the machinery of government worked.

But why I pursued this particular career path in the first place may also be an important part of the story. When I mentioned to a friend some months ago that I was embarking on my next book on the South African economy, he asked me why and how I became an economist. My answer was that the reason had its origins in an anecdote my father shared with me long ago.

When I was a young boy of about ten living in the Western Cape, my father (who was a successful local businessman and farmer) took me with him on a visit to the local 'township'. On looking around I asked him: 'Why are the people here so poor?' He replied: 'I don't know. You need to be an economist to explain it.' 'Well, then,' I apparently responded, 'I want to be an economist.' I have no personal recollection of this exchange but I did develop an interest in economic history at school. Later I enthusiastically opted for economics as the major subject in my first degree, a BCom at the University of Cape Town, so my intrinsic interest in the subject obviously remained.

It was therefore perhaps inevitable that, as a young academic in the late 1960s, I found myself increasingly drawn to economic policy issues in South Africa, rather than to pure economic theory. Policy challenges in a country like South Africa, given its complex economic and political history, piqued my interest. Apart from the run-of-the-mill monetary and fiscal policy decisions that all economies need to make, South Africa's apartheid system obviously posed challenging questions. This gradually captured my serious attention, although the apartheid era had not at that stage quite reached its apogee. I felt a strong urge to be drawn into the policy-making process – to see if I could make a contribution.

Whether South Africa could develop a more inclusive economy was my driving thought at the time, though, at that juncture, my immediate ambitions were more limited. I needed to identify what career path would allow me to get closer to the 'engine room' of policy in South Africa and then over time hopefully enlarge my professional sphere of influence. Two obvious priority areas or entry points were fiscal and monetary policy, both conventionally 'big-ticket items' in economic analysis. But there was a problem. At the time, institutions like the Ministry of Finance (as it was then called) and the South African Reserve Bank (SARB) were, of course, Afrikaner strongholds. I, nonetheless, decided to apply for certain modest positions that had been advertised.

I was, however, prudently warned that, although prospects of a junior appointment to the two institutions might exist, being an English-speaking citizen in South Africa in those days was a career-limiting qualification in the public sector. We are, of course, talking about several decades ago. The chances of promotion in that era were therefore not good or at least highly uncertain. Given this reality, I reasoned, where was the next best place to be if I wanted a seat somewhere in the cockpit of policy?

After I had consulted widely, I was advised by several mentors to 'go into organised business'. 'Chambers of commerce and chambers of industries are the structures regularly consulted by the public sector,' said one leading business person at the time, 'and you can help to shape the critical economic input they give to government.' This, I felt, was practical and good advice. Hence I soon found myself appointed to the staff of the Federated Chamber of Industries (FCI) as an economist. And so began my decades-long career in organised business.

Here may I repeat three pieces of advice I was given by an eminent past president of one of the major business associations at the time. He said, firstly, that a person was no good in organised business unless they had had three years' training in frustration – after that they would find the right way to go about things instead of constantly knocking their heads against brick walls; secondly, very few were preoccupied with important matters, for what always received prior attention was what was urgent; thirdly, the first obligation of a key adviser was to keep the president out of trouble! This was hard to believe then, but I subsequently came to appreciate the advice.

Another important lesson I learnt was the difference between a good economic adviser and a bad one. The first keeps asking, 'Would it not be better to do this?', or 'Have you realised that?', while the second buries himself or herself in the preparation of long and pointless memoranda that no one has enough time to read. It was important to anticipate events in the policy process as far as possible.

I retained my academic interest by lecturing part-time at the University of the Witwatersrand in South African economic history. My predecessors as lecturers in this course had been Helen Suzman and George Palmer, then editor of the *Financial Mail*. In the end, competing professional demands on my time inevitably meant that I could only offer the course for a few years before having to pass it on to someone else.

As the years unfolded, I was fortunate enough to be the only person who ended up in a senior executive capacity serving, in total, 'organised industry' (the FCI), 'organised commerce' (the Association of Chambers of Commerce of South Africa, or ASSOCOM) and ultimately (following the 1990 merger between ASSOCOM and the FCI) 'organised business' as a whole (the South African Chamber of Business, or SACOB, now the South African Chamber of Commerce and Industry, or SACCI). More recently I was also involved in Business Unity South Africa (BUSA), holding the position of deputy CEO until 2013.

These career developments also coincided with a series of watershed developments in South Africa's political economy, with organised business as a whole enjoying a key vantage position at major shifting points in South Africa's political and economic history. These various structures – together with other organisations such as the National African Federated Chamber of Commerce (NAFCOC), the Black Business Council (BBC) and the Foundation for African Business and Consumer Services

(FABCOS) – have over a long period been the main national multisectoral bodies representing South African business in interactions with the public sector at various levels.

My commitment to organised business also steadily drew me into key structures such as the Economic Advisory Council (EAC), the National Economic Forum (NEF) and subsequently the National Economic Development and Labour Council (NEDLAC). During my own involvement in wide-ranging policy-making activities, I was privileged to gain unique experience in the dynamics of apartheid, transition and democracy in South Africa. The trajectory of my career has enabled me to develop a distinct perspective on the role of business in South Africa – covering 'the good, the bad and the ugly'.

In the process I have developed a better understanding of the dynamics of organised business in particular, its strengths and weaknesses, its strategies and the important role it has played in South Africa's political economy over many years. So when I wandered into economics and organised business, I had hoped it would prove useful in real life as well as offer satisfaction. Reality has – perhaps alas? – more than fulfilled my youthful hopes.

When I look back, I believe that this involvement in organised business and public policy has been hugely beneficial for my own mental and spiritual development. It is true that I had less contact with the more technical side of economics for several years. Only through recent academic appointments at the University of the Witwatersrand, the University of Pretoria and North-West University have I again come to feel at ease in the predominantly analytical field of economics.

But in every other respect the experience has been one of almost pure gain. It has given me an opportunity to rethink the fundamentals of my subject in terms of a range of policy applications that were crying out for change. It has given me an insider view of the machinery of government and those policy-making techniques used in tackling problems. It has allowed me to make new contacts and friendships in the public sector, in business and in labour. And by often working side by side with officials and professional colleagues whose background and outlook have frequently differed considerably from my own, it has deepened my insights and hopefully helped to find common ground.

The study of how institutions are formed, how they operate and change, their possible decline and their influence on behaviour in society has increasingly become the focus of economic, political and social studies. We need to understand the diverse nature of institutions that develop to promote human cooperation or to hinder it, whether in business or elsewhere.

But what of organised business? The overarching goal of organised business in South Africa has been to provide an amplified voice for business on policy matters, often controversially so. It therefore seems possible, looking through the prism of my business experience over a number of decades, to provide fresh perspectives on several vexing and contentious issues in South Africa's economic and business history. These include the relationship between capitalism and apartheid in the past, how best to articulate a 'voice for business', the proper role of market forces, the current preoccupation with 'white monopoly capital', the part that business could be playing in bringing about 'radical economic transformation', and why organised business structures today seem weak and divided even compared with earlier years.

At present there does not appear to be a strong voice for business in South Africa; instead, there is an ever-rising cacophony of overlapping messages emanating from bodies with competing acronyms. Does this apparent heightened fragmentation in organised business serve the interests of policy-making, or indeed business itself, over the long haul? What has gone wrong? Can the Humpty-Dumpty of organised business be put back together again? Is there still scope for business to display more institutional effectiveness and to help put South Africa on a path towards more sustainable and inclusive well-being? But we run ahead of ourselves.

There are many misconceptions about the brands, products and institutions that denote organised business. When it comes to the term 'chamber of commerce', for example, confusion and erroneous assumptions are even more likely, though almost everyone has heard of the term. One vintage response to the question of what chambers of commerce do is 'they hold meetings'. This lack of understanding is in large part self-inflicted because chambers in various towns, cities and regions, and even nationally, often focus on different things and actually frequently operate in different ways. We will return to the structural question concerning chambers and organised business in more detail in Chapter 7.

Chamber origins

Let us then take a few steps back to create a context for the general history of organised business and where all these issues fit in. In the very beginning there were trade routes, commerce and guilds. But the modern history of 'organised commerce' or 'organised business' can be traced back to 1599, when the term 'chamber of commerce' appeared for the first time in business history, in Marseilles, in France. The Marseilles Town Council was persuaded that it was no longer possible to combine commercial and municipal functions and what was wanted was a new, separate organisation set up by merchants. The council also stipulated that the trade representatives should be 'worthy, well-to-do, dignified and solvent'. And thus it all began.

When we study the history of chambers of commerce, for example, it is interesting to note the extent to which anger was originally a binding motive force in spurring business activism. Anger made business leaders set up chambers and invest the considerable time needed to make them effective. A chamber of commerce created a new institutional model to channel anger and protest over time into more sustained business lobbies to address the authorities at various levels. Modern business lobbies therefore evolved from protest into respected and mostly orthodox components of the policy process in various countries, including South Africa. The historical reasons for protest and criticism of government now often lie shallow below the surface for many businesses, unless provoked by a serious threat to their interests.

This concept of a chamber of commerce as an institution or instrument of civil society gradually spread both nationally and internationally, as business increasingly felt it needed to protect its trade and investment interests. Hence economic and financial developments over several centuries encouraged the evolution of organised commerce or organised business as a role player at local, regional, national and international levels.

Yet collaborating in associations was driven by the desire for a better quality of life in some societies. In his book *Democracy in America* Alexis de Tocqueville said:

> In the United States, they associate for the goals of public security, of commerce and industry, of morality and religion ... Americans

of all ages, all conditions, all minds constantly unite. Not only do they have commercial and industrial associations in which all take part, but they also have a thousand of others ... If it is a question of bringing to light a truth or developing a sentiment with the support of a great example, they associate.[1]

This ability to, in effect, self-organise in Tocqueville's view not only meant that government did not always have to impose order in a hierarchical, top-down manner. It also taught people cooperative habits which they could carry over with them into economic and public life. In modern parlance, it is about the contribution of 'social capital' and cooperative behaviour to societal outcomes.

Today there are about fifteen thousand chambers registered in the official World Chambers Network registry. The global umbrella body for the chamber movement is the International Chamber of Commerce (ICC), founded in 1919 and located in Paris. It has ICC national committees in its member countries throughout the world and seeks to represent business on a variety of issues at the global level. South Africa has played an active role in the ICC over the years. Sam Motsuenyane, former president of NAFCOC, and Judge Mervyn King, of corporate governance fame, have been among its esteemed past chairpersons.

But the ICC would not necessarily include the many other trade associations and sectoral bodies that have also developed to promote and lobby collectively for business interests. Hence a business-led civic and economic advancement entity operating in a specific space may describe itself in different ways – but ultimately operate much like a chamber of commerce. Chamber 'missions' thus vary across the world, but basically the core mandate of these structures is to further the collective interests of their business members and often to advance community interests.

There is a broad diversity of administrative and legal models in the global system of chambers, mainly due to the nature and evolution of national legal and political systems, and also to traditions and cultures. They come in all shapes and sizes and project different levels of efficacy in serving wide or narrow interests, as we shall later see.

And while most chambers may wish to see policies that are 'pro-business', not all would necessarily be 'pro-market' in their approach. It is recognised that a number of their activities might well degenerate into rent-seeking or restrictive practices. We must therefore always be on our guard against collusive action in the economy, from whatever source, even a chamber of commerce. But the more broadly based the membership of such structures, the greater the checks and balances and the lower the risk of this happening.

A narrow approach would also not be in line with the traditional philosophical commitment of chambers of commerce to open markets and to uphold the competitive system. Fortunately, empirical research confirms that in a wide range of developed and developing countries most business associations' activities are in reality market supportive and contribute to economic efficiency. Under certain conditions business associations and chambers can even contribute to economic development without intending to do more than defend their members' interests, just as trade unions can do.

And in South Africa?

In the case of South Africa, the first chamber of commerce was established in the country's first major town – Cape Town – in 1804. Other chambers evolved slowly as the country developed economically from a pastoral base through to mining, industry and, more recently, services. The national body, ASSOCOM, was established in 1892, the FCI in 1917, the Afrikaanse Handelsinstituut (AHI) in 1942, NAFCOC in 1958 and the previous BBC in 1996. The last-mentioned was re-established as a separate entity a few years ago when several black business organisations broke away from BUSA.

The record shows that, although efforts have been made from time to time to 'rationalise' and 'deracialise' organised business in South Africa, such attempts have been only partially successful. These multisectoral representative business bodies were nonetheless reshaped and streamlined to some extent by the creation of SACOB in 1990 (now SACCI) when ASSOCOM and the FCI were merged, and by the establishment of BUSA in 2003. BUSA was intended to create a truly non-racial 'confederal' structure to unite the major business organisations under one roof and to make business more inclusive. But its foundations were fragile through no fault of its own.

MEMORANDUM OF ASSOCIATION

OF THE

Association of Chambers of Commerce of South Africa.

NAME.

The name of the Association is "THE ASSOCIATION OF THE CHAMBERS OF COMMERCE OF SOUTH AFRICA."

1. The objects for which the Association is established are:—

   a. To discuss and consider questions concerning and affecting Trade and Commerce, at Meetings of Delegates from Chambers of Commerce; and to collect and disseminate information from time to time on matters affecting the common and separate interests of such Chambers and the Commercial interests of South Africa.

   b. To communicate the opinions of the Chambers of Commerce, separately or unitedly, to the various Governments in South Africa or to the various departments thereof, by letter, memorial, deputation, or otherwise.

   c. To petition the respective Parliaments and Volksraads on any matter affecting Trade and Commerce.

   d. To prepare and promote in the respective Parliaments and Volksraads Bills in the interest of Trade and Commerce, and to oppose measures which, in the opinion of the Association, are likely to be injurious to those interests.

   e. To attain those advantages by united action which each Chamber would have more difficulty in accomplishing in its separate capacity.

2. The income and property of the Association whensoever derived shall be applied solely towards the promotion of the objects of the Association, as set forth in the Memorandum of Association.

3. Every Chamber of Commerce subscribing to the Association undertakes to contribute to the Assets of the Association in the event of the same being dissolved during the time it is a Member, or within one year afterwards, for payment of the Debts and Liabilities of the Association, contracted before the time at which it ceased to be a Member, such amount as may be required not exceeding (£5) Five Pounds.

Memorandum of Association (*Presidents of the Association of Chambers of Commerce of South Africa, 1892–1980*, p. 5)

ASSOCOM meeting 1898 (*Presidents of the Association of Chambers of Commerce of South Africa, 1892–1980*, cover)

The organised business landscape in South Africa has historically always been populated by a plethora of structures divided by race, language or other superficially different interests, and has therefore been less governable. ASSOCOM and FCI were representative of mainly English-speaking business people, while the AHI represented the Afrikaans-speaking business community.

Business is of course not monolithic. But a more unified and coordinated voice of business in South Africa would certainly have enhanced its impact on the course of events. It is not the intention here to unpack the labyrinth of other efforts that have come and gone over the years to promote greater solidarity across the South African business landscape. Later we will examine what might have been some of the causes of this problem and suggest possible solutions.

It must again be emphasised that to expect a single voice for business anywhere in the world is unrealistic in view of the inherent business competition built into the market system. We must remain realistic about what can be achieved. But a more unified voice is possible if the right boundary conditions are set and observed in mobilising business opinion effectively. Indeed, if this were not possible, chambers of commerce and associations would not exist at all. The history of organised business both in South Africa and elsewhere shows that, if properly structured and led, chambers of commerce and associations can effectively advocate and lobby on a range of socio-economic issues. It is this track record and potential that we should examine further in South Africa.

To understand the various beliefs and business institutions in whose milieu these forces have prevailed, we need to re-examine some of the fundamental economic forces that have shaped South Africa's development. We therefore need to unpack certain decisions that have faced the business community in the socio-economic environment in which it has found itself. Given an economic history of conquest, discrimination and development in South Africa, the ominous shadow of apartheid permeated all business decision-making. This means that for many years South African business probably faced bigger challenges than its counterparts in many other parts of the world.

That said, what was done to ameliorate the situation? What did the organised business community seek to do? How was the policy environment changed, if at all? What was the institutional strength and capacity of business associations in South Africa, given the socio-economic challenges facing the country? To answer these questions, we need to revisit what actually happened in some instances. The purpose is to provide a broad but at the same time selective overview of the role that business in general, and organised business in particular, have played in South Africa's recent economic and political history. South Africa's particular historical trajectory does not easily fit into an archetypal Procrustean bed of 'capitalism'.

Many of these scenarios have been more than adequately covered in multifarious books and articles, both academic and journalistic, and even in recent public debates about 'white monopoly capital' in South Africa. To the extent that it can be avoided, we do not wish to traverse this intellectual, political and institutional ground again. However, in reviewing some of the academic research over the years on organised business and business in general in South Africa, we must confess to a certain disappointment at the gaps that still remain and the consequent lopsidedness of the analysis.

Much of the academic and other writing has offered no particular insight into how organised business actually operates. Instead, it has often displayed strong preconceived notions and revealed little or no attempt to interview leading players at the heart of policy-making in organised business itself. Too many academic treatises on the role of business in South Africa have come across as theoretical ruminations from a distance on subjects in which the authors had not fully steeped themselves empirically.

At this point in the narrative there is a choice. One option is to traverse all the old ground again, providing a new broad survey of the role of business under apartheid. As previously indicated, this has been well covered over the years by other scholars and analysts from both left- and right-wing schools of thought. The other (and better) option is simply to provide a case study of what certain elements of organised business in particular said and did during the heyday of apartheid, which allows for more detailed and rounded treatment. There is also much business documentation that has not yet been placed in the historical record, as subsequent pages will reveal. Readers can then form their own judgement.

This focus, of course, is not intended to detract from the sterling efforts of other business associations and groupings like NAFCOC, FABCOS, the Consultative Business Movement (CBM), the Urban Foundation, Business Against Crime, and leading business people pushing to varying degrees for change and reform. It was indeed a collective effort that was often mutually reinforcing, but admittedly sometimes also contradictory.

But did these economic and business pressures ultimately make a difference? Did they help move South Africa towards the eventual ending of apartheid and the shaping of a new democracy? This is the hardest test for any institution to pass, given the dynamics of change in South Africa. It is impossible to demonstrate that economic and political conditions would necessarily have been very different if business had remained supine, or indeed ponder what other 'ifs' of history might now be worth exploring if business had acted differently. We can only look at the record of some of those business efforts and form a view.

The business leaders and chambers that pushed for change over the years indeed believed that economic and other factors could, and should, be more strongly mobilised to oppose the apartheid system. They were not always popular with their rank-and-file members, but they were able to supply strong leadership as a basis for engagement with the government. They were willing to persist in their efforts, despite frequent rebuffs from the apartheid leadership. This should not be airbrushed from South Africa's business history.

And this was the message that SACOB sought to convey to the Truth and Reconciliation Commission (TRC) when it gave evidence on these matters to that body in November 1997. The exchange at that TRC hearing between business and the commission provides an important framework and perspective for many of the complex processes and issues raised subsequently in this book. It enables us to use the TRC as a fulcrum to put both the pre-TRC and the post-TRC developments into structured perspective and to review the TRC outcomes twenty years later. It thus provides the major peg for the extended analysis in Chapter 2.

2
Apartheid and capitalism in South Africa: Good or bad business?

The journey between 1960 and 1994 was a long and terrible one, wasteful of human life and of human potential. Yet it was a path that everyone travelled.
– Truth and Reconciliation Commission (1998)

Historia magistra vitae [history is life's teacher] – but she had bad pupils.
– Anon

Historical development which would normally take centuries was compressed into two or three decades.
– Rosa Luxemburg,
The Accumulation of Capital (1913)

As this chapter will testify, the 'journey' between 1960 and 1994 was also a long one for business in South Africa. 'History', CV Wedgwood says, 'is lived forward but is written in retrospect. We know the end before the beginning and we can never wholly recapture what it was to know the beginning only.'[1] This remains true as we revisit the parameters of 'apartheid and capitalism' in the South African context. The economic and business history of South Africa confirms that there is no finality in human affairs, whether in this country or elsewhere. There is no static perfection or non-improvable wisdom to be achieved which cannot be bettered as time moves on.

We need not spend too much time defining 'capitalism', but should rather find a workable definition that will serve our purpose from here on. Capitalism is a system of governance for economic affairs that has emerged in different settings and continues to evolve over time. As a result, it defies simple definitions. But the *Macmillan Dictionary of Modern Economics* usefully outlines capitalism as follows:

> Political, social and economic system in which property, meaning capital assets, is controlled for the most part by private persons. Capitalism contrasts with an earlier system, feudalism, in that it is characterised by the purchase of labour for money wages as opposed to the direct labour obtained through customs, duty or demand in feudalism; under capitalism, the price mechanism is used as a signalling system which allocates resources between users. The extent to which the price mechanism is used, the degree of competition, and the level of government intervention distinguish exact forces of 'capitalism'.[2]

The conception of economic freedom flowing from this definition is not a closed one laid up in heaven, deducible from a few simple concepts and capable of being transcribed onto a couple of tablets of stone. Rather it is an evolving system, part natural growth, part artificial, continually adapting itself or being adapted to new conditions and new knowledge. Its only main criterion is that it leans towards freedom, rather than away from it, supported by appropriate rules and policies. Practically, this is its great strength.

Conceptually it remains a condition of action, not a criterion thereof. Clearly, some free acts are good and some are bad. At its heart lie the role of entrepreneurship and the freedom to expand personal initiative to underpin economic dynamism or what one famous economist called 'animal spirits'. This should mean that it is from the spontaneous actions and choices of ordinary people that 'progress' springs, or what the National Development Plan (NDP) would call 'an active citizenry', rather than from a predetermined end under the pressure of an impersonal force known as 'capitalism'.

As it happens, the publication of this book coincides with the bicentenary of the birthday of Karl Marx, the great critic of capitalism. It is therefore fortuitous that we should be assessing where capitalism is now going in South Africa. We can recall that in his classic book *Capitalism, Socialism and Democracy*, Joseph Schumpeter warned that capitalism and democracy were an unstable mixture. According to him, successful business people would conspire to bar the entry of new rivals, government bureaucrats would simply smother enterprise with taxes and regulations, and hostile intellectuals would attack capitalism's natural flaws, while singing the praises of alternative systems that would entail a huge loss of individual freedom. His fear was that 'bourgeois society' was spawning its own gravediggers, as Marx had predicted. In his view, the entrepreneur, the creative force in capitalism's success, was under attack.

And since the Great Recession of 2008 and the general preoccupation with significant inequality in various parts of the world, including South Africa, questions about the sustainability of the capitalist system continue to arise. Such books as *Saving Capitalism from the Capitalists* and, more recently, *Capital in the Twenty-First Century* highlight the challenges to the economic system and make suggestions for reform. Even if the present anti-business sentiment in South Africa is a passing wave, are the foundations of the pro-private enterprise system here secure?

Hence key studies such as *Why Nations Fail* have highlighted why more inclusive economic institutions create inclusive markets, which not only encourage people to make the best use of their abilities and skills, but also provide a level playing field which enables them to do so. And to do so, economic institutions must secure private property, uphold the rule of law, and provide public services that facilitate and support economic transactions. This is what apartheid failed to do. It also helps to explain why too many South Africans have come to view today's capitalism not as their friend, but as their foe.

In South Africa's case, with its mixed economy, the capitalist economy under apartheid was complicated, skewed by the government's role and interactions along racial lines. The apartheid economy, which rested peculiarly on capitalist foundations, was nonetheless an exclusive one, not an inclusive one. A skewed political system meant lopsided economic development, the legacy of which South Africa is still trying to overcome.

Whatever wisdom we may have acquired is therefore a small matter compared with what is possible and desirable. We need to be dynamic, adaptable and pragmatic if we want to learn from our past mistakes and build a better future. It is commonplace that good historians do not judge statements from the past by their own standards. We need to create the right perspective.

So whatever interpretations of history or the economy we may have, even those we deem most important are unlikely to last forever. The essence of good historiography is doubt or, as philosopher Karl Popper once put it, 'conjecture and refutation'. Modification and revision are always possible in the light of new or additional evidence. Business's views about South Africa have also changed over time, as it has acquired new insights. And even if we imagine that our interpretations of history are eternal truths, the future is likely to make a mockery of them, as the current situation in South Africa shows.

Cocksure certainty in some circles is the source of much of what is wrong in South Africa today and is something of which the contemplation of history ought to cure us. Of course, we should hold our beliefs and act on them if necessary. But underneath it all there should always be that wider historical perspective that sets limits to our actions and helps to sensibly shape the road ahead. It also helps to inject elements of pragmatism into reform programmes and decision-making, whether in the public or private sectors.

In seeking solutions and shaping policies it is therefore not helpful to be trapped in extreme 'isms'. Both Marxism and free market fundamentalism, while useful conceptual frameworks, basically represent a reluctance to acknowledge that these theoretical models are simply analytical tools used to better understand economic phenomena. They merely suggest possible means of achieving certain ends, without being the ultimate word or an insuperable obstacle to compromise and good decision-making.

Both extremes embody a refusal to accept the discipline of empirical and evidence-led observation, trial and error, and piecemeal rather than utopian change, as evincing the real complexities and trade-offs facing decision makers. The big, long-running debate about business's role in society, be it in South Africa or elsewhere, is still caught between two contrasting, and rather tired, ideological positions. We can still detect rumbles of ideological thunder. We need to update it. 'I don't hate capitalism,' says income inequality guru Thomas Piketty, 'I just want to fix it.' And history matters and remains broadly relevant when we put a repressive system like apartheid on trial. So those who enjoy controversy need not fear the horrors of perpetual peace.

Although in retrospect it looks improbable, with the opposition to apartheid steadily growing internally and externally, the demise of the apartheid system was not originally a foregone conclusion. The adage that we must never forget that there was a time when events now in the past were still in the future has considerable relevance here. There were a number of contingencies, such as the breakdown of leadership and changes at the top of the apartheid government, which, had they gone the other way, might have delayed the dismantling of apartheid by some time. It is but one of the 'ifs' of history to enquire what might have happened if PW Botha had not suffered a stroke early in 1989 and had continued as President, as seemed likely, into the 1990s. What course would that decade then have taken in South Africa?

It required a combination of pressures to contain these hazards and ensure an eventual successful outcome. The process of change in South Africa therefore did not operate so inevitably or in such a clear direction as it might seem in posterity. The eventual overturning of the apartheid system was the outcome of thousands of choices, several of which, if taken differently, could have delayed the demise of apartheid. It is only in hindsight that the outcome seems inevitable. Change does not move in a straight line, whether in South Africa or elsewhere. At each stage of the journey towards a democratic South Africa, there were turns and forks – which had to be taken for better or worse.

Revisiting business and the TRC: 'A story within a story?'

That said, the work of the Truth and Reconciliation Commission (TRC), other institutions and investigations, academic analyses and personal memoirs over many years have painted a wide-ranging picture of the apartheid era. It remains well-populated territory and cannot all be repeated here, as the literature on apartheid is vast and impressive. The TRC was specially instituted in 1996 'to establish the facts about the causes, nature and extent of gross violations of human rights under apartheid', and it represents a watershed assessment for all interested stakeholders, including business.

The TRC rightly chose 1960 as its commencing benchmark for the interrogation of the apartheid system. It wanted to keep the magnitude of its task manageable. 1960 was a momentous year in which both South Africa and the world changed dramatically. Internationally, social change, especially the decolonisation of Africa, was gathering speed. But South Africa, under the leadership of Prime Minister Hendrik Verwoerd, instead moved towards the intensification of apartheid and increasing international isolation because of its racial policies.

Yet what was the role of business in all this? What was its collective response to apartheid? Apartheid was a path that business had also travelled and, as with all journeys, it revealed many signposts. A good departure point, therefore, more than two decades after the TRC hearings, is to revisit and update the evidence given to the commission by business. And in revisiting the question of the role of business under apartheid, there may indeed be 'a story within a story' to be discerned, a credible narrative within the broader picture of the evils of the apartheid system, as revealed by the TRC and others.

Although there were doubts expressed about the methodology and subsequent findings of the TRC, business was among those that accepted that the commission served an invaluable and necessary purpose in exposing as much of the truth about apartheid as was possible in the circumstances. It was necessary for business to be included by the TRC and to be interrogated about its role. The noted journalist Max du Preez said that 'despite the many dark suits and striped shirts, one could at times be forgiven for thinking that this was a meeting of anti-apartheid movements … especially when powerful companies like Anglo and Barlow Rand claimed to have always opposed apartheid'.[3]

But the problem here, as Nicoli Nattrass said, is that the TRC and many commentators concentrated above all on the systemic relationship between the business sector and the apartheid regime. All business – large, medium and small – was covered by a blanket of 'collective guilt'.

> The TRC found that some sectors of business were more involved with the apartheid regime than others, but that most businesses were culpable by virtue of having benefitted from operating in a racially structured environment. Whereas apartheid agents were granted amnesty in return for free disclosure and encouraged to

seek reconciliation with their victims, the TRC proposed that wealth taxes be considered as appropriate restitution with regard to business. The TRC thus shifted from a focus on individual perpetrators to a systemic analysis that equated any profitable activity with prospering under apartheid and drew a line between benefitting from the system and moral culpability for it. This systemic approach directed attention away from those whose involvement with the apartheid regime was of graver moral concern than that of others, and took the heat off wealthy individuals who, by virtue of personal contracts and financial muscle, might have been able to effect change faster had they acted more decisively.[4]

Hence, certain 'bad capitalism' examples have been well documented by Hennie van Vuuren in his recent authoritative book, *Apartheid, Guns and Money*. His work highlights the profitable and corrupt networks that developed under apartheid and sanctions – the convergence of intelligence sectors, governments, certain corporations, arms producers and political parties. It is a compelling narrative. Several of Van Vuuren's conclusions may be too sweeping, given his apparent deep dislike of capitalism in general. But his claim that 'corruption, a secret economy and a network of international allies [under apartheid] have for too long been shielded and obscured' is a valid exposé of where business went bad. It contains some key lessons about the circumstances in which corruption spread, and provides a catalogue of business sins that have been trenchantly revealed. Unfortunately, efforts by both SACOB and the AHI (as early as 1992) to roll back proposals to increase defence spending, as it would increase corruption, were unsuccessful.

Then there is the well-documented evidence of the socio-economic evils arising from the migrant labour system and the prolonged maintenance of other racial barriers which inhibited full participation of all citizens in the economy. Although apartheid was removed in 1994, South Africa still has one of the most unequal income distributions in the world, and this remains a serious challenge. None of this must be swept under the carpet.

But the nagging question remains about how capitalism in South Africa collectively performed under apartheid. Has all the evidence been properly weighed? Was business always as bad as it seemed? The purpose here is to explain, not to exonerate. In retrospect, the question whether business was nonetheless able to 'do good' under a bad system (and in a mixed economy) needs to be placed in a different perspective.

Even an astute and respected journalist like the late Allister Sparks could still write of that period:

> I found myself at increasing odds with the business community's lack of interest in the politics of apartheid. Big business was largely in the hands of the English-speaking community, while Afrikaners dominated the political arena. Most business leaders, with some notable exceptions, seemed content to leave it that way; they would utter ritual criticisms of apartheid but declined to get involved in politics or even speak out collectively against it.[5]

Either Sparks seldom read the business pages of the publications with which he was associated or his conflicts with a conservative media management gave him a rather lopsided view of other business opinion. As this chapter seeks to demonstrate, there was certainly no 'lack of interest' on the part of organised business in the 'politics of apartheid'. But Sparks was certainly not alone in his view. Many other analysts have also either ignored or distorted what business did, or did not do, under apartheid. These perspectives need to be revisited.

What business said to the TRC

The TRC had in any case arranged special business hearings in 1997 at which business organisations and individual business people were invited to testify. Business organisations included SACOB, NAFCOC, the AHI and FABCOS. All business witnesses were critically interrogated about their role and expectations under apartheid. NAFCOC in particular rightly emphasised the extent to which the apartheid state systematically undermined black business.

It would be reasonable to say that, although the business representations were given a fair hearing, the darkest suspicions were understandably entertained in the TRC's questioning about the participation of (mainly white) business in the apartheid system. As indicated, the TRC's conclusions about white business and apartheid were extremely negative.

Even though there might have been agreements about the facts, there were inevitably differences about their interpretation, both by the TRC and others. In fact, the submissions by business itself revealed a wide range of perceptions. Organised business nevertheless believed it had assembled evidence that many business people had a better track record in opposing apartheid than might originally have been presumed. It sought to convince the TRC of this reality, against the bigger canvass of an unacceptable and repressive system. Capitalism could no more be judged by its aberrations than democracy dismissed because of its defects.

Without going into detail, in its findings on the business sector the TRC in a nutshell argued that business was central to the economy that sustained the South African state during the apartheid years. It also said that certain businesses, especially in the mining industry, were involved in designing and implementing apartheid policies. The TRC saw that most white businesses benefited from operating in a racially defined context. In general, the TRC was critical of white business in its actions during the apartheid years. It said the overall impact of apartheid had also 'perniciously' damaged emerging black business. The TRC believed that, overall, white business had gained from apartheid, in contrast to the view expressed by business that it had regularly opposed apartheid and that the system had had an increasingly adverse impact on the economy.

But was this the whole story? Is there a single business story? Or, as suggested earlier, is there 'a good story within a bigger, bad story'? To explore this, let us examine what SACOB said to the TRC. The stance taken by SACOB is singled out here, partly because at the time it was the premier business organisation, partly because it was broadly representative of a cross section of business interests, and partly because it claimed a longer and wider track record in opposing apartheid.

At this stage it should furthermore be noted that business, in its response to apartheid legislation, emphasised in its TRC submission that it used terms common at the time that are not currently acceptable, and so were not intended to offend – as indeed they are not intended to in this book. The various business milestones nonetheless need to be recorded. Inevitably there is also a degree of repetition in the narrative, which emphasises how difficult it was for business to grapple with a highly formidable system of racial engineering.

Let us begin, then, with business and the TRC. In its submissions to

The SACOB delegation at the Truth and Reconciliation Commission in Johannesburg, November 1997

the TRC in November 1997 SACOB, led by its president, Humphrey Khoza, gave its 'message' with the following introductory clarifications:[6]

- The submission by SACOB also embodied the previous business history of ASSOCOM and the FCI. SACOB was the outcome of a merger between those two organisations, which came into effect on 1 January 1990. The principal reasons for the merger were to develop a more unified, more effective and financially stronger voice for business, given the new socio-economic challenges emerging as the country moved towards democracy. (SACOB at the time 'represented' about 35,000 enterprises in South Africa.)
- With the benefit of hindsight, SACOB accepted that the enormity of apartheid required stronger responses from business, for the lack of which it apologised. It acknowledged that apartheid had done great damage to the human dignity of the majority of fellow South Africans. It recognised that business had had a mixed record under apartheid and many white business people had indeed benefited under the system. It was therefore a matter of deep regret to SACOB if businesses operating under the umbrella of SACOB, or its predecessors, had acted in violation of the stated official policy positions of these organisations. But the organisations had nonetheless sought to provide business leadership for change in extraordinarily challenging times.
- There could be no 'collective responsibility' on behalf of business as a whole. SACOB could only speak for the policy decisions taken by itself or its predecessors (ASSOCOM and the FCI) and not for any

other organisations. 'Good' and 'bad' capitalists could not be subsumed under a generic 'collective guilt'. The chamber movement in South Africa had also developed on the Anglo-Saxon model, which provided for voluntary, rather than statutory, membership of enterprises. This had important implications for factors such as the resources available to the institution, its level of autonomy from government, the balance between big and small firms, the degree to which it represented all businesses, and the ability of constituents to compel their members to act in a particular way. Persuasion and leadership were the only instruments available to influence business.

Against this background, if we then review the catalogue of actions taken by ASSOCOM, the FCI and SACOB over the years, we see that they can be conveniently divided into four main categories:
- *Oppositional actions* – saying 'no' to what the apartheid government was doing, or intending to do, to enforce racial discrimination.
- *Exploratory steps* – signalling a preparedness to cooperate and extend government reform initiatives as they later unfolded.
- *Defensive strategies* – dealing with political violence and economic sanctions.
- *Proactive initiatives* – promoting social dialogue, economic restructuring and constitutional options for South Africa.

At the end of the day a deep, if unspoken, driving force behind thoughtful business leaders was that if capitalist friends did not change the system, its opponents would do it for them.

The organised business 'track record' in retrospect

Within this context it is now worth re-examining the impact of the most important elements of apartheid legislation on the business sector, and the response of ASSOCOM and the FCI to the introduction and enforcement of such legislation. Even though many pieces of legislation were introduced prior to 1960, which constituted the start of the period of the TRC's investigations, there was – in the motions passed at ASSOCOM congresses – evidence of concern at their impact and opposition to their introduction from as early as 1949.

It should be noted that reference to motions passed is intended to be illustrative of the thinking within the two organisations, rather than provide a comprehensive analysis. Many of the themes contained in these motions originated at the level of local chambers of commerce and industry and were repeated at national, regional and local level by the leadership of the respective organisations in speeches, press releases and discussions.

But, more importantly, what action was taken? The tools available to organised business then, as now, were mainly those of advocacy and lobbying. The motions and resolutions were regularly taken up with the Prime Minister or President of the day and relevant Cabinet ministers, and there were frequent clashes with authorities at the highest level. The business congresses were open to the media and usually received good coverage.

To begin, the Group Areas Act was promulgated in 1950 and, in conjunction with the Population Registration Act, sought to control the acquisition of immovable property and the occupation of land and premises by legally defined 'groups' – 'whites, natives and coloureds'.

The effect of the Group Areas Act on business was to move workers further away from their places of work, thereby increasing their travel time and impacting negatively on their productivity while they were at work; severely limit the ability of 'white' capital to move into 'black' areas, thereby undermining the development of significant areas of the country; prevent the development of a black middle class, with resultant implications for the motivation to train and be trained; and inhibit the emergence of black business.

In response to this, the chamber movement passed a series of congress resolutions which sought, firstly, to emphasise the importance of the 'native' population to the economy of the Union of South Africa, and then to urge the authorities to make land available for 'native housing' in urban areas and to press ahead with the provision of such housing on an economic basis in accordance with proposals put forward by chambers of commerce and associated bodies.

In 1952, a resolution was passed deploring the failure of local authorities to tackle the black housing problem, and calling on the government to ensure that there was 'no hindrance whatever' to the provision of this vitally important requirement. Then in 1958, a resolution was adopted calling for compensation to be paid to traders suffering loss of business or damage as a result of the application of the Act.

In its 1960 Statement of Policy, ASSOCOM urged that South Africa be developed as a single economic entity, and called for the progressive relaxation and ultimate withdrawal of restrictions preventing members of any race from conducting business in any part of the country. The response of Prime Minister Verwoerd was to accuse the chamber of aligning itself with the opposition parties and of inappropriately involving itself in the political process. Verwoerd denounced ASSOCOM as 'traitors paving the way to black domination'. In retaliation, he withdrew from addressing a forthcoming ASSOCOM national congress. Verwoerd also instructed his Cabinet to minimise contact with ASSOCOM.[7]

In practice, this did not mean that all interaction between ASSOCOM and the government ceased. But the recollection of those who were involved at the time was that for a period the relationship was polite but distant. There is a big difference between formal consultation and effective consultation. The impression gained by ASSOCOM representatives in dealing with the government immediately after the Verwoerd letter was one of cordial formality, with little to show by way of outcomes in response to representations.

In spite of this coolness, there were a number of resolutions passed by ASSOCOM in the late 1960s and early 1970s that sought to undermine the Group Areas Act by calling for, among other things, a review of the policy relating to the provision of health clinics and a relaxation of restrictions on the provision of banking facilities in black areas.

A similar theme was repeated in a key 1976 ASSOCOM motion which was submitted jointly with the FCI and which called for:
- the government to move with greater urgency towards the elimination of racial discrimination, especially in the economic sphere;
- recognition of the presence of, and need for, all racial groups in urban areas and the need for all racial groups to be permitted to own property in urban areas;
- the removal of restrictions on black business people;
- the setting aside of mixed trading areas in which all races could trade freely;
- the relaxation of restrictions on employment of other races in white-owned businesses; and
- the establishment of mixed restaurants in central business districts.

As a result of this motion, both organisations were again attacked, this time by Prime Minister John Vorster in his opening speech at the ASSOCOM annual congress in 1978, for meddling in the political affairs of the country. 'Efforts to use business organisations to bring about basic change in government policy will fail and cause unnecessary friction between the government and the private sector. You cannot ask me to implement policies rejected by the electorate and in which I do not believe.'[8]

This did not prevent a business delegation at the congress from pointing out to Vorster there and then that the much-trumpeted official deadline of 1978 for 'turning back the tide of black urbanisation' had come and gone with no prospect of success, given the realities of the situation. Reference was also made to an interview that Steve Biko had given in 1972. Discussing the apartheid government, Biko had said that if they were intelligent, they could 'create a capitalist class society'; that South Africa was one country in Africa where blacks might compete favourably with whites in industry, commerce and other professions.

In 1980, following the Carlton Hotel meeting between Prime Minister PW Botha and business leaders, the ASSOCOM congress passed a resolution stating that the success of the government's economic policy would depend on the degree to which the rights of economic opportunity and property were given 'to all population groups' so that shared prosperity could emerge.

During the mid- to late 1980s, calls for the scrapping of discriminatory legislation, and particularly the Group Areas Act, became more strident, with a number of motions to this effect being adopted. The 1988 motion on economic growth and reform drew attention to the direct link between economic growth and political progress, and called explicitly for the dismantling of the Group Areas Act and all remaining discriminatory legislation.

It may be recalled that the Bantu Education Act of 1953 had brought all schools under government control and required that an inferior curriculum be used in black schools. It also established new 'black' universities and subjected black enrolment at 'white' universities to government control. The net effect of the Bantu Education Act was to exacerbate the skills shortage in South Africa and to raise the wage levels of skilled and semi-skilled white workers at a faster rate than that of productivity growth.

It also served to prevent the development of a significant black middle class and thereby also impacted negatively on the growth potential of the domestic economy.

The poor standard of teaching provided under the system of Bantu Education made it significantly more difficult and costly for trade and industry to train workers and integrate them into the economy. Together with job reservation it created a hothouse effect in respect of skilled labour – the impact of which is still evident today in the competitiveness (or otherwise) of South Africa's manufacturing sector, the (still) relatively high tariff levels, and the significant skills deficit in the country.

Even prior to the promulgation of the Bantu Education Act, ASSOCOM and the FCI had urged that every possible step be taken to enable blacks to acquire skills, and had requested that an investigation be launched into the question of enhancing their employability and productivity and increasing their vocational training and guidance. In the early 1970s additional motions were passed calling for improvements in education facilities and the establishment of training institutions outside the homeland areas, while in 1980 there were calls for a significant increase in education spending on black, coloured and Asian education.

In 1981, an ASSOCOM–FCI resolution was adopted calling for the urgent provision of equal education opportunities for all. This theme was repeated again in the 1988 resolution on education, which called for a single ministry of education; equal, affordable and compulsory education for all; and the more rapid implementation of equal treatment in teacher training and the award of qualifications.

The Reservation of Separate Amenities Act, which was also promulgated in 1953, served to enforce separate but unequal public amenities for different racial groups. These requirements were echoed in other pieces of legislation, such as the Shops and Offices Act and the Factories Act. Apart from imposing added capital costs on businesses, which were forced to build duplicate facilities, the Separate Amenities Act also had a negative effect on motivational levels, and soured relations between the different elements of the workforce. In 1978, a motion was passed at the ASSOCOM congress calling for the repeal of those sections of the Shops and Offices Act and the Factories Act that required the provision of separate facilities for employees of different racial groups, in order to permit employers to move towards the provision of integrated facilities.

In an attempt to stop the growing reliance of industry on black labour, the Industrial Conciliation Act of 1956 enabled the Minister of Labour to reserve jobs for specific racial groups in any industry, trade or occupation. A subsequent amendment also empowered the minister to make determinations against the wishes of the industrial councils established for specific industries. In 1970, the Bantu Laws Amendment Act extended job reservation provisions still further. Apart from being a violation of economic rights, the impact of these pieces of legislation on business was particularly costly.

The innocuous title of the Physical Planning and Utilisation of Resources Act, passed in 1967, hid a far more sinister motive. Sections 2 and 3 of the Act were used to coerce industries in white areas to observe job reservation requirements. The Act gave government wide powers to control the establishment and expansion of factories in the major centres (where expansion was defined as any increase in the number of black employees), while at the same time attempting to encourage investment in decentralised areas close to the homelands.

Together with the additional administrative burden that compliance with this Act placed on industry, the Act was not applied uniformly. Although there was widespread failure within commerce and industry to comply with job reservation requirements, the Act was used in an ad hoc way as a weapon against individual businesses – sometimes on the basis of the political views of their owners and managers. Uncertainty over whether they would be allowed to continue or expand their operations also contributed to a significant fall-off in private manufacturing investment over time.

The opposition to the Physical Planning Act by both the FCI and ASSOCOM was sustained, despite threats from various government ministers, on the grounds that 'forced' decentralisation, among other factors, ran contrary to sound economic principles. Successes in eliminating job reservation requirements also resulted in the benefits of decentralised industry being eroded.

It should now be clear that apartheid was not conducive to the growth of either skill-intensive sectors – such as manufacturing – or sectors needing a large domestic market – such as commerce – nor did racial restrictions promote the development of black business. Black entrepreneurship and opportunities were severely hampered by apartheid legislation, which organised business regularly opposed and sought to repeal or modify. Over the years organised business took the consistent line that not only should economic development be inclusive, but that an enterprise-driven economy could only survive if all citizens were given a stake in it to uphold and defend especially business rights.

How did all this affect South Africa's overall economic performance? Although the country did experience relatively high rates of economic growth during the 1960s, this was in many respects a function of the strong growth in primary exports arising from the expansion of developed economies elsewhere. This correlation started to break down in the early 1970s as a result of South Africa's growing isolation and the shift towards higher value-added growth patterns in industrialised and industrialising countries. It could also be argued that there was a time lag between the introduction of certain racially restrictive economic measures and the impact of their real effects on the economy.

In addition to these factors, Merle Lipton identified the following reasons for South Africa's relatively good economic performance during the 1960s: the natural resource endowment, for which international demand intensified during the pre-1973 oil crisis period; the availability of capital, technology and skilled labour, from both foreign and domestic sources; relatively high standards of entrepreneurship and management; and political stability.[9]

While we will never know for certain, there is a strong view that South Africa's growth performance could have been even better in the 1960s, and significantly better in subsequent decades, if apartheid had been dismantled sooner and a stable democratic political order established. This must remain another one of the 'ifs' of economic and political history in the country.

It should also be noted that over the period covered by the TRC's mandate, both ASSOCOM and the FCI increasingly took issue with those aspects of economic policy that imposed significant economic and social costs on the economy through their 'inward-looking' nature – thus also making the South African economy progressively less competitive. As the South African economy became more sophisticated because of industrialisation and enhanced infrastructure, so too did the human and economic costs of apartheid and exclusion become more apparent.

Attitudes towards trade unions, collective bargaining and labour relations

Both the FCI and ASSOCOM took early positions in favour of allowing workers from all races to organise and bargain collectively, and, through their representatives on the Economic Advisory Council, pushed for the establishment of a commission to investigate the issue. This ultimately led to the establishment of the Wiehahn Commission to review and normalise labour relations in South Africa.

While it must be said that commerce and industry's opposition to apartheid's labour laws was based in large part on survival and enlightened self-interest, there was, within the leadership of both ASSOCOM and the FCI, also a principled view that the organisations could not simultaneously advocate a private enterprise approach without acknowledging the importance of basic human rights and recognising black aspirations to achieve inclusiveness.

Calls to 'free up' the labour situation were met with significant opposition, and in 1958 the Minister of Transport warned:

> It is very dangerous for businessmen to enter the political arena in an organised manner. Speeches made at the [FCI] Convention were nothing more than a reflection of the [opposition] United Party's integration policy. The integrationists among industrialists ... wish to go against the stream of an overwhelming White Volkswil. The Prime Minister asked them cordially to reconsider. If they continue ... the Volkswil must be called against them.[10]

As early as 1958, ASSOCOM passed a resolution stating that it was in the national interest to bring about an increase in the wages of unskilled black workers as this would lead to increased productivity and a better utilisation of labour resources. This motion highlighted the importance that was placed by organised commerce and industry on increasing participation in the domestic market and the concern surrounding the distortions and deprivation of rights which were being created within the labour market.

In 1970, ASSOCOM and the FCI joined other major employer bodies and leading business people in denouncing the Bantu Laws Amendment Act, which gave the government carte blanche to extend job reservation.

It was recognised that the successful erosion of the job bar would have far-reaching implications for apartheid: indeed, the concessions made by government in 1973 were regarded in some quarters as the most significant victory against apartheid policies since 1948.

However, the FCI and ASSOCOM still believed that progress in removing job reservation was too slow, and in order to mobilise business opinion more effectively, the South African Employers' Consultative Committee on Labour Affairs (SACCOLA) – in which both organisations played a leading part – was re-established. In 1976, the employer organisations participating in SACCOLA accepted codes of employment which committed them to the elimination of racial discrimination from all aspects of employment.

Although there was a lack of unity in the early 1960s within the FCI on the issue of black participation in unions – resulting in a somewhat ambivalent approach, which favoured such a development in principle but suggested that 'now is not an appropriate time' – the organisation did push for the representation of black workers on industrial councils. However, as time progressed, there was growing recognition and acceptance of the importance of being able to negotiate with representative unions in order to secure industrial peace.

It must be acknowledged that, prior to the Wiehahn Commission, the attitude towards workers (and black workers in particular) in even the more progressive businesses and within organisations such as ASSOCOM and the FCI was highly paternalistic and ambivalent. To counter this, the business organisations encouraged their membership to develop codes of employment practice to change attitudes.

The labour relations dispensation that ensued after the Wiehahn Commission submitted its reports succeeded in moving the business sector away from this paternalistic approach towards the adoption of a far more participatory, inclusive and consensual framework for negotiation and decision-making at the firm level. The publication of the Wiehahn Report emboldened business to 'normalise' labour relations sooner rather than later. In the wake of the Wiehahn Commission, calls from both ASSOCOM and the FCI for more fundamental political reform intensified.

At both the regional and national levels the chamber movement also denounced detention without trial, which was often used by government against union leaders. The two national organisations urged their members not to penalise workers who joined the strike to mourn the death in detention of trade unionist Neil Aggett in 1982, and ASSOCOM also registered its protest against the death of Aggett with the relevant authorities.

In spite of the fact that many of the new unions were slow to register, both business organisations recommended a flexible and pragmatic approach to the question of union recognition, arguing that representativeness, rather than registration, should provide the basis for recognition. The FCI leadership also urged its membership and the other members of SACCOLA to move away from a reliance on the authorities towards a mutually accepted structure for bargaining with workers themselves. This set the stage for future negotiations between SACCOLA and the unions over the eventual proposal of changes by the National Manpower Commission (NMC) to the Labour Relations Act.

These negotiations culminated in a major agreement, titled the Laboria Minute, between business and the unions, which was later endorsed by the Cabinet and provided the basis for much of the new Labour Relations Act of 1995 as well as for the worker and employer rights that are part of the new 1996 Constitution. This also helped to lay foundations for a more structured and inclusive social dialogue.

The role of ASSOCOM and the FCI in particular in the 'total onslaught' (1980–1990)

The 'total onslaught' era – which extended from the early 1980s to 1990 – was characterised by an acceleration in political reform, increased international isolation, a significant deterioration in economic performance, rising political and social instability, and the growing use of the security apparatus against dissent. During this period the business community was caught between the recognition of the inevitability and desirability of significant political reform and a range of developments which resulted in a great deal of instability and uncertainty.

The response of both the FCI and ASSOCOM to this acute dilemma was, on the one hand, to try to speed up the reform process and facilitate contact between the different political interests – both within and outside South Africa – and on the other, to fight a rearguard action against the sanctions and disinvestment campaigns, and the rising levels of violence which threatened the economy and job creation efforts. However, as much as business was resistant to economic sanctions, it successfully resisted an official proposal to use certificates of origin, which chambers issued to traders, in a covert way to evade sanctions.

In addition to trying to lobby the politicians for change, a key focus of attention for organised business during this period was on educating its membership to prepare them for the changes that were coming and on mobilising thinking behind the development of a human rights culture. This was also a period in which individual companies were encouraged to focus on 'social responsibility' initiatives by enlarging their mandate to promote economic transformation.

One of the reform steps taken in the 1980s that divided the business sector was the introduction of the Tricameral Parliament, which gave political representation to coloureds and Indians, but not to black Africans. Organised business was split between those who saw it as unacceptable that Africans were excluded and those who felt it was, with reservations, 'a step in the right direction'. This was a split view in business, rather than a general business view. ASSOCOM did, however, press for a clear ruling on black citizenship rights and for common citizenship to be expedited.

Nevertheless, when Dr Van Zyl Slabbert eventually resigned from Parliament in 1986 as leader of the opposition in protest against the tricameral constitution, he rightly complained that 'most of the business establishment' had been willing to support a yes vote in the whites-only 1983 referendum on the tricameral proposals. In hindsight, ASSOCOM and the FCI members should have taken a stronger line at the time and looked to the long term in a more inclusive way. In retrospect, business lagged behind the curve on that issue.

However, in recognising that there was much unfinished business on South Africa's political agenda, ASSOCOM then immediately commissioned a research study of constitutional options which would encompass a full democracy beyond the tricameral system. The 1985 ASSOCOM research study looked at the fundamentals of economic and political change in South Africa from a business perspective. Titled 'Removal of Discrimination against Blacks in the Political Economy of the Republic of South Africa', it was drafted by Professors Jan Lombard and Andre du Pisanie after wide consultation. The goal of the Lombard Report, as it came to be called, was to promote business and public debate about future constitutional options. It also called for negotiations to commence on a new political order in South Africa as soon as possible.

Later in 1985, a 'Manifesto for Reform' was published by several major employer bodies, calling for universal citizenship and meaningful political participation for the black population. The Manifesto for Reform was used by all the major employer bodies on a series of international trips in 1985 aimed at persuading foreign countries not to impose sanctions on, and foreign companies not to disinvest from, South Africa, with a view to bringing about peaceful change. These overseas forays culminated in a joint presentation by ASSOCOM, the FCI, the AHI, NAFCOC and the Urban Foundation to the United Nations public hearings on the activities of transnational corporations in South Africa in September 1985.

In January 1986, following the imposition of a state of emergency and significant business disappointment at the lack of concrete reform measures in President Botha's so-called Rubicon speech, the FCI released a Business Charter and an Action Programme for business in the reform process which, it was hoped, would serve as 'a significant rallying point for negotiation and national unity in the present climate of widespread prejudice and mistrust'.

The Action Programme committed business to supporting the rapid implementation of the objectives contained in the Manifesto for Reform, and to assisting in the creation of a climate for negotiation using the lessons learnt in the industrial relations field. It then went on to outline the actions that would be needed from government to establish its credibility, including a significant focus on black housing and the immediate implementation of freehold title for black householders, the cessation of forced removals and the opening up of central business districts to all races.

Botha reacted angrily to the persistent pressure from organised business, until he eventually took retaliatory action. It is not entirely clear whether the publication of the Business Charter and the subsequent removal of the representative business bodies from the President's Economic Advisory Council (EAC) were linked, but many regarded the latter move as an attempt to 'punish' these organisations for their views. Also, by limiting business representation on the council to individuals, the government may have believed that it would encounter a less significant and more divided opposition (see Chapter 3).

ASSOCOM also organised a number of delegations to countries such as the United States, the UK, Belgium, France and Germany during the latter half of the 1980s. In addition to arguing against the imposition of economic sanctions, international views and concerns over such diverse issues as the 'Sharpeville Six', the Foreign Funding Bill and the National Council Bill were discussed with international politicians and business people.

At this time, meetings were also held between some local chambers and representatives of outlawed organisations, such as the African National Congress (ANC). These meetings resulted in strong calls from certain chambers for the unbanning of these organisations and the release of their leadership – including Nelson Mandela – from prison, as necessary for political negotiations leading to the election of a democratic government to get under way. This call was later reinforced at the national and international levels.

In spite of their frustration with the slow pace of reform, both organisations viewed the issue of economic sanctions as being largely consistent with the strategy developed during the 1960s – namely, that rapid and inclusive economic growth offered South Africa the best chance of ridding itself of apartheid, while also ensuring that a new political dispensation did not inherit an economic wasteland. At the same time businesses, which were generally on the receiving end of economic sanctions, had a vested interest in wanting to avert their imposition.

In 1989, in order to give the political reform process more momentum, a high-level delegation from ASSOCOM went to Lusaka to hold talks with the ANC leadership. Apart from discussing domestic political developments, these talks focused on the South African economy and the attitude of the ANC towards some critical economic policy issues. The intention was to assist (alongside other similar initiatives such as the Dakar Conference) in making dialogue with the ANC legitimate, especially on economic questions.

As previously noted, it was a strategic decision by the leadership of ASSOCOM and the FCI to merge and form SACOB as from January 1990. Organised business wanted to be in a stronger position to enlarge its sphere of influence as an agent of change in a period of pending political transition. An interesting negative political reaction to the intended formation of SACOB was reflected in the 19 October 1988 edition of *Die Afrikaner*:[11]

> The big capital interests in South Africa are busy establishing a political united front. This is evident from the attempts by ASSOCOM and the FCI to merge into one organisation. Although their interests often clash, Prof J Poolman of RAU is trying his utmost to make the merger work, even if only at national level and not at local branch level.
>
> The purpose of the merger is – as Anglo America's journal 'Optima' explains the political role of the business sector – to make individual business undertakings the focal points for the accommodation of Black aspirations. The rebuke which the head of First National Bank, Mr Chris Ball, had to endure has led to tremendous frustration among businessmen, in a business community that is one of the most politically conscious in the world and in contrast to the business sector in other countries, is leftist oriented, says 'Optima'.

Hence the comments by many analysts that in the apartheid years business in South Africa was 'well to the left' of the government. It might be said, though, that given the enormity of the apartheid system, this was not a difficult position for enlightened business people to take.

The role of SACOB during the political transition phase (1990–1994)

Although President FW de Klerk's address to Parliament on 2 February 1990 unblocked the political logjam, the political transition phase that it heralded continued to require active participation by the business community in the process, often in areas well outside its normal sphere of expertise. In addition to reviewing many of the policy stances of its predecessors, SACOB, whose 'birth' predated the speech by only one month, found itself involved in a number of other developments. These were aimed at extending democracy and upholding and defending the interests of its members against what was perceived as a potential attack against the private enterprise system from the ANC and its allies. Once again, the business strategy followed was one of engagement with both the emerging and the established political leadership in order to influence developments.

The first significant policy document released by SACOB in 1990 was a revised version of the FCI's Charter. Economic factors fully merged with political ones. Titled the 'Charter of Economic, Social and Political Rights', it restated the SACOB membership's commitment to a series of fundamental economic, social and political rights which were largely consistent with accepted democratic norms and with the Bill of Rights finally adopted. The chamber also undertook to promote, propagate and implement these rights among its membership and commerce and industry in general, as well as among all political parties and groups.

Because of the perceived threat to the private enterprise system – which SACOB saw as a key ingredient in securing South Africa's economic and political future – the chamber followed up the Charter with a discussion document titled 'Economic Options for South Africa'. This document attempted to reconcile the social needs of the country with the most appropriate delivery mechanisms and a strong, inclusive economy. It was already clear that enormous expectations about delivery had been created by the putative democracy – a challenge that is still apparent today.

Another area in which SACOB and the chamber movement became actively involved during the transition phase was in promoting peace and reconciliation, through the National Peace Accord process headed up by John Hall, then president of SACOB. South Africa went through a cycle of violence and setbacks before the democratic elections in 1994, which impacted negatively on the environment within which many businesses had to operate. In mid-June 1993, the Consultative Business Movement released a special set of guidelines on how private companies should adopt peace-building initiatives and participate in peace structures. Local chambers were deeply involved in this process.

Various chambers of commerce and associations of industry ensured that their representatives participated in local and regional peace committees. These business representatives often played a crucial role in brokering and maintaining the peace.

One of the reasons that peace was restored to Alexandra was because business around the township got involved. Money and resources were poured in and the peace structures became effective. Businesses around Thokoza and Katlehong have done very little, with one or two exceptions, like Dulux. No reconstruction, apart from some individual work by people living in the township, has been embarked upon and peace structures need greater support.[12]

What is often overlooked is the role played by SACOB as an independent mediator and 'honest broker' aiming to keep the parties talking and to remove obstacles to progress during the political roller-coaster ride of the early 1990s. High-level delegations from the chamber visited all the major political parties on more than one occasion during this period – when the CODESA talks had deadlocked – and early in 1994 senior members of SACOB facilitated a meeting between Nelson Mandela and the head of the Inkatha Freedom Party, Dr Mangosuthu Buthelezi, in an attempt to unblock the impasse that had developed. The CBM played a crucial role in this period in pushing out the frontiers of change on behalf of business.

Recognising that the transformation of South African society extended far beyond the political arena, SACOB was one of the first organisations to address the issue of affirmative action, firstly by commissioning a study of the international experience in the field, and secondly by drawing up guidelines in 1993 for its membership on how they should address the issue within their respective organisations. A critical part of these guidelines was an emphasis on the need to provide adequate support and training to previously disadvantaged employees, and to avoid token appointments.

During the constitutional negotiations at CODESA, SACOB followed the role played by its predecessors and made a number of submissions on those elements of the Constitution that were regarded as having the most direct relevance to the economy and to business in any new dispensation, ranging from property rights to monetary policy. Several of its inputs were ultimately reflected to a greater or lesser extent in the final Constitution.

Since business had long been subjected to unequal application and enforcement of racial legislation, a key element of these submissions was the need for a return to the rule of law and to secure the independence of the judiciary and the Reserve Bank. In line with a resolution favouring as much devolution of power to provincial and local levels of government as possible, SACOB also urged that a double ballot be used in the 1994 elections to facilitate this outcome.

A more concrete area of involvement in trying to ensure a relatively smooth transition was voter education. With financial support from some of its members, SACOB commissioned the production of a voter education video – titled 'Let's Vote' – which explained the electoral process and the importance of participating in the elections. The video, which was widely acclaimed, was produced in five different languages, and members of the chamber were encouraged to allow their workforce – the majority of whom had never voted in an election before – to view it.

SACOB also strongly supported the 'tripartism' process – first through the National Economic Forum and subsequently through the NEF's successor, NEDLAC. It has been argued that the seeds of these structures were sown in the industrial relations arena following the implementation of the Wiehahn Commission's recommendations. Although there were concerns within the membership that participation in these structures would amount to co-option and would not be in the interests of the business community, these fears were partly allayed by the consensus reached on a number of key economic issues.

Summing up

It must again be emphasised that what cannot be overlooked in this narrative are the parallel key activities of some other business associations and business-driven structures like the Urban Foundation, the Consultative Business Movement and the National Business Initiative, as well as those of individual business leaders. No one contribution can be seen in isolation.

What can be said is that by 1990, although the overwhelming challenge of shaping a prosperous and democratic post-apartheid society still lay ahead, most of the legally structured apartheid laws referred to in this chapter had been abolished, except for a few notable exceptions. There are many claimants taking credit for ending apartheid and there is no doubt that a combination of factors eventually produced the desired outcome, with no excessive claims by business.

The record therefore does not suggest that business played a heroic role in mounting the barricades at each and every opportunity to oppose apartheid. Indeed, business people are not usually of activist 'barricade material'. The agenda of organised business also focused on a wide range of bread-and-butter practical issues of normal concern to the business community. But economic pressure, as often articulated by business, nonetheless played its part in moving the country towards better socio-economic outcomes.

In an authoritative article (whose authorship regrettably cannot now be recovered), the role of business was described as follows:

> Our focus has been on one of the tectonic plates: business; principally white big business. The reason is not that it was the most important, but rather that its performance has not been fully appreciated. Business played major roles in reshaping the perceptions and agendas on both sides of the political divide; in creating social support for a transition to the new order; in building trust and then repeatedly rebuilding it when negotiations staggered and collapsed; in managing spoilers who sought to derail the transition; and in ensuring that the founding elections took place as scheduled and that all parties accepted the result. This does not readily translate into some percentage of the variance in explaining democratic transitions, but it does help us to see why there are obstacles to transitions that no one else will be likely to remove. Understanding what it took for South African business to succeed helps evaluate political transitions, both where business has been involved and where it has not.

Put more simply, in an article published immediately after the elections in 1994, the *Financial Mail* – commenting on various business initiatives, including those of SACOB – stated: 'Indeed, the business sector has come to play a part in national affairs that is surely without parallel in the world. It has oiled our transition to democracy.'[13]

Yet the weight of apartheid history nonetheless lies heavily on business in South Africa.

3

The Economic Advisory Council: Doing good by stealth?

> A Prince, therefore, ought always to take counsel, but at such times and reasons only as he himself pleases, and not when it pleases others; nay, he should discourage everyone from obtruding advice on which it is not sought. But he should be free in asking advice and afterwards regards the matters on which he has asked for it, a patient hearer of the truth – and even displeased should he perceive that anyone, from whatever motive, keeps it back.
> – NICCOLÒ MACHIAVELLI

WHAT ABOUT BUSINESS AND THE Economic Advisory Council (EAC)? As many governments do, the apartheid government created or used various structures to promote economic development. Some of these structures had a patently political agenda, like the National Regional Development Council (NRDC) and the Bantu Investment Corporation (BIC), while others had a more conventional role, such as the Council for Scientific and Industrial Research (CSIR) and the South African Bureau of Standards (SABS). At the economic policy level, there were the traditional monetary and fiscal policy functions vested in institutions like the South African Reserve Bank and the National Treasury respectively. Business representatives, in the ordinary course of events, would be involved in several of these structures.

Many countries in the world utilise one or other form of organised external economic advice. Among the most well-known in advanced economies are the Council of Economic Advisers in the United States (established by the Employment Act of 1946), the German Council of Economic Experts (sometimes called the 'wise men', set up in 1963) and Canada's Council of Economic Advisers (established in the 1960s). A developing country example is India's Economic Advisory Council (reconstituted in 2017 after being rendered defunct in 2014).

Over the years the approach to economic policy planning has shifted more towards 'indicative' than 'prescriptive' (especially after the demise of the command economies of Eastern Europe). The time frames have also become shorter, although we still find long-term perspectives as in South Africa's National Development Plan (end year 2030) and Ghana's recently introduced National Development Plan (2018–2057). Invariably, the policy perspectives of, and inputs from, economic and other policy advisory bodies tend to evolve in line with these changing approaches.

It is particularly important to note that a cross section of economic advisory bodies show significant differences in terms of the extent of their independence. For example, the Canadian Council of Economic Advisers has always enjoyed a high degree of independence. South Africa's EAC found itself quite far in the opposite direction, largely confined to producing internal reports and press statements which had to be approved by government, although in practice its processes became more flexible over time.

But in South Africa the role of the Prime Minister's or President's Economic Advisory Council, a top-level key advisory structure in policy-making, has so far not been sufficiently researched or analysed. The EAC, of course, worked under tight rules of confidentiality. Yet it existed for 34 years, from 1960 to 1994, and served Verwoerd, Vorster, Botha and De Klerk as Prime Ministers or Presidents. Clearly, at different times it was either used by government to attempt to reinforce the status quo or mobilised by private sector representatives to accelerate change.

In December 1959, Verwoerd appointed Dr Hennie Steyn as his Economic Adviser and as chairman of the Prime Minister's Economic Advisory Council. The EAC met for the first time in July 1960. Steyn served in these dual capacities until 1965 when he was succeeded by Dr Piet Riekert. Dr Simon Brand took over in 1978. The chairmanship changed again when the EAC was reconstituted in 1985 and a business person was appointed to occupy the position in a part-time capacity, though he was not designated as Economic Adviser to the President.

From the outset the EAC's second chairman, the formidable Dr Riekert, sought as far as possible to keep the EAC debates under narrow control and confined to 'safe' issues by tightly managing the agenda. The council normally met quarterly for two days and initially consisted of 65 members. In a primitive way, as the EAC included both government and trade unions, reflecting the political set-up of the day, it recognised the principle of 'tripartisim' between government, business and labour, but there is no record of such a term being used at the time.

The private sector, as it was then organised, was strongly represented from the outset (except for a certain period later). It will be recalled that the EAC was established by Prime Minister Verwoerd in the same year that a serious breach occurred between him and ASSOCOM over racial policies. Nonetheless, ASSOCOM was given two seats on the council, together with other employer bodies.

Verwoerd could hardly have expected a compliant ASSOCOM in the EAC's deliberations, but it is difficult to gauge at this distance in time how hard certain elements of organised business might have pushed the government initially. Then, as subsequently, business leaders were left in no doubt as to both the apartheid government's preparedness to take steps if necessary to pull them into line and the negative consequences of business activism.

Certainly, Verwoerd initially insisted that 'politics' be excluded from the EAC when he opened the council in 1960. Thus, early meetings of the EAC concentrated mainly on matters such as border industries (close to the homelands) and various aspects of 'apartheid economics'. In any case, representatives of organised business needed time to find their feet in the new structure and the EAC debate gradually opened up as the rules of engagement became more flexible. Events such as the Sharpeville massacre and South Africa's departure from the Commonwealth inevitably permeated EAC discussions. The rules of engagement at the EAC would be modified over the years as socio-economic pressures mounted. The author served on the council for several years during the second half of its existence, initially on behalf of ASSOCOM and later representing SACOB, and recalls several robust debates in that period, not all of which had positive outcomes.

However, only a limited review can be given here of the genesis and role of the EAC during the apartheid era, pending further research.

Clearly, the dearth of information about the inner workings of the EAC is strongly linked to the secrecy accompanying most of its activities. Its post-meeting media statements were inevitably bland and generic and did not reveal the real substance of the debates. It was only in the second half of its existence that the EAC became slightly more demographically representative, such as with the inclusion of NAFCOC representatives (for which the existing white employer organisations also lobbied). But it remained almost entirely white-dominated for most of its existence, although a coloured and an Indian representative were appointed in their personal capacities in the late 1970s.

What the author can say is that, whatever official documents or even EAC minutes may have reflected, ASSOCOM and (later) SACOB representatives on the EAC always prepared a highly confidential report after each meeting. This was circulated on a very restricted basis to only the top five office-bearers in the organisation, and it usually gave a reliable if discreet impression of the EAC's proceedings. It also provided an indication of what policy issues might need to be followed up by business or pursued with the authorities on the strength of EAC discussions – sometimes with the leverage of an EAC debate. The report could also be used as a basis for strategising for the next EAC meeting. Participation in the EAC also enabled organised business representatives to identify over time the more responsive policy-makers in officialdom.

These insights also assisted in shaping the documentation that organised business submitted to the EAC at subsequent meetings and that increasingly, as time passed, influenced the EAC agenda itself. One of the advantages brought by organised business was ensuring permanence in its nominated EAC representatives, thus building institutional memory and credibility with the passage of time. A stage was also reached later in the life of the EAC when like-minded EAC members would often caucus in advance of a meeting.

With growing demands for change, and as the apartheid government began to retreat from many of its positions, more holistic strategies were needed to promote reforms. Piecemeal reform had become problematic. As Merle Lipton has said, 'the system hung together'.[1] This started to become apparent in EAC discussions. As a purely advisory structure, the EAC was nevertheless able to facilitate and encourage processes that would initiate changes at other levels or, by throwing its weight behind proposals, to enhance their chances of being accepted and possibly implemented.

Discussions at the EAC therefore helped to get two significant commissions appointed in 1977: the first, under Wiehahn, to look into all aspects of labour relations, including trade union rights, and the second, under Riekert, to consider other aspects of the use of labour. Both reported back in 1979 and their work led to a series of key reforms. The Wiehahn Commission in particular broke new ground in recommending a tripartite structure in labour relations, to be called the National Manpower Commission.

There were also various 'summit' meetings, especially in the 1980s, between government and the private sector in an effort to make the best of shrinking differences over economic strategy and racial policies. Then, as now, there were excessive expectations as to what such large-scale 'talk shops' could achieve. But in such cases EAC documentation provided valuable background input to the discussions. Although comprehensive and balanced, the documentation remained devoid of any contribution from the black majority in the population. Often high-level economic analysis from the EAC staff simply overlooked the reality on the ground.

In the 1980s the Governor of the Reserve Bank, Dr Gerhard de Kock, played an especially valuable role in advocating a generally more market-oriented approach to policy, which contrasted with the direct control approach preferred by some key players both inside and outside the EAC. A stage had indeed been reached when some EAC reports – and the government's response to them – seemed to reflect more of an argument among officials themselves than a real exchange of views between the government and the business sector.

In particular, there were the Carlton (1979) and the Good Hope (1981) 'summit' conferences between PW Botha and the private sector, to which the reaction of business was hopeful but cautious. It is noteworthy that trust steadily declined between business and the Botha government as the 1980s drew to a close, despite these high-level initiatives early in the decade.

In November 1981 almost six hundred business and community leaders gathered in Cape Town at the invitation of Prime Minister PW Botha, in what came to be called the Good Hope Conference. This probably represented the pinnacle of 'consultation' between the government and the private sector at the time, surpassing even the previous Carlton Conference in Johannesburg. It was chaired by the Governor of the Reserve Bank, Dr De Kock. Although a common theme running through the Good Hope Conference was business's continued willingness to support reform, there was also an underlying warning message from several business people about the way ahead.

The remarks of some of the leading white business people of the time, who were present, included:

- 'There is a certain degree of disappointment about the results of the Carlton meeting ... We must at this Conference talk in much plainer and precise terms ... An important reason for the disappointment among business people is that government appear either unwilling or unable to act on the facts of the situation as they see them.' (Harry Oppenheimer, Anglo American Corporation)
- 'Peace and progress demand less discrimination, equal opportunities, open trading arena and neutral zones ... Once an urgent problem has been identified and a solution found, one should not allow implementation to be delayed by red tape.' (Dr Anton Rupert, Rembrandt Group)
- 'But the private sector is concerned at the pace of change. It feels that the government is "marking time" on certain aspects of reform; and that the many statements of intent were not always followed through by sufficient action.' (Mike Rosholt, Barlow Rand)
- 'While people of colour are now destined and permitted to play a rapidly increasing role in the economy, there seemed to be reluctance on the part of government to implement those socio-political measures which all acknowledged to be essential if people of colour were to participate fully in the system and support it.' (Gavin Relly, South Africa Foundation)
- 'There is perhaps one essential difference between the audience of the day and the electorate who gave the government a mandate at the polls. Businessmen had to take decisions swiftly, in order to survive. Therefore, they were keen to see change taking place faster than those on whose support at the polls the government relied.' (Dr Fred du Plessis, Sanlam)

In his reply Botha broadly endorsed the key role of the private sector, despite recognising political differences. He intended asking the EAC (to which he said he attached 'much importance') to take up several of the suggestions and recommendations with the various ministers concerned to expedite the implementation of certain reform measures.

Nonetheless, the pace of reform vacillated considerably under Botha, culminating in the notorious Rubicon speech in 1985. It fell so short of expectations that it precipitated a large capital outflow and a debt crisis requiring international negotiations to guarantee the rescheduling of South Africa's foreign debt. Unusually, South Africa made use of a prominent Swiss banker, Dr Fritz Leutweiler, to act as a mediator between the country and its creditors to facilitate the new financial arrangements that were urgently needed. These developments, of course, inevitably also found resonance with the EAC agenda at the time. What occurred within the EAC increasingly mirrored external political contestation.

In lighter vein this prompted the author to compose and circulate to EAC members a financial verse entitled 'SA's Foreign Debt Problem – dedicated to Dr Leutweiler':

We hereby pledge our hassled nation,
By rescheduling and co-operation,
By showing creditors a degree of deference,
And consistent with our terms of reference,
To swell each asset, prune each liability,
And thus regain our financial viability.

We also swear with hand on heart,
That SA will give it all it's got,
By '86 we'll be back in financial heaven,
Or if not '86, well then, '87,
Since failure will bring us little solace,
It's up to Leutweiler to find the dollars!

Another top-level conference with business leaders was called by Botha in November 1986. This time the main purpose was to evolve an economic strategy in the light of the sanctions imposed by the United States that year – but neither sanctions nor reform was to be directly discussed. Sanctions, in particular, were to be left to the 'experts', to be considered secretly and with the minimum of publicity. (As previously indicated, in his book

Apartheid, Guns and Money, Hennie van Vuuren outlines the corrupt consequences of this secretive environment.) Three main documents were submitted to the conference for discussion and debate, covering a proposed long-term strategy, emanating from the EAC; privatisation; and the government's reaction to the EAC approach.

Although the 1986 conference was also an attempt to repair relations with business, which had been damaged by the state of emergency and the Rubicon speech, it failed for two main reasons. Firstly, business resented the restricted terms of reference imposed on the conference and, secondly, it became clear that the government at that point was less open to being influenced on matters of concern to business. Business wanted a more frank recognition of the economic and human costs of continuing with political policies that had in fact resulted in sanctions being imposed in the first place.

Although the various reports assumed that a free enterprise, market-based economy was the best model for South Africa, at no time did they consider that the non-participation of blacks in the entrepreneurial sector, and their general deprivation, predisposed them to ideologies that were hostile to the promotion of such a model. Nor did they foresee that there was little likelihood, even if the identified goals were to be fully realised, of black attitudes on these matters changing in the foreseeable future. They completely ignored the fact that black attitudes were likely to be heavily tilted towards redistribution, not economic growth.

It may seem strange that the business representatives on the EAC allowed these omissions and imbalances to appear in the document. It may have been that, as by now business people sat on the EAC in their personal capacities, they did not necessarily have sufficiently strong backing or clout to insist on changes to the official documentation. Or perhaps the documents were heavily influenced by the narrow terms of reference of the conference itself. But the larger blame must lie with Botha and his Cabinet for not giving the necessary political guidance and opportunity, which would have enabled these aspects to be properly discussed at that particular conference.

PW Botha was widely regarded as a head of state who began well but lost his way by failing 'to cross the Rubicon'. Shortly after he became Prime Minister, Botha said that 'we are part of Africa and we must play that role or we will die'. 'Botha was a determined, energetic and purposeful leader,' said Hermann Giliomee, 'but was also impetuous, impatient and rash. He was a leader who was prepared to adapt, but he was also more than ready for a fight ... He would intimidate people and made them comply.'[2] Dr Frederik van Zyl Slabbert described Botha as a 'mixture of sentimentality and intolerance ... The ferocity of his vindictiveness and irrationality, when angered, never failed to amaze me.'[3] And Helen Suzman, reviewing her experience of a number of National Party leaders, said: 'then came PW Botha, an unintelligent bully as far as I was concerned! I had no respect for him!'[4]

ASSOCOM and the FCI had several bruising clashes with Botha. But a personal anecdote shows how occasionally the brusque, domineering PW could be temporarily disarmed and his sentimentality evoked. With the prospect of a meeting taking place between ASSOCOM and Botha in February 1987, the nature of the reform agenda that ASSOCOM wanted to submit was bound to lead to an explosion at the meeting. ASSOCOM, together with other business associations, had also been expelled from the EAC and, as mentioned above, in the post-Rubicon era relations between business and government were at a low ebb.

Nonetheless, in an effort to find a way to ameliorate the likely hostile mood at the meeting, the author (who was then the chief executive of ASSOCOM) conceived a personal strategy more likely to improve the meeting atmosphere. In the meantime, Botha had called a general election for 6 May 1987. The author noticed that 6 May happened to be Mrs Botha's birthday and coincidentally also his. This seemed to be an opportunity, knowing that Botha and his wife were like Darby and Joan, to manoeuvre for a more constructive meeting.

The dialogue between ASSOCOM and Botha in his office in Cape Town in February 1987 went as follows, after a frosty welcome.

RP: Mr President, before we begin on our agenda for today, I would just like to preface our representations with a personal perspective, which may interest you.

PW (glowering): Oh! What is that?

RP: Well, Mr President, you have called a key election for May 6, where you are putting important reform issues on the table. Then it is Mrs Botha's birthday that day, and it also happens to be my birthday. A happy coincidence – you can only be lucky in your endeavours for May 6!

PW (lighting up like a lamp): Is that so! That's wonderful and I'm glad to hear it. It is a good omen. I will tell Elize all about it!

After that, strange as it may seem, the delegation sailed through the controversial ASSOCOM recommendations for reform and enjoyed twice as much time as normally allocated to a presidential meeting. Action was again, in ritual fashion, promised on the issues raised. (Postscript: Botha *did* go home and tell his wife after the meeting, because on 6 May the author received birthday congratulations from 'his birthday mate' in the Presidency. 'Sentiment' could occasionally be mobilised, after all, to move things along.)

But the EAC was clearly not by any means all plain sailing. The increasingly critical role played by organised business, especially ASSOCOM and the FCI, both inside and outside the EAC, began to irk and annoy PW Botha in the early 1980s. He suddenly reconstituted the EAC in 1985, without formal consultation with the private sector. It is rumoured that, for his own reasons, the prominent businessman and economist Dr Fred du Plessis, chairman of Sanlam and a founder member of the EAC, influenced Botha to revamp the council.

Under the guise of streamlining the EAC structure, organised business was removed and replaced by senior business people in their personal capacities. Also excluded were private sector economists and some government representatives. Membership was reduced from 65 to 44. An executive committee of nine members was established to liaise between the EAC and the Cabinet. According to a 1991 *Financial Mail* article, 'the omission of organised business was seen as a deliberate snub following the failure of the Carlton and Good Hope Conferences to generate enthusiasm for the policies'.[5]

Whatever the extraneous reasons for the change in composition of the EAC in 1985, it weakened the effectiveness of the EAC to the extent that:
- business people on the EAC spoke only for themselves and escaped the discipline of being mandated by the mainstream of business;
- it weakened overall policy coherence in the sense that the government still interacted with organisations like the FCI and ASSOCOM outside the EAC, leading to official messages that conflicted with what might be said by individual business people on the council;
- the absence of organised business structures on the EAC meant that skills in mobilising consensus among the business representatives were lacking; and

- the EAC was given too much of a 'big business' image, and looked more like a 'business council' than an economic advisory council.

On the positive side, the EAC agenda always included an informative, in-depth and authoritative debate on the economic situation and outlook. This was usually introduced by the Governor of the Reserve Bank, followed by inputs from various EAC members, often based on their own prior written submissions. As mentioned earlier, the EAC was often riven with ideological differences between those who supported the market-oriented policies of the Reserve Bank Governor, Dr De Kock, and those who favoured the more interventionist stance of Dr Du Plessis of Sanlam. On monetary policy the EAC eventually favoured the appointment of a commission of inquiry into monetary matters (chaired by De Kock) which, unsurprisingly, came down on the side of market-oriented outcomes.

The EAC was also the formal initiator – but not the author – of a key planning instrument which itself served as an opportunity for information exchange: the Economic Development Programme (EDP). The EDP – of which several revised versions were produced at regular intervals – was developed by economists and other specialist staff of the government planning branches in consultation with sectoral advisory committees. Although the private sector EAC representatives participated fully in EDP discussions, their engagement was often tinged with a degree of scepticism about the EDP's real intentions.

Not that Cabinet members were always enthusiastic about the role of the EAC. In terms of overall policy formulation, the EAC did not always sit comfortably with Cabinet ministers and their various portfolios. The ministers often resisted the recommendations of the council as originating in bodies that wanted to assert control over their departments. Hence much depended on the power and influence of the EAC chairman, such as Dr Riekert, to enforce coordination where it was required, with the backing of the Prime Minister or President. The private policy sector often took extra steps both to ensure that positive recommendations from the EAC registered where it mattered and to insist on policy coordination.

As coordination and coherence in policy remain serious problems in South Africa today, we need to retain perspective. Although uncoordinated decisions are bad or costly, coordinated decisions may also be so. There is no magic about a plan that transforms the quality of decisions beyond the virtue that coordination lends.

The general view of the EAC is perhaps best outlined in this broad recapitulation:

> The EAC was established in 1960 in a period of political and economic uncertainty and arose out of the need to promote greater cooperation between government and the private sector. At that stage the government required the cooperation of the private sector in the implementation of policies such as the industrialisation of areas bordering on the envisaged black homelands. The EAC consisted of officials from key government departments and members of the public, organised business and then-recognised organised labour, as well as some prominent economists. The EAC provided a forum for extensive interest group interaction and lobbying on policy issues but initially consisted of whites only.
>
> During the 1980s representation was expanded to include representatives from the coloured and Asian communities as well as black business, but the EAC was never a fully representative body. Although the EAC was corporatist in design or form, it was also never a fully corporatist body which reflected the views of different interest groups. It can at best be described as a form of 'soft' corporatism. Nevertheless, it had a significant impact on policy-making, especially insofar as pressing issues, often of a structural nature, were identified and kept on the agenda until action was taken. Examples include the changes to South African labour legislation during the late 1970s and early 1980s and the successive Economic Development Programmes that emphasised the need for structural change to improve the growth and job creation potential of the economy.
>
> Towards the middle of the 1980s the EAC was reconstituted (based on the ridiculous rule that the number of representatives per kind of economic activity would be determined by each sector's contribution to GDP!). The chairperson was a part-time private business person and the EAC no longer had full-time technical back-up. This institutional arrangement reduced the EAC to a lobbying forum for the captains of industry and did nothing to

enhance economic policy-making during a period when the State Security Council ruled supreme. Although the EAC still reflected corporatism, its influence waned and more representative bodies (such as the National Manpower Commission) gave a more meaningful voice to interest groups, particularly certain sections of organised labour (which did not participate actively in the EAC).[6]

When he became President in 1989, FW de Klerk immediately reinstated organised business on the EAC, and also further diversified its membership. One suspects he may also have realised the extent to which the support of organised business would be invaluable for the strategic political decisions that still lay ahead.

4
Business and social dialogue in South Africa

Whatever you do for me without me, you do against me.
– Mahatma Gandhi

Whence social dialogue?

It will be evident from earlier chapters that business in South Africa became increasingly involved in social dialogue structures, both in their earlier forms and subsequently, culminating in the formation of NEDLAC. This interaction ebbed and flowed over the years and was inevitably driven forward as events unfolded. This chapter therefore describes the political and economic setting in which the origins of South African social dialogue and NEDLAC can be found. Ideas tend to take root when the soil has been fertilised by social and economic trends – and, in South Africa's case, by political developments as well. This helps to explain both the emergence of 'institutionalised social dialogue' in this country and the extent to which it had its roots in workplace issues.[1]

First of all, though, what do we mean by 'social dialogue'? The concept is an elusive but pervasive one. Globally it sails under a number of flags. These include 'social capital', 'civil society', 'civil engagement', 'tripartism' and 'corporatism'. A growing body of literature has accumulated around these separate but related concepts, especially since the end of the Cold War. For many economists the term social capital, like other, related concepts, does not have clear parameters and its role in economic development is no less hard to pin down. Social dialogue is apt to mean different things to different people.

A comprehensive working definition of institutionalised social dialogue was provided by the International Labour Organization (ILO) in 1996 as follows:

> All types of negotiation, consultation or simply exchange of information between, or among, representatives of governments, employers and workers, on issues of common interest relating to economic and social policy. It can exist as a tripartite process, with the Government as an official party to the dialogue or it may consist of bipartite relations only between labour and management (or trade unions and employer associations), with or without indirect government involvement. Concertation can be informal or institutionalised, and often it is a combination of the two. It can take place at national, regional or at enterprise level. It can be inter-professional, sectoral, or a combination of all of these.[2]

The ILO report went on to say that 'the main goal of social dialogue itself is to promote consensus-building and democratic involvement among the main stakeholders in the world of work'. This implies that social dialogue is now generally viewed – characteristically and historically, and in more inclusive terms – as tripartite. Yet we must accept that there are still conceptual and other difficulties surrounding the issue of social dialogue which have not yet been resolved.

This is probably one of the main reasons why the debate around social dialogue in South Africa is often at cross-purposes. Yet any measurement or evaluation of the impact of social dialogue depends on how the concept itself is understood, and therefore what is generally expected of its associated processes and systems. As we have no unequivocal measure of economic development, no clear-cut analytical framework exists that links national institutions and overall performance. Given that development studies in recent years have acquired new dimensions, it is even unlikely that there is only one formula for 'social dialogue in democracy', thus leaving scope for different interpretations of its potential role.

In 1972, the prominent UK political scientist Bernard Crick published an influential book, *In Defence of Politics*. He argued that the art of political horse-trading, far from being deplorable, allowed people of different views and beliefs to live together in a peaceful, prosperous society. He maintained that ideally in a liberal democracy nobody gets precisely what they want, but everyone has the freedom to live the life they choose. However, in the absence of information exchange, civility and conciliation, societies resolve their differences through coercion or violence. But the world, and South Africa, no doubt have fallen far short of Crick's ideal, and this may explain why institutionalised social dialogue in South Africa has evoked scepticism and criticism.

We should therefore recall that, ever since it was launched on 18 February 1995, NEDLAC has often been the subject of controversy, with a number of critics having expressed the view that it would fail to achieve the goals set for it at its inception. There has been considerable scepticism in many quarters. In spite of this, NEDLAC has to date produced agreements on a wide range of economic and social policy issues, and has completed numerous useful reports.

Of course, tripartism often finds critics at a more conceptual level. Some equate tripartism with corporatism, as they feel that the social partners are merely induced to toe the government's socio-economic line. Others argue that because tripartism excludes the unorganised citizens who constitute the majority of the population, their interests can never be adequately protected in such structures. There are also those who contend that tripartism usurps the parliamentary functions of the duly elected representatives of the people and that the social partners lack the mandate to represent the people's interests. These are pitfalls to be guarded against.

But while it is true that the NEDLAC process imposes some structures and disciplines on the process of policy-making, the fact that all social partners neither view it nor treat it as the sole decision-making body in the country, and that any party within or outside NEDLAC is free to approach both Parliament and other policy-making structures directly, undermines accusations that NEDLAC is a closed shop. The requirements of the NEDLAC Act are simply that participants should have a proven constituency from which they can obtain a mandate. There is nothing to prevent any new representative organisation from joining the policy-making process in NEDLAC, provided it can meet these requirements.

Proponents therefore regard tripartism as a well-structured means of reaching essential consensus on economic and social issues for the benefit of society as a whole – as opposed to, and certainly preferable to, coercion. The term 'tripartite consultations' is used here in its broadest possible sense to include consultations which, while not necessarily trilateral in themselves, contribute (often on a bilateral basis) to an overall process of dialogue on, and active participation in, national socio-economic policy-making, which ultimately involves the government and employer and worker organisations.

At the national level, social dialogue can help to achieve an acceptable balance between sectoral interests and national objectives of growth and development. Whether as a process of negotiation, consultation, discussion or information-sharing, or otherwise as a means of achieving consensus on policy options, social dialogue can help to diffuse opposition to policy proposals and dissolve damaging deadlock. Where there are institutions that allow the effective participation of interest groups in the formulation and implementation of policies that affect them, social dialogue can offer an effective means of raising productivity and economic competitiveness and also help to minimise the social costs of globalisation and ensure equitable access for all to its benefits.

To assess and understand NEDLAC's establishment and role in what remained of the twentieth century – and thereafter – it is first necessary to refer to some prior developments leading up to its creation. We must locate our historical bearings. It will be recalled that 1990 was the crucial year in which Nelson Mandela was released from prison, unleashing the various political and social forces that ultimately culminated in a negotiated full democracy in 1994 and, with that, the end of the apartheid system in South Africa. To that extent, at least the advent of representative democracy and the development of institutionalised social dialogue can be said to have converged in South Africa. For good or ill, it was decided that corporatism would be a valuable approach to follow given South Africa's circumstances.

Stepping stones to NEDLAC

Let us begin, then, with historical notions and origins.

Although NEDLAC eventually arose from a merger between the National Economic Forum (NEF) and the National Manpower Commission (NMC), the genesis of tripartism in South Africa can be traced back to the labour relations arena, which developed in the wake of the watershed Wiehahn Report in 1979.[3] The acceptance by the National Party government of most of the recommendations of the Wiehahn Commission was significant, because it paved the way for the legitimisation of black and multiracial trade unions in South Africa and their subsequent recognition by commerce and industry. It was a major step forward at the time to normalise labour relations in this country.

We should not, at this remove, underestimate the impact that the Wiehahn Report made on the political and socio-economic circumstances then prevailing:

> The recommendations of the Wiehahn Commission – appointed in 1977 – produced a veritable watershed in labour relations in South Africa. It was unique in its consequences. It constituted the first crack in the wall of apartheid. After Wiehahn nothing would ever be the same again ... No other official enquiry had as incisive an effect on the South African economy as the Wiehahn report has had. An independent study found that more than eighty percent of the recommendations had been positively reacted upon by the Government.[4]

In this process, power relations within the South African economy started to shift from a highly paternalistic framework – which essentially had government deciding what was best for the country, and employers deciding what was best for their workers – towards a more inclusive and consensual framework of decision-making. This shift predated, but would in many respects be seen to have been synchronised with, South Africa's gradual movement towards a democracy that would place value on, and give full recognition to, human rights.

The experience gained by both organised business and organised labour in the post-Wiehahn industrial relations system – such as through the NMC – equipped individuals within each of these constituencies with the necessary tools to act as facilitators, mediators and negotiators, and, in doing so, made a more collaborative decision-making process possible. Although South Africa had officially withdrawn from the ILO in 1967, informal links with that body were maintained by some stakeholders – and these were also of assistance in this period.

However, this is not to deny or make light of severe tensions between business and labour in the post-1980 period – especially since the apartheid system had created a political vacuum which the new trade union movements understandably attempted to fill. This resulted in some, if not all, major unions assuming political roles that extended far beyond the general framework of an inclusive collective-bargaining system. Leaders in organised business realised that commerce and industry would continue to bear the brunt of these pressures unless there was meaningful political reform. As a consequence of this, calls from the organised business community for a political settlement grew more insistent and there were increased attempts to promote a broadly based commitment to fundamental human rights in South Africa.

It might therefore be argued that, in spite of the mounting exogenous pressure on the industrial relations system during the latter half of the 1980s, significant pathways of trust slowly emerged between the different constituencies. Unfortunately, much of this trust developed between individual personalities involved in the industrial relations process – rather than at an institutional level – so that then, as now, the consensus-building exercise was subject to the vagaries of leadership moving into different spheres of activity.

By 1988, the government tried to roll back some of the advances made since the Wiehahn Report. Pressure from both organised labour and organised business resulted in a historic agreement being reached in 1990, which was subsequently endorsed by the Cabinet and signed by the Minister of Manpower. Apart from providing the foundations for a new Labour Relations Act, the important Laboria Minute – as the agreement came to be known – also made provision for the formation of an appropriate forum to discuss the impact of labour relations on the economy. However, the trade unions interpreted this provision more widely, arguing that the forum should discuss, and even negotiate, all micro- and macroeconomic policy issues. This was an important breakthrough as far as the Laboria Minute was concerned.

At the time, there was a great deal of scepticism within the business sector about the motivation of the unions for such an interpretation. Some business people argued that the unions and their political allies merely wanted to use the forum to put additional pressure on the government of the day. Others again saw it as a ploy on the part of organised labour to set their ideological battle with business in a more rigid framework, one that would ultimately land business in positions that it would not otherwise have countenanced.

Although many business people were in any case strongly convinced that political change was essential, as the negotiations over a new political dispensation developed – and it became clear that the African National Congress (ANC) and its allies would assume the dominant role in any future government – so uncertainty grew within business over the extent of the ideological divide, the kind of economic policies that might be adopted, and business's own ability to influence future policy-makers. The rising number of strikes and boycotts instigated by the unions was also damaging the economy and business. There was a growing need to move away from a dominant culture of adversarialism in the socio-economic arena towards one of consultation and dialogue – and perhaps even one of forging agreements to help overcome the legacy of apartheid.

Emergence of the National Economic Forum (the 'golden triangle') and NEDLAC

Against this background, both organised business and organised labour began to see advantages in having a negotiating forum for constructive engagement. The Consultative Business Movement played a key role in facilitating this process. As a result, a series of meetings between labour and business took place, and agreement was reached on the creation of a forum to discuss economic issues. The next step was to get a hesitant government on board in the early 1990s.

What contributed to the reluctance by government to join the forum process was the ongoing trade union hostility at the time to the introduction of value-added tax on a wide range of basic foodstuffs, which were previously exempt from general sales tax, and the firm, opposing stance adopted by the Minister of Finance, Barend du Plessis. However, when Du Plessis resigned in April 1992 and was replaced by Derek Keys (who came from the business community), this obstacle to government's participation was removed.

Following a summit meeting between Keys and a joint business–labour delegation, the Cabinet agreed to the formation of the National Economic

Forum (NEF). The founding documents were soon drafted and the NEF was established administratively. Keys referred at the time to the 'golden triangle' of government, labour and business. Both Keys and Alec Erwin (then a senior economic spokesperson for the alliance of the African National Congress, South African Communist Party and Congress of South African Trade Unions (ANC–SACP–COSATU) and subsequently a Cabinet minister in the Mandela- and Mbeki-led governments) played significant roles in the establishment of the NEF.

The NEF was an informal structure set up with two working groups – one of which focused on the short-term issues, while the other was to have dealt with longer-term policy matters. However, because of the changing power relations in the country at the time, and the inability of the government to address long-term policy matters, the focus of the NEF's activities was very much on short-term issues affecting day-to-day economic governance. There was little success in developing a common vision for South Africa's economy. But by keeping the economic policy wheels turning, and by diverting political agendas away from the shop floor, the NEF played a highly constructive role in the country's transition at that stage.

Several participants believed that the NEF's strength at the time lay in its informality. The creation of the NEF in 1992 had been seen as the result of a needs-driven, voluntary process mainly initiated in its early stages by labour and business, reflecting a political will to make it work and deliver. It was not a statutory body, yet it bound its key players to important agreements. The role of informal discussions, and the combination of constituency mobilisation (sometimes in the form of strikes) and tough bargaining at the NEF, created a platform on which the future social dialogue framework would be built.

In addition, the NEF provided the various constituencies with some understanding of the perspectives and problems of the other participants, and helped to develop some capacities among them. Although labour was very good in the areas of process and negotiation, it had as yet little understanding of the implications of proposed policies, while in the case of government, certainly in the conditions prevailing in the 1990s, the reverse was closer to being true.

Somewhere between the capacities of labour and government stood business – with some individuals having experience of processes and negotiations, and others with a clear understanding of policy implications.

The trick lay in combining these skills. Fortunately, most of the constituency leaders were able to meet this challenge in order to further social dialogue.

Most obvious of all, but no less significant, was that the mere process of establishing or improving cross-cultural human relationships must have done something – and perhaps did quite a bit – to facilitate the formation of social capital at a crucial stage. If so, a large part of its genesis lay in workplace changes. There was also significant personal chemistry among the key participants, which, in a sense, was carried through to the eventual establishment of NEDLAC. The transitional NEF provided a good apprenticeship for the more formalised NEDLAC which still lay ahead.

At about the same time that the NEF was established, the National Manpower Commission (NMC) was restructured, with commissioners being selected on the basis of representativeness rather than expertise – as had previously been the case. While the focus of attention of the NMC continued to be on the labour market and the labour relations system, it also became an embryonic tripartite negotiating structure along similar lines to the NEF.

As previously indicated, another source of renewed cooperation and trust-building lay in addressing the endemic political violence which characterised the early 1990s and which threatened to derail the political negotiations. Apart from the start of trilateral engagement around workplace challenges, critical developments also unfolded on a broader political level which began to involve other formations, such as organised labour and business in the National Peace Accord. The negotiated Peace Accord was an important mechanism for keeping contemporary political violence to manageable proportions and it involved more or less the same actors as were participating in the NEF. They were all linked, to a greater or lesser extent, to the tough and tumultuous political process then under way.

After the 1994 elections and with the formation of the Government of National Unity (GNU), many of the labour participants in the NEF moved into senior policy-making positions within government, and carried with them a generally favourable view of tripartism. Yet on all sides it was also recognised that deep, unresolved differences of opinion between the three participants remained an obstacle to the development of a national vision. This vision was perceived to be essential for both national reconciliation and the realisation of South Africa's economic potential – and as a means of countering the negativity of sceptics abroad. The gains to be had from compromise therefore continued to look attractive.

As a result, there were elements within all three constituencies – but particularly in labour and business – that were favourably disposed to the formalisation of the NEF process. In this period several informal processes were poised to have significant formal consequences. Soon after the elections in 1994, business and labour met with a number of Cabinet ministers in the new government, seeking to formalise the structures of institutionalised social dialogue. Events then moved to the drafting of the NEDLAC legislation. The process leading up to the launch of NEDLAC was characterised by robust and intensive negotiations.

On all sides, there was a real commitment to make NEDLAC work – spurring a group of constituency leaders to advocate a social dialogue structure that could help in addressing South Africa's serious socio-economic challenges. These included the challenge of transforming the economy from one that had become inward-looking, uncompetitive, excessively protected and isolated from the world economy into one that would be open, competitive and growing – no less, in other words, than to reintegrate South Africa into the international economy and the globalisation process in the post-sanctions era.

It was thought that sustainable development might be more assured when key stakeholders were involved and committed to decision-making, while implementation of policy might be made easier when stakeholders were able to invoke the participatory process. Thus, irrespective of the state of the economy, social dialogue would provide a veritable voice to the key actors to convey their concerns on policy issues and, by so doing, align their views with those of the new government. Policy issues in which the relevant actors participated in such articulation would then mirror the needs and views of the broad spectrum of society and thus stand a greater chance of effective implementation.

In other words, quite apart from enhancing its own legitimacy, the mechanism of social dialogue broadened the decision-making process as well as the scope to facilitate the evolution of socially acceptable policy. The promotion of institutions driving such dialogue could possibly contribute to economic democracy. Moreover, social dialogue could help to forestall social instability and obstacles that might arise if affected stakeholders were not consulted or if their views were not taken into account in policy decisions. These remained the arguments in favour of intensified social dialogue.

Given that both the NEF and the NMC had effectively developed along tripartite lines representing the same constituencies, it was logical for any new structure to incorporate the two bodies. Discussions in the latter half of 1994 centred on how this could best be done. NEDLAC was then established as a statutory body with its structure, operational powers and characteristics being prescribed in the NEDLAC Act of 1994. The NEDLAC Act was one of the first pieces of legislation passed by the new Parliament.

In summary, therefore, it could be said that the four main stepping stones to the creation of NEDLAC were the Wiehahn Report, the NMC, the Laboria Minute and finally the NEF. When the economic history of this period comes to be written, special recognition must be given to the significant and decisive role played by the NEF at the time. It proved to be a distinctly important institutional bridge between the old and the new regimes and an important means in the building of social capital in South Africa.

Launch of NEDLAC

It is perhaps understandable that many of the tributes to Nelson Mandela have tended to focus on the reconciliation philosophy and strategy that he presented, while downplaying the fact that this was inextricably linked in his mind to nation-building. He believed in creating strong institutions to underpin and sustain democratic processes on a long-term basis. Hence his belief right at the outset that social dialogue, as embodied in an institution like NEDLAC, was necessary to provide the social and economic dimensions to the reconciliation and nation-building to which he was so deeply committed.

NEDLAC came into being on 18 February 1995. It was officially inaugurated by Mandela, whose speech and demeanour on the occasion reflected his great pride in the establishment of this key institution. As he warned at the NEDLAC launch, 'our democratic gains will be shallow and persistently threatened if they do not find expression in food and shelter, in well-paying jobs, and rising living standards'.[5]

SACOB banquet at which President Nelson Mandela was the guest speaker, Johannesburg, 30 August 1994. From left to right: SACOB President Cedric Savage, SACOB Director-General Raymond Parsons and President Nelson Mandela (Author's personal collection)

About NEDLAC, the author recalls an anecdote in this connection which once again, in a small way, throws a big light on the nature of the man. While the author was driving by car to Pretoria in 1994, the car phone rang. It was Madiba on the line. 'Raymond, I want to talk to you about the negotiations around NEDLAC.' Then, hearing the background noise of the vehicle, he asked, 'Where are you?' 'Travelling on the highway to Pretoria,' was the response. 'You pull over immediately and stop, otherwise I'm terminating this conversation!' he said. The author recalled nothing of the subsequent conversation, but was struck by the concern that an important political leader had for someone's personal safety, at a time when he was preoccupied with much more important matters.

High expectations and enthusiasm in many quarters surrounded the launch of this institution. NEDLAC was to be a major instrument of post-conflict rehabilitation. It was intended to inaugurate a new era of inclusive consensus-seeking and, ultimately, decision-making in the economic and social arenas. The enabling legislation formally spelt out NEDLAC's task to pursue the goals of growth, equity and participation. As the legislation indicated, NEDLAC was committed to a broad scope of activity covering all aspects of social and economic policy- and decision-making.

At NEDLAC's inception, its five objectives – which would shape its agenda – were specifically outlined as follows: to promote economic growth, participation in economic decision-making and social equity; to seek to reach consensus and conclude agreements on social and economic policy; to consider all proposed labour legislation relating to labour market policy before it was introduced into Parliament; to consider all significant changes to social and economic policy before it was implemented or introduced into Parliament; and to promote the formulation of coordinated policy on social and economic matters.

From the outset it was acknowledged that for the negotiation process in NEDLAC to succeed, the first prize would be to secure agreements. To start with, it was necessary to develop a work programme that would identify the key issues on which the social partners needed to seek agreement. The work programme itself would have to evolve out of a consensus on the socio-economic priorities for South Africa. This, in practical terms, would largely be distilled out of the economic agenda of the governing political alliance.

NEDLAC therefore drew heavily on the experience of its predecessors, the NEF and the NMC. It also modelled itself to a large extent on successful institutions of social dialogue in other parts of the world, notably Holland and Ireland, but with adaptations to take into account the development challenges of South Africa.[6] It was also hoped that the formalised process of information-sharing at the national level would enable participants to strengthen their commitment and build trust.[7] Social capital provides data which can make further cooperation possible. This collective knowledge could become a valuable asset in decision-making and in finding workable compromises in order to lower transaction costs.

Compromise, of course, did not necessarily mean the surrender of one side to the others. All parties had to make a contribution. Up to a point, an agreement might represent a genuine accord which had developed out of conflict or controversy. Short of that point, the contribution made by one or other side within NEDLAC would, on the whole, depend on the respective strengths of the parties and the skill of their negotiators at any given time. It was granted that there could be compromises that were weak or difficult to defend. Often social dialogue outcomes would result in policies being those that would secure agreement, rather than those that would efficiently achieve a given set of objectives. This is partly why many critics dislike NEDLAC 'compromises'.

NEDLAC was, and remains, institutionally distinctive in several ways. It is the most representative policy body South Africa has ever had, since it includes government, labour, business and the 'community'.[8] It is an agreement-making body of broadly equal partners and not merely an advisory body. Of the roughly fifty countries – mainly developing ones – that have NEDLAC-type institutions, South Africa is unusual in that NEDLAC is a negotiating body and not only an advisory one.

NEDLAC also requires mandated representatives, which means that constituencies are held accountable for the consequences within their own sphere of influence. South Africa has therefore developed its own hybrid system of social dialogue through NEDLAC – the 'golden triangle' having now become a quadrilateral or a quadrangle by including the community constituency at certain levels but not in all the chambers. There were special reasons at the time for this particular configuration.

And what was social dialogue intended to do? Ideally, institutionalised social dialogue was needed to help undo the damaging legacies of apartheid and address the challenges of economic performance, more especially with reference to growth, job creation and poverty alleviation. Pitched at its highest level, NEDLAC was intended to provide the socio-economic dimension of the reconciliation and nation-building to which President Mandela was strongly committed. The main participants in NEDLAC – predominantly the ANC-driven government, business and labour – all had their reasons for engaging in the NEDLAC process. From their various perspectives they all hoped that, in one way or another, NEDLAC would help to keep the country 'governable' and maximise their own influence in the process.

Although NEDLAC was regarded at the time as an agreement-making body rather than an advisory one, it was recognised by all participants that the NEDLAC process was not supposed to be a substitute for Parliament. While agreements could be reached between the social partners, such agreements were not intended to be binding on the country's elected representatives and certainly could not, in the absence of parliamentary debate and adoption, result in changes in the laws of the land.

Furthermore – and especially given the contemporaneous political power balance, which included a formal alliance between the ANC,

COSATU and the SACP – the fact that the parties likely to be most affected by proposed legislation had reached agreement on it was expected to significantly reduce the likelihood of parliamentary opposition to its enactment. That said, problems did soon develop in the relationship between NEDLAC and Parliament – the perception that there appeared to be two parliaments – and these difficulties persisted for some years.

In the early years of NEDLAC the government delegations tended to play a dominant role in setting NEDLAC's agenda. But this changed over time, and the social partners are now more proactive in shaping policy agendas. Experience soon suggested that the influence of negotiators depended on more than representational status. Technical expertise was important, persuasiveness counted a great deal, diplomacy, a sense of timing and experience in social dialogue mattered – all had an impact. None of these requirements is prescribed anywhere in NEDLAC documentation, yet they have often proved decisive in securing workable outcomes.

The engine rooms of NEDLAC today remain its four chambers, in which the social partners discuss issues related to the specific portfolio of each chamber. These are the Labour Market Chamber, the Trade and Industry Chamber, the Public Finance and Monetary Policy Chamber, and the Development Chamber.

All in all, the NEDLAC arrangement ('tripartism plus') is more inclusive than those of most other similar institutions elsewhere. In other words, social dialogue and civil dialogue are not as compartmentalised as they are, for example, in the European Union. This inclusivity has both advantages and disadvantages for the functioning of NEDLAC. It has undoubtedly had an important influence on the policy areas to be covered and in the setting of the NEDLAC agenda. It also has protracted the processes and complicated the outcomes.

One of the biggest problems facing the NEDLAC process has been in the arena of communication and mandating. This arises because of the relatively long and complex communication chains and the large number of filters and gatekeepers along the way, which result in something of a 'broken telephone' problem and a lack of understanding of both the issues and the implications of certain policy proposals at the grassroots level of the different constituencies.

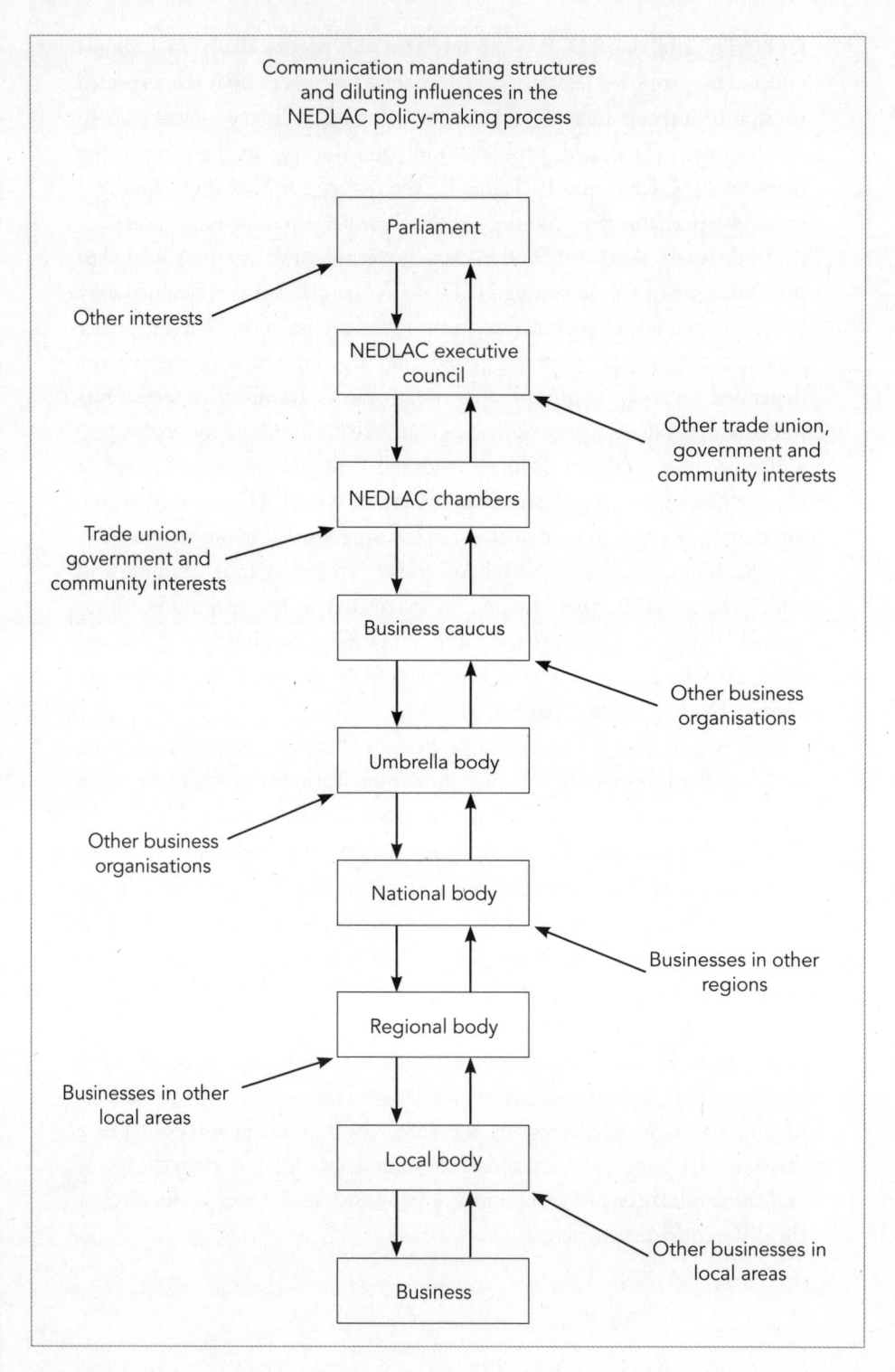

Communication mandating structures and diluting influences in the NEDLAC policy-making process

- Parliament
- NEDLAC executive council
- NEDLAC chambers
- Business caucus
- Umbrella body
- National body
- Regional body
- Local body
- Business

Diluting influences:
- Other interests → Parliament
- Other trade union, government and community interests → NEDLAC executive council
- Trade union, government and community interests → NEDLAC chambers
- Other business organisations → Business caucus
- Other business organisations → Umbrella body
- Businesses in other regions → National body
- Businesses in other local areas → Regional body
- Other businesses in local areas → Local body

Selective overview of NEDLAC's formal outcomes[9]

During NEDLAC's first few years, its main focus was on negotiating the introduction of the government's new labour market policy and legislation. While NEDLAC's labour market processes enjoyed a correspondingly high profile, the Trade and Industry Chamber also began to do important work in the spheres of trade liberalisation, preliminary discussions on the formulation of an industrial strategy, and competition law reform. NEDLAC's agenda slowly broadened over time to include a range of socio-economic matters.

But labour issues predominated. Soon after the 1994 elections, the Labour Minister, Tito Mboweni, initiated a complete overhaul of the South African labour market. Intentions were spelled out in the Department of Labour's five-year plan and commenced with a comprehensive review of the Labour Relations Act (LRA) and the appointment of a Presidential Commission into the Labour Market, on which business was represented.

Due process required that any legislative proposals resulting from either initiative would have to be referred to NEDLAC in due course. However, the proposed far-reaching changes to both the LRA and the Basic Conditions of Employment Act (BCEA) were prematurely rushed into the NEDLAC process – the LRA redraft even before the Presidential Commission had been appointed and the BCEA before the commission had reported.

The first important issue addressed by NEDLAC in 1995 was therefore the draft amending legislation (to revamp the LRA). It proved to be a stern test of the fledgling organisation and, by the same token, of future 'quadrilateralism'. Pressure to reach agreement was heightened by the Minister of Labour setting short deadlines for the completion of negotiations. Less than three months were allocated for the respective parties to reach consensus, a time frame which in the circumstances was rather inadequate. Labour market changes, after all, lay at the crucial intersection of economic, social and political policies and were bound to be a heavily contested terrain requiring careful strategic planning and an integrated approach.

There are two aspects of this early experience in NEDLAC that still need to be stressed. Firstly, the policy underlying the LRA was never properly considered by the Presidential Commission, either on its own terms or as part of the labour law reform process as a whole. Reform of the LRA and the BCEA accordingly went ahead without a thorough labour market evaluation – either in respect of their particular subject matter or in respect of the linkages to other aspects of the labour market, such as skills development and social security.

Secondly, the phased nature of the negotiations precluded presentation and negotiation of a single and coherent package of labour reforms. In part these errors and omissions can be attributed to high expectations that a broad social accord was in fact emerging at the time; in part it was doubtless considered that the early introduction of meaningful reforms would demonstrate the government's commitment to protecting workers in any social accord. As we have seen, there had already been a positive history of social dialogue up to then – and hence there was the real expectation of a broader social accord to stabilise and drive the post-apartheid economy.

The overall accord never materialised. Accordingly, the labour law reform process, albeit always tripartite in composition, was segmented – its different facets being separately introduced and negotiated. Many of the recommendations of the Presidential Commission never saw the light of day. And those recommendations that were introduced (such as the amendment to give the Minister of Labour the discretion to extend sectoral collective agreements) were withdrawn in response to fierce opposition from organised labour. The effect therefore was that the labour law reform process – although necessary – dissolved into piecemeal negotiations, from which several serious unintended socio-economic consequences emerged in subsequent years.

Another important strategic 'gap' in the early days of NEDLAC's operations was that attempts were made to reach agreement on various issues in the absence of an overall framework for economic policy-making. Similar tensions accompanied other elements of the Ministry of Labour's five-year labour programme – such as the BCEA – even after the release in 1996 of the Growth, Employment and Redistribution (GEAR) strategy, which referred to 'a more flexible labour market'.

A decision was taken at the highest level that the implementation of GEAR as a 'stability pact' was urgent and that consultation at various levels would be kept to the minimum. GEAR was regarded as 'non-negotiable' and withheld from NEDLAC. 'I confess that even the ANC learnt of GEAR far too late – when it was almost complete,' Nelson Mandela later said.[10] Whatever the reasons, GEAR did put considerable strain on the NEDLAC processes. If economic policy becomes an ideology, it turns practical matters into issues of principle.

The organised labour constituency felt its positions were indeed being threatened by several of the policy choices made in GEAR, which it considered too market-friendly. Union leaders began to use their influence within the ANC-led alliance to reopen negotiations on the strategy.[11] The fact that certain Cabinet ministers were known to be ambivalent about the GEAR strategy gave organised labour additional leverage. Comments made at the time by some senior government representatives at COSATU meetings suggested that organised labour had some success in generating equivocal official attitudes about GEAR. It also frustrated the work of the Public Finance and Monetary Policy Chamber in NEDLAC for several years. Within NEDLAC this chamber became the lightning conductor for opposition to GEAR.

While the lack of an overall shared vision has not prevented the development of a problem-solving approach by NEDLAC participants to specific policy issues, it has often generated considerable tension in NEDLAC. Yet a dialogue that becomes problem-solving and practical can produce limited consensus, even where there are deep underlying conflicts of interest, and even where there may be no shared understanding at the outset. Experience also suggests that adopting that approach to achieving consensus in one sphere often encourages a similar attitude towards other areas of policy. NEDLAC has been both a steep learning curve and a strong intellectual challenge in policy-making.

Hence, over the past twenty-three years, NEDLAC – as the portal of entry into social dialogue in South Africa – has found itself driven into an ever-widening socio-economic agenda as its processes have developed. It probably has the most complex agenda of any public institution in South Africa. It has had both successes and failures and has undoubtedly also been a source of deep frustration for NEDLAC participants. In practice, it was not only to become an institution in which to reach formal agreements, but also to evolve into a potential instrument of consultation and coordination regarding several policy issues.

Emergence of the Millennium Labour Council

One of the spin-offs from the broader commitment to social dialogue in South Africa was the formation of the Millennium Labour Council (MLC) in 2000. In its bilateral business–labour interaction, the MLC has been a source of both cooperation and conflict in the social dialogue process.

In the late 1990s Charles Nupen – student leader, activist, lawyer and mediator – took a group of labour and business leaders on a trip to two countries in which social dialogue had contributed to both economic growth and social cohesion. The countries were Ireland and Holland. These visits clearly made a deep impression on these leaders, who included on the business side Anglo's Nicky Oppenheimer and Rembrandt's Johan Rupert. In July 2000, the group established the MLC, which was officially launched by President Thabo Mbeki. In the agreement establishing the council these business and labour leaders noted: 'The current unemployment, job losses and lack of job creation constitute a deepening crisis in South Africa that requires urgent action. Current levels of poverty and inequality are unacceptable and new initiatives are needed to promote improved quality of life and decent work for all.'[12]

The council's first chairs were Zwelinzima Vavi (COSATU) and Leslie Boyd (SACOB). More recently, FEDUSA presidents Koos Bezuidenhout and Godfrey Selematsela have chaired for labour and Bobby Godsell for business respectively. The council has about twelve members from business and labour who serve in their personal capacity. It meets four times a year.

Since its inception there has been tension between this leadership group and NEDLAC. Inevitably, those not involved in MLC meetings are suspicious of what transpires behind those closed doors. The purpose of the MLC is to promote social dialogue, but not to enter into formal negotiations or reach binding agreements. Again, this produces an uncomfortable tension. Nevertheless, the council has played an important role in occasionally helping to unblock negotiations in NEDLAC when necessary.

At present the MLC is doing homework on four issues which could eventually feature in formal negotiations around the concept of the National Development Plan's proposed 'social compact'. These four issues are higher levels of inclusive economic growth; workplace transformation; gender and race-based violence; and governance and leadership, particularly in the state-owned enterprises.

The MLC is seen as a fragile structure. Given the deep divisions in the society that it serves, the fact that it has survived for eighteen years is surprising. Its lack of decision-making powers is a frustration to some members. However, the lack of mandated positions and ritualised negotiating tactics provides opportunities for frank and often spirited debate, and this is viewed as a strength. Also, the continuity of membership has built both personal relationships and trust.

Evaluation of the role of NEDLAC – and its future

Any assessment of NEDLAC's role since its formation in 1995 would be bound to reflect an overall perspective on the South African economy, politics and society in the intervening years. NEDLAC and social dialogue over this period have undoubtedly attracted critics; and to give the most strident of them their day in court, the most sweeping of all possible questions must be posed: Would South Africa have been better off without NEDLAC?

While much more empirical analysis is clearly needed to evaluate NEDLAC's interventions in specific policy matters, and how they may have influenced policy outcomes over the years, the interim and overall qualitative answer must be no. Without the conflict management potential of a structure like NEDLAC, the transition to a successful democracy would have been, to say the least, trickier than it proved to be, given South Africa's political history.

Indeed, it could be argued that the recurring spectacle of labour and capital sitting down together to discuss policy under the auspices of NEDLAC was reassuring to investor confidence at the time. It has rightly been emphasised that South Africa has been broadly able, through sound monetary and fiscal policies, to inject more certainty and predictability into the policy environment. Less credit, however, has been given to the contribution of institutionalised social dialogue to perceptions of stability.

Economies are vulnerable during their transition phases. There are difficult perceptions to handle, in what are often periods of acute uncertainty. We must accept that – in moving from a 'closed' regime to an 'open' one – a country usually has to go through a transitional period that may require its leaders to expend huge amounts of political capital with no guarantee of success. NEDLAC helped make a difference here. While NEDLAC did not govern the country, it arguably helped to keep it governable.

It is nonetheless evident from an analysis of the NEDLAC experience over this period that there are a number of quite fundamental issues on which the NEDLAC constituencies have remained divided. But there have been policy areas – as the agreements already reached and reports issued amply confirm – where there has been a high degree of commonality of interests and views, and it has therefore been worth the trouble of placing them on the NEDLAC agenda. Social dialogue must be seen as a means to an end, not an end in itself.

Has social dialogue made a quantifiable difference to South Africa's economic performance since 1994, at least in the formative years? It is extremely difficult to link a specific institution or feature on the national landscape to a particular set of economic results. It is really not possible to establish a direct correlation between extensive peak-level social dialogue and higher economic growth rates or a rising human development index. All that can safely be said of South Africa is that the average economic growth rate was negligible in the early 1990s and rose to about 2.5 per cent in the six-year period post-1994 – and, furthermore, that the acceleration of growth over, say, the period 2003–7 is arguably an extremely significant reflection of the groundwork that took place in the earlier period.

To the extent that certain processes, such as NEDLAC, promoted social stability and reduced perceived country risk, they must have made a positive contribution. South Africa's international credit ratings (delivered by, for example, Moody's, S&P and Fitch) did slowly begin to improve in the early years and subsequently returned increasingly favourable verdicts on the South African economy. These are developments, in a period that has been historically designated as one of 'consensual stability', to which NEDLAC contributed. Consensual stability helped to reduce uncertainty and raise expected returns on investment.

But economic and political circumstances have changed. Every opportunity has to be taken to reassess the role of institutionalised social dialogue and NEDLAC in South Africa. How well has NEDLAC done? Where has NEDLAC failed and why? What are the boundaries of social dialogue in South Africa? Do we still need NEDLAC? Have institutions like NEDLAC, in other countries, been tested by differences as deep as those that still exist here? How should NEDLAC in future structure its contribution to policy, and is the institution adequately resourced to carry out its mandate? Does NEDLAC sufficiently publicise its successes? Should it still be located in the Ministry of Labour or should it now be moved to the Office of the Presidency or Deputy Presidency?

We must acknowledge the recent strong criticisms that have again been levelled against NEDLAC:

- According to Michael Spicer (Vice-President of BLSA), 'NEDLAC has been "suicidal" for the country ... NEDLAC confirms all the bad biases of the economy and exacerbates unemployment, but it buys you the appearance of stability. So, for short-term peace you end up undermining the long-term stability of the economy.'[13]
- As stated in Claire Bisseker's *On the Brink*, Roger Baxter (CEO of the Chamber of Mines), 'agreed that NEDLAC, as construed then, was a total waste of time. It entrenches the positions of big business, big government, big labour and one has to ask, as Pravin Gordhan did in NEDLAC on the February (2016) budget, whether, by each constituency continuing to hammer on about the same issues from the narrow perspective year after year, we are really making progress?'[14]

These criticisms of social dialogue in general, and NEDLAC in particular, should be read and pondered by all who want to promote social cohesion in South Africa – even if some of the readers decide not so much to share their critics' assessment, as to make sure they are proved wrong.

But have diminishing returns now set in for NEDLAC? Has the 'golden triangle' of earlier years become a Bermuda triangle? At least two in-depth studies of NEDLAC (2006 and 2013) led by Professor Eddie Webster of the University of the Witwatersrand have traversed the terrain of social dialogue and NEDLAC thoroughly, and made recommendations for constructive changes. Organised business, together with labour, made wide-ranging inputs to improve the functioning of NEDLAC, reflecting their concern that NEDLAC was operating sub-optimally.

Financial Mail, September 1995 (Author's personal collection)

In their 2013 report titled 'Repositioning Peak-Level Social Dialogue in South Africa: NEDLAC into the Future', Professor Webster and his colleagues warned:

> In light of the shift in the policy-making processes post-Polokwane, the global economic crisis that began in 2008 and the growing wave of unrest, both workplace and around service delivery over the last five years, this report revisits the 2006 External Review of the National Economic Development and Labour Council (NEDLAC). Indeed, some commentators have attributed the growing unrest to a failure of social dialogue. NEDLAC constituencies, in particular government and business, are increasingly concerned about whether the costs of NEDLAC outweigh its benefit as a peak-level social dialogue institution.

Based on the in-depth interviews with key NEDLAC informants, we have identified the main challenges facing NEDLAC. We presented the first draft of the report and recommendations to each of the four NEDLAC constituencies separately and incorporated their feedback into the report. We conclude that NEDLAC is an institution that could help to overcome the current policy stalemate. To move forward, all social partners need to recognise this impasse. Until this happens, the kinds of shifts that are necessary by all constituencies will not take place. One of the roles of NEDLAC is to provide an independent space for all the partners to develop a common vision on the way forward.[15]

There remains a serious message here about the functioning of NEDLAC. For if function declines, so also do status and influence. NEDLAC still needs to identify the bottlenecks and constraints in the institution's functioning that generate frustration within and between its main stakeholders. There is no doubt that key changes are needed if NEDLAC is to deliver on its mandate and remain relevant to the national agenda. In particular, ways must be sought to ensure that NEDLAC becomes an active driver of effective dialogue, rather than just its passive custodian. The fact that social cohesion in South Africa has deteriorated to the extent that it has in recent years inevitably raises fundamental questions about the efficiency, relevance and credibility of NEDLAC in the critical current times.

As pointed out earlier, NEDLAC is only one of two social dialogue structures globally that are negotiating instead of advisory bodies. The question must be posed whether many of the problems that have developed around NEDLAC's role and effectiveness have arisen from its commitment to negotiation, with all the logistics that this involves. It is not something to be dogmatic about, but it would be useful to debate the advantages and disadvantages of the two approaches in respect of NEDLAC's efficacy and capacity to meet deadlines.

There is also the long-standing problem that business perceives as arising from the fact that COSATU, as a major participant in the labour constituency, has been in a formal political alliance with the ANC and the SACP. This has proved problematic over the years, in that a key labour component like COSATU has doubled up as a social partner at one level. This perceived lack of a level playing field in NEDLAC has helped determine how business has come to see NEDLAC. From the business perspective this has contributed to the difficulties experienced in arriving at consensual outcomes in NEDLAC.

The ability and capacity of the constituencies in NEDLAC, including business, to respond effectively to NEDLAC's expanding agenda – and to do so within strict time frames – has also become a severely limiting factor in NEDLAC's efficacy. Additional pressure has arisen from the differing schedules of NEDLAC, the Cabinet and Parliament and the failure to coordinate them. This has hampered NEDLAC's outcomes. Despite reaching a landmark agreement on a national minimum wage (which still needs to be implemented), NEDLAC does not usually enjoy a good press.

Professor Mzukisi Qobo of the University of Johannesburg believes that NEDLAC has reached its 'sell-by date' and that a new organisation, consisting of a looser formation of business, government and labour, should take its place. 'There are tensions among the social partners and a trust deficit, which means that the mechanisms in place, such as NEDLAC, are no longer relevant. It was a transitional arrangement, but now we need a social compact.'[16] Ultimately social cohesion can only be gained if all stakeholders are prepared to adopt a longer-term perspective and accept the need for some sacrifices to attain it.

The National Development Programme (NDP) proposes a 'social compact' marked by equity and inclusion, for which it says a number of conditions need to be in place. As is apparent, it is the absence of many of these requirements in South Africa that has so far hampered the maturing of social dialogue in general and the proper functioning of NEDLAC in particular. A successful social compact will require a much greater degree of convergence on aims and means than has hitherto been possible in the country. The NDP rightly concludes that this says a great deal about the history of the country and the general lack of trust.

The quality of social dialogue in South Africa undoubtedly needs to be enhanced. Social dialogue should not just be about what various participants demand of each other, but also about how they can add value to longer-run solutions in the face of otherwise seemingly intractable situations. Nonetheless, trust must extend beyond the formal institutions that espouse it, as important as these institutions are. Despite the lip service paid to social dialogue in South Africa, there are still too many destructive attacks on certain stakeholders, which seem to reflect a visceral hostility towards them. The effect of the use of pejorative codewords like 'white monopoly capital' is that they dismiss rather than refute. One problem is that much of the demonisation of business does not lend itself to factual settlement and is in fact a proxy for other issues.

One of the major lessons of a mixed economy is that capital and labour need to coexist, which means they must get beyond caricatures and narrow self-interest, and seek to fundamentally understand each other better. They remain too important and too interdependent to do anything else. Power, shared accountability and responsibility require cooperative behaviour from all participants.

There is indeed a time for robust and sharp debate, but there is even greater potential for constructive cooperation on issues of common interest. This must be the mantra for the future. The breakdown of trust into unpredictable and negative behaviour turns too many processes into a game in which all lose. Consensual stability needs to be restored. Corporatism must generate sufficient consensus in ways that reduce conflict. Success depends on minimising disputes, not winning them. This is how someone experienced in the methods of advocacy and compromise expressed it colourfully some decades ago:

> I suggest [he said] that things get done gradually only between opposing forces. There is no such thing as self-restraint in people. What looks like it is indecision ... It may be that truth is best sought in the market of free speech, but the best decisions are neither bought nor sold. They are the results of disagreement, where the last word is not 'I admit you're right', but 'I've got to live with the son of a bitch, haven't I?'[17]

In the bigger picture, South Africa is not so much at a crossroads as at a T-junction, and we will now need to make key choices about the future direction of our economy and our society. We need to find within ourselves the magic with which to transform and direct our economy towards the 5 per cent, 6 per cent and even higher average growth rate, as some leading emerging economies have done. The NDP, for example, offers us a vision for 2030 that needs to be translated into reality through a collaborative effort.

We must nonetheless ensure that social dialogue does not become a smokescreen for procrastination or inaction but rather a spur to better outcomes. We need to encourage institutions and mechanisms so that, however much talk is put into one end, they grind out decisions and implement them within reasonable timelines at the other end.

The challenge facing NEDLAC and scores of other committees in South Africa which engage in endless debates without always reaching a conclusion is amusingly summed up as follows:

> Oh, give me your pity – I'm on a committee, which means that from morning to night,
> We attend and amend and contend and defend without a conclusion in sight,
> We confer and concur, we defer and demur and reiterate all our thoughts,
> We revise the agenda with frequent addenda and consider a load of reports,
> We compose and propose, we suppose and oppose, and the points of procedure are fun,
> But though various notions are brought up as motions, there's terribly little gets done,
> We resolve and absolve, but never dissolve, since it's out of the question for us,
> What a shattering pity to end our committee – where else can we make such a fuss?[18]

It is effective social dialogue that will provide the essential mechanism to reduce the trust deficit in South Africa. We need to build more trust among major stakeholders in the economy, including an active citizenry, to help provide the ideas, commitment and leadership needed to lift South Africa beyond current dogmas, tensions and disputes. In this way, we can build on our strengths and address our weaknesses as a country by tackling problems jointly.

This is not something that is merely 'nice' to do but, as the NDP emphasises, is imperative in building a climate of solidarity to achieve superior outcomes and better delivery. Globally, building trust is closely associated with stronger economic performance and social stability. In turn, there remain the irreducible elements of a shared responsibility in South Africa, because a united and cohesive society is an essential prerequisite for peace and prosperity.

What might frequently be seen as evidence of solidarity and unity in South Africa seems to be event-driven rather than organically based. Focal points like the advent of democracy in 1994, the Rugby World Cup victory in 1995, the global economic crisis in 2008, the staging of the Soccer World Cup in 2010, the death of Madiba in 2013 – these events appear to bring the nation together for a brief moment and give us a glimpse of what might be possible. Yet we appear unable to sustain it for long or to capitalise on it. It soon relapses into underlying tension, conflict and polarisation, with solidarity hanging by a thin rope waiting for the next big event to give it another temporary boost. Unity in South Africa is rather like Tarzan of the Jungle swinging precariously from tree to tree, with big spaces in between.

We need to root our sense of solidarity more deeply by strengthening the structures through which we are meant to collaborate and collectively work on an ongoing basis, thus being less dependent just on events to display intermittent unity. When assessing the imperfect and half-forged mechanisms of social dialogue in South Africa, we should always pause and ask the question: What is the alternative? The reform or restructuring of an institution like NEDLAC needs to be seen in this broader context if it is to make its maximum contribution to social cohesion.

5

From organised to disorganised business: What has gone wrong?

> Do not judge me by my successes, judge me by how many times
> I fell down and got up again.
> – NELSON MANDELA

AFTER A PROMISING START IN THE 1990s with the roll-out of the new democratic dispensation in South Africa under the leadership of Nelson Mandela, organised business has become more and more fragmented as time has gone by. In fact, the level of instability in the organised business movement today is at an all-time high, with several multisectoral bodies at the national, provincial and local levels having overlapping or conflicting interests and mandates. This has created a fair amount of confusion in the marketplace.

According to Joan Warburton-McBride, chief executive of the Johannesburg Chamber of Commerce and Industry (JCCI), 'The level of splintering and competition within the organised business movement in South Africa is unprecedented given the size of the country.'[1] Not surprisingly, this has weakened various organisations' influence and called into question their future sustainability. What has gone wrong?

A country divided

The fragmented character of the organised business movement in South Africa is in many ways the inevitable by-product of the significant schisms in society. The last decade has been far from easy for the country and large swathes of the population. Battered by strong and unpredictable political and economic headwinds, South Africa has veered well off the path that was laid out for it in a series of socio-economic plans, especially the National Development Plan (NDP).

Today South Africa remains a seriously conflicted country. Many opposing ideologies are circulating over what economic system and governance standards should prevail, and what contribution private businesses and state-owned enterprises should be making in growing the South African economy and redressing past injustices. Racial tensions are ever present and social cohesion is an elusive goal. Even the ruling party, the ANC, has become increasingly divided in recent years, while its once-solid alliance with COSATU and the SACP is under considerable strain.

Fanning the flames of discontent have been the growing revelations of corruption – often at the highest levels – with state-owned enterprises in particular being at the centre of brazen (and often successful) attempts by a political elite to enrich themselves at the expense of the people of South Africa and of the country's economic future. Corruption, of course, is not new. It has been a feature of all previous administrations in South Africa. But the fact that it has become so pervasive and so blatant points to the virtual collapse of ethical governance and oversight in the country. Whether for political expediency or from a sense of outrage, people from across the political and socio-economic spectrums have not been reluctant to express their anger, fears and frustrations over what has become an untenable – but in many ways preventable – situation.

Corruption is often referred to as a cancer, with the phenomenon of state capture having emerged, like an ugly growth, as one of its nastiest and most destructive manifestations yet. State capture, however, does not paint the full picture, since many businesses and individuals have clearly been captured as well, in a complex web of dubious or illegal transactions involving powerful people in government and the private sector who have abused their power.

And the extent to which in recent years key law-enforcement agencies have been undermined has increasingly had an impact on the private sector. If senior persons in the public sector escape criminal sanctions for wrongdoing, it also means that bad acts in the business sector have a better chance of avoiding detection as well. The 'policemen of the marketplace' may also have become compromised.

South Africa has reached a critical point. A few short years after the death of Nelson Mandela, who used to be a constant reminder of what could be achieved if there was a steady focus on reconciliation, South Africa has been witnessing growing divisions between groups of people on the basis of ideological principles, political loyalties, race and socio-economic circumstances. It is as if previous attempts to heal the wounds of the past have been exposed as too superficial, with pent-up hurt and resentment resurfacing – only this time with a new level of ferocity.

The loss of focus on nation-building and the fallout evidenced in rising unemployment and deepening poverty and inequality have been taking South Africa backwards, whereas – with its gift of hindsight – the country should be setting an example to other countries that are trying to move out of a torrid political past. Organised business could and should be one of the leaders of such a process, working from an agenda that sets out to help dissolve, not aggravate, tensions in the country.

Resource limitations

Being an effective representative of business requires financial, human and physical resources. Although not a universal norm, in South Africa membership of a chamber or business association is voluntary. This invariably leads to limited funds for operations or expansion, a small staff complement to carry out what might be quite a broad and complex mandate, and a relatively small membership base. In a weak economic climate when downsizing and cost-cutting are the order of the day, membership numbers tend to dwindle even more. The growing dysfunctionality of many municipalities (and frequent service delivery protests) can partly be attributed to the deterioration in organised business coverage in many parts of South Africa and the erosion of links with relevant tiers of government.

Given the frequent need to supplement the revenue from membership fees and commercial services with external grants – such as research funding from the International Labour Organization (ILO) or South Africa's National Skills Fund, which inevitably steers work programmes in particular directions – chambers and business associations run the risk of their attention being diverted from the immediate needs of their constituencies. This could prompt a further decline in membership if there

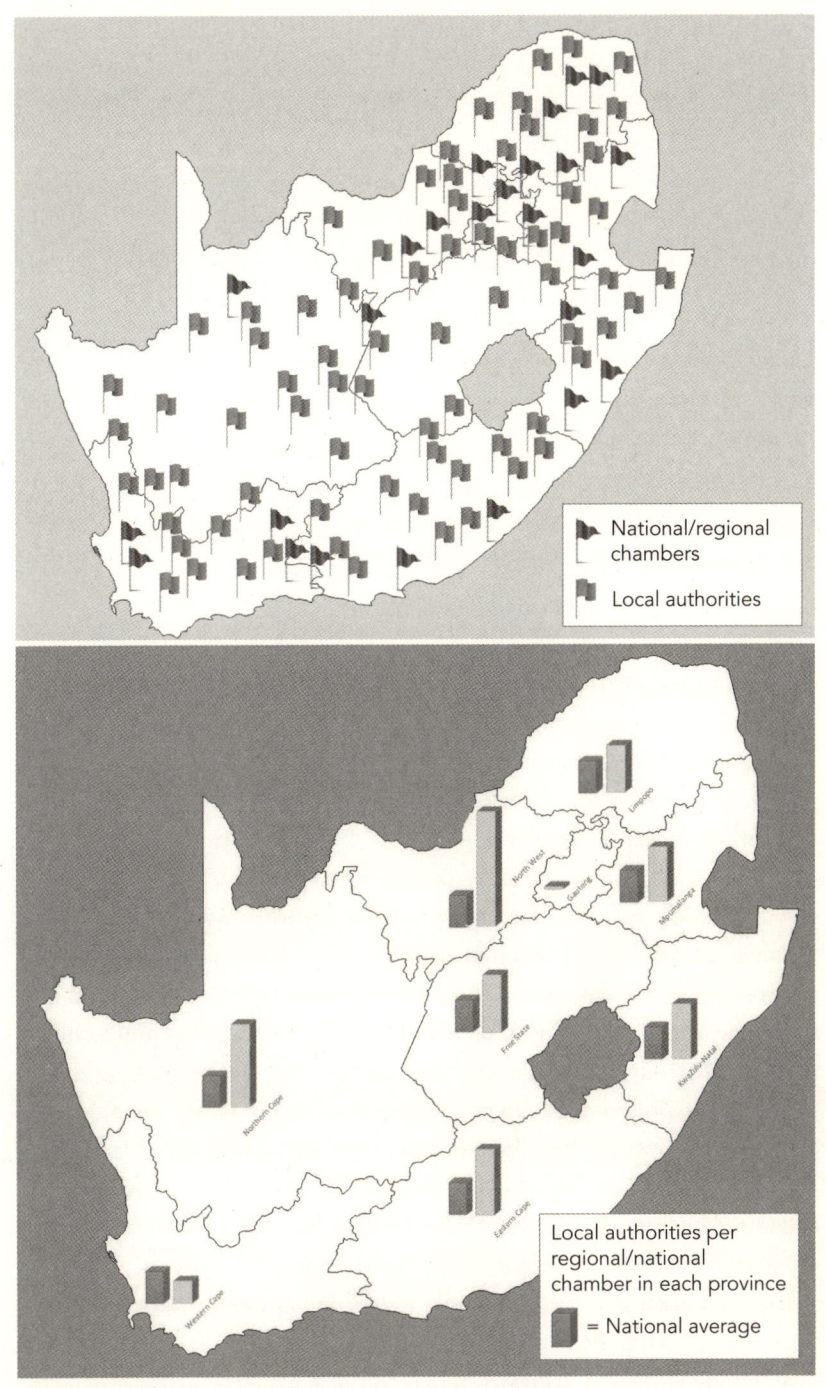

Maps indicating disproportionately low representation of national/regional chambers to local authorities (a ratio of 1:7)
Source: Jacob van Rensburg, North-West University Business School, 2018

is a perception that key focus areas are the object of neglect. Even when there is a sizeable membership base derived from a confederation structure – such as in BUSA's case – there are many gatekeepers, whose presence elongates and compromises communication channels and dilutes impact.

With generally thinly stretched resources, organised business entities often find it difficult to meet their members' expectations. Not only do members require chambers and other representative bodies to be attentive and to keep them apprised of important issues and events, they also expect them to deliver value for money by continually adapting their services to keep pace with industry and technological developments.

For example, the increasingly dispersed approach to production in the world today, which is a hallmark of the global value chain phenomenon, and the ever-expanding array of business opportunities in different regions call for a more tailor-made, as opposed to a standardised, approach. The tailored approach, though, can consume considerable resources, which is not always feasible for a small organisation.

Although recent years have seen organised business representing a shrinking proportion of businesses in South Africa, a number of new structures have nevertheless sprung up, catering to different interest groups with different mindsets and expectations. This has placed even greater pressure on the already limited talent pool from which presidents and other board members are drawn. Board positions in organised business structures in South Africa are voluntary, that is, they offer no remuneration, but they do carry fiduciary responsibilities under the Companies Act. As a result, it is difficult to find willing candidates.

Top positions are particularly prone to high turnover. Many years ago, when the organised business movement in South Africa was more unified and made stronger inroads into the government policy-making space, leaders of representative bodies typically occupied their positions for stable periods, which helped to create continuity. The kind of leadership that came to the fore in previous years is no longer available. Today, many organised business leaders have to contend with encroaching competition from other structures (often in the same geographical area), shrinking market share, a highly uncertain policy environment, and strained relations with the government – all of which diminish their ability to effectively channel the views of business.

It is much harder to make a difference. Insufficient personal incentive and high frustration levels often play out in short job tenures and sometimes a debilitating loss of expertise to the organisation and its members. The 'revolving door' leadership pattern means that every so often much of the institutional memory is lost, with every new appointment heralding the adoption of a new management style and fresh attempts at understanding and serving the constituency in question and reaching out to the government and other social partners. It makes it difficult to build credibility.

Generally, resource constraints and frequent leadership changes have made it difficult for several organised business bodies to carve out or retain a clear identity for themselves, and to develop meaningful traction with their natural constituencies. In such a climate, name changes are quite common (which need not be a problem unless introduced too often), with certain organisations opting for an identity overhaul. For example, SACOB changed its name to SACCI some years ago, while the Afrikaanse Handelsinstituut (AHI) recently became the Small Business Institute (SBI), with a new mandate to represent the interests of South Africa's small and medium-sized businesses and with a new slogan: 'Big voice of small business'.

Changing market requirements

As society evolves, multisectoral bodies like SACCI, JCCI and others face the ongoing challenge of conveying relevant and in-demand information and advice. Twenty years ago, before information was as freely available as it is today, chambers of commerce and business associations were an important source of information on industry trends, market opportunities and government regulations affecting different economic sectors. Sourcing such information used to be time-consuming and costly for many companies, with the result that they valued the varied information offerings that formed the basis of chambers' membership and supplementary service packages.

With so much more information now accessible via the Internet, thanks to great leaps in technology – particularly on the digitisation front – people are increasingly relying on their own research skills to access information. Alternatively, they approach sectoral bodies (which are not the focus of this book) for more specific, sector-relevant information. Even the value of some chambers' and other business associations' networking events are diminishing as people gravitate more and more towards social media as core information and business tools.

The growing popularity of social media has changed the way people associate with one another, eroding the perceived value of and demand for traditional, face-to-face consultations and networking events. Furthermore, the fact that many of the businesses that organised business is designed to serve compete with one another makes it difficult to determine a common vision and harmonised set of needs.

Yet over and above their information-dispensing role, chambers of commerce and other representative bodies have a duty to promote the interests of the businesses they represent – particularly at the policy-making level. In this regard, they should act as conduits for raising awareness about generic or even sector-specific needs and challenges, and as promoters of innovative solutions that resonate with the country's growth and development goals. This, though, inevitably gives rise to the 'free-rider' problem where non-members derive benefits from a chamber's efforts (together with government) to, say, streamline business registration procedures or improve public service delivery in a certain geographical area.

These days, too, large and influential businesses are finding it less necessary to work through a representative organisation in order to connect with foreign investors, local municipalities or national government – many will approach them directly. With policy-making – via NEDLAC and other policy-driven structures – having drifted into the ambit of 'big business', organised business has lost ground. Contributing to this is the growing belief that organised business is no longer able to roll back ill-conceived policies and excessive regulatory burdens because it lacks sufficient political clout.

The informalisation of work is another factor denting the appeal of joining chambers and other multisectoral bodies. In South Africa, a growing number of people are taking up pursuits in the informal sector as opportunities in the formal economy dwindle. However, by operating under the radar as unregistered producers and traders, informal businesses remain largely unrepresented and marginalised at the policy level. From street waste pickers to tailors and painters, the informal sector could play a much more significant role in recognised supply chains, but they often remain in the shadows and operate independently with a limited and sporadic customer base and poor growth prospects.

Another factor at work could be the extent to which urbanisation over the years has steadily drained rural towns of the leadership and participation needed to sustain local chambers. But there is no evidence to suggest that urban or peri-urban chambers have been correspondingly strengthened.

Underperformance of the small business sector

According to the Small Business Institute (SBI) chairman, Bernard Swanepoel, the small business sector accounts for 95 per cent of all businesses in South Africa and contributes at least 40 per cent to the country's GDP. Small business development is a popular topic on policy agendas, while several government agencies and private sector organisations profess to promote the interests of, and provide support to, small businesses. But even a simple repeated commitment, for example, requiring the public sector to pay its bills to suppliers within 30 days has proved hard to implement, although it remains important for the cash flow and survival of small enterprises.

Most small businesses, though plentiful in number, continue to underperform and few make the transition into more sizeable operations that are able to take on additional employees on a sustainable basis. The failure rate in the early years is also high due to insufficient funding and business or financial management acumen, and a lack of awareness of or access to market opportunities. As small businesses – often collectively referred to as SMMEs (small, medium and micro enterprises) – make up a sizeable proportion of the actual and prospective membership or client base of chambers of commerce and business associations, their general incapacity is another factor that works against the attempts of organised business to swell its membership numbers. In fact, the general instability in the SMME sector means that the membership of chambers and business associations is continuously under threat. In such a climate, it is difficult to make representations on behalf of SMMEs.

There is no clear-cut definition of an SMME but it generally refers to a business entity that operates with limited resources and generates modest returns in comparison with larger corporates and multinationals. A common (though imperfect) criterion for determining whether a business falls into the SMME category is the number of employees it has. In South Africa, an SMME is typically viewed as a business with up to 100 employees, with a medium enterprise employing between 50 and 100 people, a small enterprise employing between 10 and 50 people, and a micro enterprise employing fewer than 10 people. The difficulty in arriving at a reliable picture of the SMME sector lies in the fact that it has an extremely diverse character, is very fluid (because firms come and go), and is made up of many informal businesses whose activities are not easily tracked.

The dearth of research material and formal statistics on the SMME sector is a serious problem because policy-making flows from very broad and possibly unreliable assumptions. On the subject of SMMEs, Bernard Swanepoel has said: 'We don't know how many exist, how many people they employ, whether they are growing or contracting, what sectors they dominate and what challenges they face.' Adopting the right policy positions, therefore, is extremely difficult. Anecdotal evidence suggests that onerous regulations and procedures constitute a major factor in SMMEs' inability or unwillingness to expand their operations.

We would imagine that with SMMEs accounting for such a sizeable slice of the total business pie, more determined efforts would have been made to peel away the layers of red tape that often confront these firms, both when starting out and later when their businesses are up and running. However, progress has been slow. Swanepoel adds that, very often, in government's attempts to assist SMMEs, more layers of bureaucracy are added. There needs to be a much closer relationship between small business, or the organisations that claim to represent them, and the Ministry of Small Business Development.

The World Economic Forum's 'Global Competitiveness Index 2017–2018' highlights how poorly South Africa fares in terms of its regulatory efficiency. For example, under 'Number of procedures to start a business', South Africa ranked 70 out of 137 countries (compared with Rwanda at 36/137 and Mauritius at 53/137); under 'Time to start a business', South Africa ranked 125 out of 137 countries (compared with Rwanda at 12/137 and Mauritius at 35/137); and under 'Burden of government regulation',

South Africa ranked 89 out of 137 (compared with Rwanda at 3/137 and Mauritius at 51/137). Against the first two measures, South Africa's performance has deteriorated sharply over the past two years.

Business success in South Africa should not have to depend on the extent to which it has to navigate a morass of regulations and interactions with bureaucracy. 'Smart tape rather than red tape' should be the maxim. The regulatory environment with which SMMEs have to contend has proved to be particularly harsh in certain sectors. The private higher education sector in South Africa is a case in point, as little attempt has been made by government to differentiate between small educational institutions, which are often legally constituted as non-profit companies, and large, well-resourced ones.

In terms of current legislation, private higher education providers – if they wish to offer programmes that lead to qualifications – must be registered and accredited with the higher education and quality assurance authorities. These are very costly and time-consuming exercises. Providers are also subject to complex annual reporting requirements, which include having to produce a formal financial guarantee (with bank-supported evidence) to the effect that a sizeable percentage of the value of the tuition fees for a calendar year is available in a special bank account, which can be withdrawn at short notice should anything happen to the institution in question and students have to be compensated for not being able to complete their studies that year.

For small providers, this requirement has often been crippling from a cash-flow point of view and has forced many to diversify into non-qualification educational services. It is a tragedy that the private education sector (which plays such an important role in building knowledge and helping firms to enhance their competitiveness) has had to bear the brunt of such ill-advised regulations – particularly as these regulations have not appeared to generate useful or accessible data which might contribute to a better understanding of the small business sector in South Africa. Other sectors have been similarly affected by poor consultation processes and unbalanced decision-making.

Where South Africa should be providing a supportive environment for small businesses, fear of the cost and time involved in formal business registration and ongoing regulatory compliance has driven many entrepreneurs and small businesses into the anonymity of the informal sector. The recent creation of the SBI out of the old AHI seems like a good idea, since having a business association in the small business sector's corner will be an advantage. Yet getting the formula right and delivering value to this highly diverse collection of firms will be challenging.

The proposed changes to competition law to tackle the challenge of excessive concentration in the economy in order to drive inclusive economic growth and transformation are presently under review. The aim is to open up markets to *new* small businesses, particularly black-owned businesses, to facilitate participation in the economy through a different approach to competition policy. There are two policy goals here: to keep economic power from being overly concentrated – which is relevant to transformation – and to ensure that those who control economic resources are capable of using them efficiently. These are not always compatible goals.

Growing friction between business and government

There is no doubt that the increasingly fragile relationship between business and the government over the years is one of the main reasons for the organised business sector in South Africa losing its common purpose and much of its clout. The origins of the deteriorating relationship between business and government are complex, going back many years.

The Centre for Development and Enterprise (CDE) has frequently emphasised the extent to which the root of the problems in business–government relations has been in historical fault lines, based on racism, which generate a variety of interest groups as well as organisations: the relationship seems to have moved in cycles over the decades. However, it is over the past decade that things have taken a particular turn for the worse in several ways.

Earlier chapters have revealed how, before South Africa's transition to democracy, organised business often took the lead in exerting pressure on the National Party government to jettison its apartheid policies. In the 1980s, at the height of the sanctions campaign against South Africa, the economy was dominated by a few conglomerates, including Anglo American and Rembrandt, which were very influential and more or less of the same mind when it came to knowing what was needed to bring about political, economic and social change in the country. Thus, organised business was able to communicate a reasonably holistic, streamlined message during its interactions with the government in the run-up to the 1994 elections.

The Mandela years: The honeymoon period

When Nelson Mandela was released from prison in 1990, he announced that nationalisation (of, for example, mines and banks) was accepted ANC policy. However, he was soon conveying a much more pragmatic message, saying that South Africans should respect the business sector. Having assumed the presidency, Mandela faced the challenge of rehabilitating an economy that had been severely weakened by apartheid and sanctions. The country had also accumulated huge debts from its military excursions around southern Africa. The economy therefore had to attract foreign investment and generally boost investor confidence. While economic growth and investment during Mandela's time were fairly modest, the foundations were laid for a new spirit of reconciliation in the country, which was considered the priority at the time.

As outlined especially in the previous chapter, business was widely viewed as the anchor that would help to steady the economy as well as a key player in the reconciliation process:

> Without the involvement of the private investor, the South African economy will not grow and will therefore not be able to address the needs that confront the masses of our people. Equally, we are aware that the investor will not invest until he or she is assured of the security of their investment. This and many other things have to be guaranteed to ensure that the necessary levels of investor confidence are attained.[2]

After 1994, with Nelson Mandela at the helm of the new ANC-led administration, organised business assumed an advisory role vis-à-vis the government and for a while remained active in consultative forums and policy-making circles. However, when Mandela stepped aside to make way for a new administration under the leadership of Thabo Mbeki, the cordial bilateral relationship (even in the face of ideological differences) between the government and the business sector began to shift, as did the influence that organised business structures once enjoyed.

The Mbeki years: A case of betwixt and between?

During the Mbeki era, from 1998 to 2008, business–government relationships were characterised as cordial and quite formal, becoming increasingly distant as time went by. This was despite the more business-friendly Growth, Employment and Redistribution (GEAR) strategy, which had been introduced in 1996 after the Reconstruction and Development Programme (RDP) was abandoned. The Congress of South African Trade Unions (COSATU), a member of the formal Tripartite Alliance, had persuaded the ANC to adopt the RDP in return for the support of the trade unions in the 1994 elections. Much like the South African Communist Party (SACP), the other member of the Tripartite Alliance, COSATU represented the economic left wing of the alliance and over the years has been very critical of what it has perceived to be the 'neoliberal' orientation of the ANC.

Whereas the RDP was intended to address South Africa's many socio-economic problems, which had flowed from the apartheid government's policies of racial discrimination, GEAR emphasised the pursuit of economic growth through fiscal restraint, the gradual relaxation of exchange controls, tariff reductions, tax cuts to encourage investment and stimulate business activity, and privatisation. It also advocated a smaller role for the government in the economy.

The corporate sector, in turn, underwent a restructuring process, moving to some extent away from the conglomerate approach, which had dominated the pre-transition period, towards one that attempted to pave the way for more competition and greater participation by marginalised groups. Although the introduction of GEAR drew the ire of COSATU and the SACP, it soothed (initially at least) national and international capital markets and resonated with much of the (largely white) business community.

In 1999, Thabo Mbeki established the Big Business Working Group as a vehicle for dialogue between the government and large corporates. Under pressure from other quarters, he soon formed other working groups (the Black Business, Commercial Agriculture and Trade Union Working Groups). During his tenure, Mbeki also established an International Investment Council comprising CEOs of leading multinationals operating in South Africa, which met a couple of times a year. But there were still tensions over a number of issues, such as dealing with the Zimbabwe situation and other aspects of state intervention. 'The backlash, especially from Mbeki, led to the private sector refraining from making public announcements and attempting to engage the state. Instead, they retreated to a "defiant" position where public engagement or criticism of the state did not happen.'[3]

At a more constructive level, Mbeki sponsored NEPAD (the New Partnership for Africa's Development) in which the promotion of a vibrant African private sector was emphasised. Research has suggested that the NEPAD programme had positive spin-offs for companies in Africa.

In the meantime, global and domestic economic factors moved the South African economy forward. The early part of the 2000s saw a significant improvement in the country's economic performance, which should not be overlooked:

> In the early 2000s, the government started upgrading of South Africa's infrastructure which followed fiscal consolidation. Through improved fiscal management, money was available to spend on infrastructure, with good management yielding quality infrastructure, delivered on time, within budget and which supported private corporate expansion. Fixed investment growth accelerated to double digits during this period, propelling growth to above 3% year-on-year, then onwards to above 5% year-on-year and unemployment to below 22%. Credit ratings rose, with an A+ from Moody's ... Indeed, most of the 2000s saw the highest consistent growth rate South Africa experienced in 35 years. This all ended in 2009.[4]

In 2005, Mbeki launched the Accelerated and Shared Growth Initiative for South Africa (AsgiSA). Although it was widely supported, it also formed part of the President's drive to transform South Africa into a 'developmental state'. This is not the place to discuss the applicability to South Africa of the developmental state framework, which also remains a guiding principle in the NDP. Developmental states are often associated with high economic growth and hence invite imitation. There are various developmental models (East Asian, Scandinavian, Brazilian) on offer in the world.

As another one of a series of key programmes and research projects designed to move the South African economy onto a higher growth trajectory by removing 'binding constraints', AsgiSA for a while enjoyed broad favour, including from business. But AsgiSA never got off the ground as a growth plan. And it was an OECD report on South Africa at the time which identified a fatal flaw in the programme. The OECD warned that there was a contradiction between the weaknesses of state capacity to support the goals of AsgiSA and the emphasis on state programmes to address the very same constraints. It would be bureaucratic failure that became the Achilles heel of public sector efficiency and delivery in South Africa. AsgiSA regrettably also became a casualty of this vulnerability.

Hence AsgiSA failed to gain much traction and was relatively short-lived. But the idea of a developmental state took root and has permeated government policy ever since. A number of studies have shown that the developmental state model is often the spawning ground for various forms of corruption. It seems to have encouraged a torrent of system-gaming and rent-seeking in South Africa. It may also have had the unintended consequence of making conventional business associations often appear irrelevant or neutered.

The introduction and then periodic tightening of Black Economic Empowerment (BEE) legislation provides an example of the state intervening in commercial activities in order to encourage the business sector to do more to carve up the economic pie more equitably. Transformation became a popular watchword and began to find its way into more and more policies and regulatory instruments. The early 2000s saw the government prescribe that each economic sector in the country establish a charter setting out goals and targets relating to transformation.

Owing to the pivotal role of mining in the economy and its long history, the Mining Charter was the first to receive attention. In an article titled 'Government and Business – Where Did It All Go Wrong?', Michael Spicer argued that the Mining Charter negotiations and ensuing legislation, which involved the transfer of mining rights from the private to the public sector, had seriously dented business confidence.[5]

As the years went by, more sectors experienced various forms of government intervention, which many business leaders saw as costly, unnecessarily bureaucratic and market-unfriendly. To the present day, says Spicer, state intervention remains one of the leading sources of friction between the business sector and the government. While business has continuously appealed for policy certainty and legislative efficiency, the government has often found it necessary to intervene to drive a stronger transformation agenda in the face of perceived resistance from many businesses.

The ANC government has often been accused by the organised labour movement and members of the media of following a 'talk left, walk right' strategy – in other words, of displaying a tendency to criticise the markets when speaking at various public forums but then to rely on the markets and the business community to generate the income needed to build infrastructure, provide services and address socio-economic challenges.

Government policy under Mbeki attempted to balance two opposing sets of interests: on the one side were the needs of the broader society, mainly represented by COSATU and the SACP, which were transformation and poverty alleviation; while on the other side were the needs of foreign investors and the local business community, which supported policies that promoted privatisation, deregulation, financial and trade liberalisation, and fiscal restraint. The ideological drivers of business and government were often very different.

To COSATU and the SACP, however, GEAR and then AsgiSA flew in the face of the nationalisation objective which had featured so prominently in the Freedom Charter. As their influence with the ANC declined and their feelings of being sidelined grew, COSATU and the SACP played a major role in ousting Mbeki in favour of Jacob Zuma as the ANC president at the ANC's 2007 national elective conference.

Prior to the conference, the COSATU general secretary, Zwelinzima Vavi, had criticised the ANC's policy documents, saying that they suggested that there was nothing wrong with market-driven capitalism as long as capitalists were encouraged to behave ethically and not become self-serving. He also said that the policy documents 'trivialised' the class struggle and workers' economic contribution to the country and left the ANC without a proactive role in policy-making.

One of the complaints that the government levelled against business at the time was that organised business had become increasingly fractured, complicating government–business interactions. Attempts were made in the 1990s and early 2000s to reshape certain organised business structures to better reflect the changing demographic profile of business and society as a whole. Mbeki was instrumental in encouraging the formation of a new 'peak' non-racial business association. To this end, Business Unity South

Africa (BUSA) was established in 2003. Another significant development was the establishment of Business Leadership South Africa (BLSA) in 2005, formerly the South Africa Foundation. BUSA is a confederation of South African chambers of commerce and industry, professional and business associations and sector-specific employer associations, and the result of a merger between Business South Africa (BSA) and the Black Business Council (BBC).

The BBC is an umbrella body for business and professional organisations, including the National African Federated Chamber of Commerce and Industry (NAFCOC), the Foundation of African Business and Consumer Services (FABCOS) and the influential Black Management Forum (BMF) which had formed part of the original team that crafted the first BEE legislation. In 2011, the BMF parted company with BUSA, citing a lack of influence in the organisation and priority (allegedly) given to white business interests, claims which the BUSA executive later denied.

The Zuma years: The gloves eventually come off

Jacob Zuma took office in the aftermath of the global financial crisis and as the South African economy was emerging from recession. There was a high degree of collaboration between government, business and labour to deal with the impact of the global recession. South Africa recovered reasonably well compared with many other countries. Initially, Zuma appeared keen on promoting economic continuity and stability, and it was under his watch that the National Planning Commission (NPC) and its brainchild, the NDP, came into being. He also voiced his support for NEDLAC and its work in promoting dialogue between the main economic interest groups in the country. Zuma opted not to continue with Mbeki's working groups and International Investment Council, and these ceased to function.

As time went by, economic policy under the Zuma administration became more interventionist, as reflected in initiatives like the launch of the Industrial Policy Action Plan (IPAP) and the New Growth Path (NGP) as well as the release of the Expropriation Bill. IPAP, which has had a number of iterations, emphasises the role of government in selecting and allocating resources to selected labour-absorbing sectors (from agro-processing to energy), as well as a trade policy anchored on the pursuit of industrialisation and export diversification.

The New Growth Path (NGP) was an economic plan envisaging a greater role for the state in the management of the economy. Specific focus areas included mobilising domestic investment to boost employment and enhancing social equity and competitiveness.

The subsequent National Development Plan (NDP) was launched in 2012, building on the New Growth Path as the definitive way ahead. The NGP had been the product of the Economic Development Department and had emphasised the benefits of a 'developmental state'. The NDP, in turn, was the product of the National Planning Commission (NPC) and emphasised the importance of a 'capable state'. It stressed the significant role of the private sector in generating growth and employment. Thus, it was and still is seen as more business-friendly.

Although officially endorsed by the government, the NDP has found few true proponents within the Tripartite Alliance because of its emphasis on market openness and business efficiency. It does, though, strongly advocate inclusive growth and the need to put South Africa's many accumulated socio-economic ills at the top of government and business agendas. Except perhaps for the ocean economy project and Operation Phakisa, there is not much to show for the NDP since 2012.

Although Zuma met from time to time with business (and labour), the relationship between much of the organised business sector and many parts of the government gradually deteriorated to the point where hostility on both sides was palpable. BUSA was no longer seen as the key player in organised business, greater attention being given to other business groups. Edged out of high-level consultative forums in which South Africa's economic, trade and investment performance and prospects were debated and new strategies and plans were formulated, many chambers of commerce and business associations found it difficult to play their traditional advocacy role.

What added to the general problem was the unprecedented number of ministers, deputy ministers and directors general whom Zuma reassigned or removed from their positions after short periods, leading to high levels of instability in various government ministries and departments. For example, during Zuma's tenure, the working relationship between most ministers and their directors general averaged about a year. This made it very difficult for organised business to engage productively with the relevant parts of government. The Cabinet alone was reshuffled eight or nine times. Of great concern was the frequency with which the Finance Minister was changed in recent years. Perhaps more than any other, this portfolio needs to project stability and certainty. In such a volatile climate, key concerns from various business constituencies that should receive the attention of government cannot be effectively communicated to relevant parties or acted upon. This has not helped chambers' and business associations' credibility either, as it becomes difficult to assure members that official contacts are stable and accessible for lobbying purposes.

Many of the chambers excluded from the consultative process have been accused of being 'untransformed' (in terms of staffing and board representation) or not transformed enough, or of being agents of 'white monopoly capital'. Many chambers believe that this essentially disqualifies them from serious consideration in the eyes of government.

An exception, though, is the Black Business Council (BBC). Relaunched in 2012 with its stated mission being to assist previously disadvantaged people, the BBC has positioned itself as a preferred partner of government in respect of various projects aimed at stimulating the manufacturing sector. On that note, the BBC, NAFCOC and other black business structures have increasingly seen themselves as 'developmental' agents for black business rather than promoters of broad economic and commercial policy goals typically espoused by organised business structures.

Admittedly, the transformation journey in South Africa has so far been far from smooth, with relatively few true beneficiaries and therefore limited impact overall. BEE legislation has been one of the main statutory tools used to encourage such transformation. However, one of the consequences of the legislation is that it has split businesses along racial lines as it has effectively created different business environments for black-run and white-run companies. Many companies have approached BEE as a tiresome exercise in compliance ('ticking the boxes') and put in the minimum amount of effort.

Impatient for more rapid economic transformation, the black business elite and members of the governing party have attempted to enforce greater compliance by tightening the regulatory noose and introducing harsher penalties for non-compliant companies. Sensibly, the small business sector is largely exempt from BEE requirements (because of a relatively high turnover threshold), which would be an additional cost burden.

At the policy level in South Africa, market friendliness has in recent years been replaced by a more protectionist (or, at least, very cautious) trade policy aimed at stimulating home-grown industries by shielding them from foreign competition. Such a strategy has drawn a mixed response from businesses operating at the coalface, with large firms in particular seeing their competitiveness and long-term prospects being weakened.

Without debating the merits or otherwise of South Africa's trade policy, what should be said at this point is that insufficient attention has been given to the education and skills crisis in the country, which, if not tackled aggressively, will continue to deprive young people of meaningful work and the country of sustainable trade and investment opportunities. Organised business acknowledges that the private sector could play a much stronger and more visible role here. The Johannesburg Chamber of Commerce and Industry (JCCI), for example, is very active in providing training to its members on various aspects of export market development and runs an incubator programme for small businesses, which has a strong mentorship element.

'Business has become a victim of government policy rather than a source of influence,' said Janine Myburgh, president of the Cape Chamber of Commerce and Industry. She cited property rights legislation as an example. 'We acknowledge the need for land reform but the continuing uncertainty has a negative effect on a labour-intensive industry with great export potential. Over-regulation in many areas has also created unnecessary red tape which has added to the cost of doing business.'[6]

Putting even more strain on business–government relations over the past few years were the persistent allegations of corruption surrounding Jacob Zuma and others in government and business. Of course, as they say, 'it takes two to tango', and so it is hardly surprising that many reports have come to light of complicity, on the part of a number of state-owned enterprises and private firms, in questionable state-linked contracts.

A great deal of mistrust developed between business and government, with entities such as BLSA and BUSA becoming more vocal about the glaring evidence of state capture, supported by political patronage, and the ever-faster merry-go-round of political appointments and reassignments designed to ensure that Zuma remained surrounded by loyalists.

In addition, economic growth has been constrained for some time while policy uncertainty is still high as senior government officials periodically contradict one another over plans for nuclear spend, land redistribution and bail-outs for state-owned enterprises. Not surprisingly, investors, credit rating agencies and markets have – at least until recently – reacted badly to South Africa's political and economic path. This has created the impression, unfair though it may be, that belonging to a business association or chamber of commerce serves no purpose. On the contrary, given the enormity of the challenge in South Africa, the importance of organised business pulling its weight cannot be over-emphasised.

Is South Africa unique in the challenges that business, particularly organised business, faces? 'Yes,' thinks Janine Myburgh. 'We have a government that treats business with suspicion and sometimes hostility. It has taken unto itself the role of prescribing how business should be conducted, who should be employed, and it has interfered with traditional and successful methods of advancing skills and empowering people.'[7]

Undoubtedly, the government has been sending mixed signals when referring to and engaging with the business sector in South Africa. While acknowledging that the country needs strong business entities to create employment, attract investment and grow the tax base, the government has frequently voiced its disapproval of what it has perceived to be the business sector's single-minded profit motive and reluctance to take South Africa's myriad development challenges into account in its investment decisions, expansion plans and hiring practices.

In many parts of the world, it is usually accepted that a business enterprise is primarily concerned with delivering value to shareholders through the investment of capital in production and profitable activities. However, given South Africa's political history and still deeply divided society, many business people cannot afford the luxury of turning a blind eye to the plight of millions of people who are on the economic fringes. This is not only a question of upholding human rights. South Africa's economic future hinges on more inclusive growth and wide-ranging transformation. Pravin Gordhan, who was relieved of his job as Finance Minster in March 2017 in one of Zuma's highly controversial Cabinet reshuffles, remarked in a pre-budget address that year: 'This is not a transformation to be achieved through conquest, conflict or extortion, as in our past. Our transformation will be built through economic participation, partnerships and mobilisation of our capacities. It is a transformation that must unite, not divide, South Africa.'[8]

Clearly, there is a desperate need to improve communication and rebuild trust between business and government. However, business (like the ANC and other political parties, the Tripartite Alliance and the organised labour movement) is itself far from unified and has achieved no clear consensus on the way forward. As a result, organised business structures face the challenge of having to look after the interests of firms with different economic interests and ideological standpoints and sympathies.

Even the regular calls by various business leaders in the past for the ANC to recall President Zuma and root out corruption within its ranks did not necessarily signal a meeting of minds throughout the business community or an act of lobbying in the true sense of the word. Though well-meaning and necessary, pronouncements of this nature have a relatively short shelf life and are generally not enough to effect change because of insufficient mobilisation.

Although thousands of South Africans periodically have taken to the streets in an apparent display of unity against state capture and other forms of corruption, the protesters have been driven invariably by very different worldviews. They may have been fighting a common enemy, but that does not automatically make them brothers in arms. Sometimes, though, when faced with a crisis, people do rally together, displaying unusual solidarity in order to deal with a major threat.

Looking ahead

An economy should be a strong source of inclusive growth, employment opportunities and well-being, and should be able to rise confidently above difficulties when they occur. For this, creativity and collective effort are required. Furthermore, it should never be allowed to deteriorate to a point where things appear too difficult to fix. This would be like an estate agent, on being asked what should be done to improve the sales prospects of a very run-down building, responding: 'Where on earth do you start?'

In assessing what has gone wrong, many commentators have said that South Africa has lost its moral compass – the fight now is over money, not ideology. This is important, particularly as more and more revelations surface of once-esteemed corporate entities having been complicit in questionable government-linked contracts. Equally worrying, though, is that South Africa appears to have lost its economic compass, with economic thinking and planning being short term, at best, and pulling in many different directions.

However, the all-important long-term economic vision for the country is not clear, not only because of ideological differences between the many interest groups in society but also because the growing scale of the problems that are unfolding is prompting many people to ask, 'Where on earth do you start?'

Yet deciding on a cohesive and long-term economic vision for the country – one that is realistic and not overly aspirational (a criticism that has sometimes been levelled at the NDP) – and securing widespread commitment to it is the best way forward for South Africa, even though to many this may seem like an impossible dream at this stage. Alongside the many prophets of doom, there are also inspirational individuals in government, business and civil society who are trying to get people to rally behind the idea of a new, inclusive and resilient economic future for the country. This is the idea that South Africa's new President, Cyril Ramaphosa, is promoting. He and many others realise that collective effort is required, and neither political nor commercial interests should be allowed to get the upper hand. South Africa still has resilient institutions to rely upon, including in the private sector.

Business (including organised business) therefore still has a crucial role to play in putting the economy back on track and becoming a vocal agent of change, particularly since (in many people's view) it has been too passive for too long and has often displayed tacit acceptance of policies over which it was not consulted and which had obvious shortcomings. A case in point is the extremely expensive experiment with the Sector Education and Training Authorities (SETAs), which have seen businesses (large and small) contribute compulsory levies over many years to a large and lumbering skills training system which has failed to make a difference to the country's skills crisis. There are many other examples. One of the unfortunate side effects of excessive state interference in commercial activities is that it has the potential eventually to discourage business from thinking that it can change things or make a difference.

Commenting on the depressed political and economic climate in the country, South Africa's Chief Justice, Mogoeng Mogoeng, remarked to business leaders at a function honouring South Africa's top companies in

2017: 'How can we give up hope? Why is it that there isn't much movement in the area of investment? Are you not running the risk of waiting until it's too late? The same applies to land. Why do you sit back with all the talent you have and allow a few opportunists to ruin it for all of us when you could come up with a plan to resolve this peacefully?'[9]

6
The case for a strong organised business movement in South Africa

When spider webs unite, they can tie up a lion.
– AFRICAN PROVERB

Hope in the face of difficulties, hope in the face of uncertainty, the audacity of hope.
– BARACK OBAMA

IN HIS ABSORBING BOOK, *SMART SWARM*, Peter Miller provides fascinating insights into how ants, honey bees, termites and other small creatures follow a highly organised and disciplined approach to building communal habitats, finding food, fending off danger and ensuring the survival of their species. Authority is clearly defined, resources are deployed and tasks are allocated. No one is idle, and the focus is always on the well-being of the community as a whole. Teamwork is essential; without it, important links in the chain would be broken, confusion would reign and the community would die.

Human communities, of course, do not operate in the repetitive, consistently efficient style of ants, bees and termites. Their organisational tendencies are influenced by myriad factors, and these produce highly variable results. People rely on reasoning rather than blind instinct; they also ask questions and frequently challenge the status quo. Creating a sense of cohesion among groups of people can be difficult in the face of so many different points of view and value systems. Yet to be successful, any community – large or small, human or otherwise – requires some sort of organisational arrangement. An organisation provides many benefits –

from a sense of common purpose and a roadmap for getting things done, to safety in numbers.

Although the business sector in South Africa has been buffeted from all sides in recent years, there nonetheless remains a strong cohort of organisations that have been determined not to be cowed, and have focused their energies on tackling challenges head-on and keeping the show on the road. Many companies (both black- and white-owned and -managed) have successfully injected a community-like spirit into their commercial operations, from which has flowed strong performance from committed employees, suppliers and other external stakeholders. These companies invariably have strong leaders – those who are forthright and assertive without resorting to dictatorial or bullying tactics.

But South Africa is facing one of its harshest sustainability tests yet, with a weak economy and very unstable political environment, both deterrents to investment. Business therefore needs to mobilise. But it is not only the responsibility of big business to push for the much-needed change of direction in South Africa. Just as ant, bee and termite colonies comprise complex configurations of scouts, informers, runners and soldiers, which ultimately take their direction from the main 'bug in charge', so all sizes of business should in their own way be putting shoulder to the wheel to seek robust, collective solutions to the problems the country is facing. In the words of Margaret Thatcher, 'You can't enjoy the fruits of effort without first making the effort.' Organised business still has a central role to play in coordinating these activities.

In this chapter and the next, we explore why South Africa needs a strong and cohesive organised business sector, and how even relatively small entities can punch above their weight if they organise effectively and get their service offerings and external linkages right.

Organised business under pressure globally

Given the considerable challenges that businesses in South Africa are facing – some challenges being unique and some being typical of those experienced in other developing countries – the organised business sector certainly has its work cut out for it.

As in South Africa, chambers of commerce and business associations in other parts of the world are facing questions about their relevance, particularly with the encroachment of 'do-it-yourself' societal norms, and have seen a steady decline in membership numbers. As noted previously, this has prompted frequent makeovers and mergers among business associations, with varying degrees of success.

In the United States, UK and several other Western countries, there was a time when being a member of a chamber of commerce gave a company status or credibility. With competition intensifying and businesses facing heavier regulatory burdens and financial compliance requirements, the allure of chamber membership has waned. Business people (especially in small firms) are busy and cannot afford the perceived luxury of attending information-sharing forums and networking events. In addition, whereas chambers used to be valuable meeting grounds for buyers, suppliers and service providers, businesses now find useful contacts through various other means. Across the world, therefore, tighter budgets, increasingly busy lifestyles and extra demands on people's time, and the growing predilection for personalised services have deflected many businesses' attention away from the benefits of being a member of a multisectoral body.

Those organised business structures that have been successful in maintaining healthy membership numbers and a high profile have adopted strategies that have kept their operations fresh and responsive to changing environmental circumstances – however challenging these have appeared to be. Adaptation has become a fundamental element of their business philosophy. They are willing advocates of change; are experienced in the cut and thrust of business, government and labour relations; and often have an enviable level of knowledge (which is constantly nourished) about their country's or their geographical region's economic activities and potential.

They also know that their chances of making a difference will be greater if they pull together with other actors in the broader organised business community that enjoy competitive advantages in areas where they do not. These might include a special relationship with a local or regional authority, technological prowess, a dynamic and experienced board of directors, or a strong and diverse membership base – which could be tapped by means of various collaborative arrangements.

That some organised business structures are of a confederation type creates critical mass, which should afford them a certain amount of clout. Yet the ability to truly make a difference, particularly in policy-making and regulatory circles, requires that an organisation be sufficiently representative of its constituency, which generally goes well beyond having a sizeable membership.

It has been emphasised that it is unrealistic to expect a country to have a single voice for business. Different entities represent companies with different interests, from those operating in specific industry sectors to those tethered to particular cities or regions. While it obviously makes economic sense to have more than one bank or supermarket chain to choose from in a competitive economy, the same does not necessarily hold for subscription-driven, voluntary business associations and chambers. The more concentrated and aligned the representative bodies, the surer and louder their collective message will be and the easier it will be to call the government and the business community as a whole to account. This is crucial in South Africa today in the face of weak governance standards, policy confusion and growing evidence of state capture, often with private sector collusion.

Looking back: What did business do after 1994?

The first few chapters of this book were devoted to addressing the question: What did business (and organised business) do to help rid South Africa of the apartheid system and ensure a reasonable transition to democracy up to and after 1994? While there have been a number of positive, defining moments along the way, there have also been plenty of setbacks and disappointments, with attempts to forge a more resilient economy and sense of unity among the people of South Africa often crushed by unexpected and seemingly uncontrollable events – events which recently have bordered on the unimaginable.

At this point in the narrative, therefore, it is appropriate to reflect on what, broadly, we can learn from the business sector's handling of the situation and, in turn, which parts of history should be selected and used as beacons to light the way forward. This is important because when the future arrives and we look back at this segment of South Africa's history, we want to be able to give a positive answer to the question: What did business do?

From a variety of information sources, opinion pieces and personal accounts there has emerged the realisation that scattered and relatively soft noises coming out of the business sector have largely been ineffective in changing the attitudes and behaviour of the government of the day. This has been no more evident than in the case of the intractable Zuma administration, which leapt from one economically incoherent policy position to the next, resisting attempts from beyond the inner circle to respond to the unfolding economic and social crisis in the country with logic and integrity.

In an earlier chapter, we speculated about what would have happened if business in South Africa, for example, had done more to agitate for the removal of such an unconscionable system as apartheid. Would democracy have dawned much earlier than 1994? Would the scars have been any less deep than they are today?

As Winston Churchill once wisely said: 'The further backward you look, the further forward you can see.' This message is particularly appropriate in the case of South Africa given its long and well-documented history of political conflict, economic struggle and social discord. History can teach and heal, but it can also repeat itself in cruel ways.

With the benefit of clear hindsight, the South African business sector – which has had to weather many storms (both locally and internationally) over the years – is in a unique position to apply the pressure needed to steer the country into calmer and more certain waters. To do this, it needs to know where it wants to go and to have enough support to ensure a safe passage for all concerned. The organised business sector could play a pivotal role here by being one of the champions of the cause, channelling strong and inclusive messages and reprising its role as the collective voice of business in South Africa.

The relative timidity displayed by many businesses in South Africa in recent years is to some extent attributable to a belief that business should not actively meddle in politics. But as political decisions and activities influence the economy in so many ways, business leaders and representatives must regularly concern themselves with the economic and business consequences of political factors if they wish to influence the country's socio-economic trajectory.

During the apartheid era, business (and organised business in particular) got short shrift from prime ministers and presidents like Verwoerd,

Vorster and Botha for apparently overstepping the mark and interfering in affairs of state. Yet organised business – working with various social partners – pushed ahead regardless, and was ultimately able to take some credit (however small) for the eventual demise of the apartheid system. With a new enemy in everyone's midst – what former President Thabo Mbeki recently termed the 'rapacious value systems' that have gripped the economy – strong collaboration is needed like never before.

Unity is strength
Most people have heard the expressions 'unity is strength' and 'the whole is greater than the sum of its parts'. Given the deeply divided nature of South African society today, organised business cannot itself afford to remain fragmented (owing to commercial rivalry, ideological differences or racial disharmony), with many competing 'voices' conveying a confusing array of messages to their communities and the country as a whole. This clears the way for the government to divide and rule, which essentially means exploiting coordination problems among those who are often critical of its economic stance and policies.

In her article 'From Fragmentation to Fragile Unity: Organizational Fault-Lines in South African Business', Nicoli Nattrass emphasised that it is imperative that business associations have a common vision of the world if they are to have a sufficiently powerful effect on the state.[1] This potentially introduces a number of challenges, as small representative bodies differ from larger representative bodies, while those with a largely black membership differ from those with a largely white membership, and so on.

But in its broadest sense, a common vision could relate to a society in which all stakeholders are consulted about the issues that affect them and which is structured in a way that encourages inclusive economic activity and sustainable development and wealth creation. Focusing on long-term and more holistic goals should, over time, help to collapse more parochial barriers associated with race, geography or unhealthy rivalry in the marketplace.

After the removal of Nhlanhla Nene as Finance Minister in December 2015, which signalled a new era in government domination of economic decision-making, many businesses (often for the first time) became outspoken and critical about the dangerous path that Jacob Zuma and his supporters were leading the country down during his presidency. Various organised business structures, in turn, from representatives of large businesses like BLSA to smaller chambers of commerce expressed their concerns and sometimes outrage at many of the policy choices made and laws passed, as well as the glaring lapses in leadership that were becoming increasingly evident at the different levels of government. On these sorts of matters, there was quite widespread convergence of opinion, which is a positive sign. However, convergence in views is only a rudimentary first step; committed action and positive results need to follow.

Similarly, a number of individual business people spoke out against the unstable economic and political situation in South Africa. However, experience has shown that this is a hazardous occupation for all but the most courageous because of the high risk of victimisation. Members of the CEO Initiative, for example, a business group formed to expedite socio-economic reforms, liaise with government and uphold an ethical system of governance, have apparently been subjected to close and often uncomfortable personal scrutiny in their capacity as leaders of clearly identifiable corporate entities. A strong organised business sector helps to reduce the risk of victimisation or retaliation because it engages in robust and continual lobbying on behalf of business as a whole. As it is a collective mouthpiece, it can take the punches much more easily than individuals can.

South Africa's history over the past few decades has shown that government, business, labour and civil society all need to be consulted over matters that affect them if useful results are to be forthcoming and workable relationships between the different social partners are to be maintained. As we saw in Chapter 4, NEDLAC – despite its many detractors – has tried to uphold this principle.

A classic example of how badly things can go wrong when relevant parties are not properly consulted and there is a general lack of transparency was the uproar over the Gauteng e-toll system and the National Roads Agency's poor handling of the messy saga that ensued. The e-toll system has pitched the provincial government, trade unions, and much of the business sector and civil society against national government and is on the verge of collapse, with only a small percentage of motorists still paying their toll fees. Although many may feel vindicated because – through 'people power' – a perceived symbol of corruption has been brought to its knees, the theatrics that have accompanied the unsuccessful rollout of e-tolls serve only to weaken South Africa's economic foundations and exacerbate the trust deficit between the government and many parts of society.

Of concern, too, is that resistance to specific initiatives like e-tolls and the problematic socio-economic path along which the government has been leading South Africa is largely reactive in nature. Institutional instability lies at the root of this problem. Achieving greater unity and harmony among organised business structures would lead to their empowerment, clearing the way for them to propose – in more proactive ways – strategies and plans that are in the country's or individual provinces' best interests. Taking preventive steps would also be far less costly – for all concerned – than attempting to correct unpopular decisions and actions at a later stage.

Many businesses, whose employees come from a range of socio-economic and ideological backgrounds, have voiced their anger at how things have turned out in South Africa. Business confidence has been low in the midst of unprecedented policy uncertainty. Interestingly, as mentioned in Chapter 1, a sense of anger and frustration among business leaders was the trigger for the establishment of the first chambers of commerce hundreds of years ago, and these went on to become effective vehicles for channelling businesses' concerns and demands to the authorities of the day.

Unfortunately, in South Africa's case, attempts by individual chambers and business associations in recent years to get the ear of government have reportedly been largely unsuccessful. This is a common phenomenon in developing countries (particularly in Africa) where the absence of a cohesive and therefore influential private sector reduces chambers and business associations (where they exist at all) to minor players in the economy. However, where there is a strong private enterprise ethic in a country, there is more scope for organised business structures to step up and share the load of representing firms and, collectively, to make more noise, which is not so easy to ignore. This supports the Gramscian idea that you do not have to be in power to wield power.

We know that the business sector makes an immense contribution to the South African economy and society as a whole, particularly in the all-important area of employment. Research commissioned by BLSA revealed that in 2016 BLSA members alone:

- contributed R1.9 trillion in output (more than the total value of government's budgeted expenditure that year);
- employed approximately 1.3 million people directly and nearly 2 million people indirectly in the supply chain (far exceeding equivalent numbers employed by the public sector);
- contributed R431 billion or 36 per cent of the total taxes collected in the country;
- contributed 34 per cent of GDP.

Commenting on the findings, the BLSA chief executive, Bonang Mohale, remarked: 'It's a reminder that business touches every part of South African life and has a positive role to play and [a] voice in the success of the nation.' He added: 'Business is committed to doing more to encourage inclusive economic growth and transformation ... Government must create the economic and policy conditions necessary for growth to occur, and then together business, government and civil society can work to put the South African economy back on track.'[2]

Of course, BLSA members represent big business – a sector that, while making a sizeable contribution to GDP, does not represent mainstream business in South Africa. We must also recognise that in many countries big business often becomes an elite which, while frequently supportive of mainstream business associations, nonetheless likes to have its own club or structure. This is logical and acceptable – provided it does not exercise a disproportionate influence over policy or degenerate into cronyism.

As revealed in an earlier chapter, the SMME sector also makes a significant contribution to GDP (in fact, more – in percentage terms – than big business). But SMMEs' lack of effective representation serves to fragment and dilute their economic potential, and gives the impression that the South African economy is indeed dominated by large corporates associated with 'white monopoly capital'. While financial muscle (and the leverage that comes with it) provides a solid foundation for driving change in South Africa, leverage takes many different forms – which need to be skilfully crafted into instruments of persuasion rather than left as blunt objects that are likely to deliver less sustainable results.

The immense problems that South Africa currently faces require well-conceived and well-coordinated solutions, with the involvement of all stakeholders. 'Not enough people in South Africa realise that we are all in the same canoe,' said Roger Baxter, chief executive of the Chamber of Mines. 'And the more leaks the canoe springs [credit rating downgrades, escalating government debt, corruption and capital flight], the faster we will all sink.'[3]

Today more than ever before, organised business should be at the front of the South African canoe, helping to anticipate and navigate the oncoming rapids and repair the leaks as they occur.

Contributing to a sound policy environment

The business sector has a wealth of practical knowledge of what is happening at the coalface of the economy – what works, what does not, what can be learnt from others' experiences, and so on. It therefore goes without saying that business leaders and representatives – along with their social partners – should play an active role in the official economic policy-making sphere. The organised business sector, in turn, is well placed to coordinate such involvement as it has a natural advocacy role. It also understands the dynamics of the business sector from different vantage points. This is because (to use a sporting analogy) it often has to alternate between being coach, player and referee.

There is a tendency among some South Africans to think that businesses will only be able to thrive if the policy and regulatory environment is just right – when the fuzziness has been removed from assorted policy documents, when obstacles to trade and investment have been cleared away, and when red tape has been all but eradicated. Waiting for this to happen, though, will largely be an exercise in futility because there will never be perfect conditions for business. Even in the face of heightened policy uncertainty, positive business decisions are still possible.

This is not to say that policy certainty should not be the goal of government and business alike. Hardly any economic assessment or media release from international or local financial institutions, business lobbies, economic analysts, financial journalists or credit rating agencies has appeared over the past few years without the inclusion of the words 'policy uncertainty'. Policy uncertainty has been a strong deterrent to local and international investment. This has had serious repercussions for all segments of society as it has impeded economic initiatives that could have taken the country forward on its developmental path, both in the short and longer terms. These trends have been tracked on the North-West University's Policy Uncertainty Index, which provides a quarterly assessment of the state of the policy environment in South Africa against a range of indicators. Whatever its imperfections, the National Development Plan (NDP) – had it been properly and consistently implemented since 2012 – could have provided an acceptable level of policy certainty by now.

Given the dearth of formal data on the activities of firms in South Africa, organised business entities can be valuable (though by no means exhaustive) sources of information. Such information might cover economic developments at a local and international level, different industry sectors, and the opportunities and challenges that confront them, as well as assorted best practices and success stories emanating from chambers' and business associations' engagements with their organisational networks – all of which can help to steer the policy-making process in practical ways.

In the light of this, it may appear to be a foregone conclusion that advocacy should remain the primary area of focus among business associations and chambers of commerce in South Africa, in keeping with the mandate of similar bodies in other parts of the world. This is certainly the case with so-called peak organisations such as BLSA, SACCI and the BBC. However, as chambers of commerce have found themselves increasingly excluded from policy debates, their advocacy role has declined and they have become more active in the provision of commercial services, such as training, mentoring and market development assistance.

Undoubtedly, the provision of commercial services outside a standard membership package can serve a valuable purpose for the business community, particularly where service offerings are developmental in nature and directed at building capacity and sustainability. This is especially important for the SMME sector. However, having recalibrated their operations in this way chambers and similar organisations have to compete against other providers of training, consulting and publications, a situation which then calls for a larger investment in marketing. Among these competitors are government entities (such as provincial and local authorities) which are able to provide some equivalent products and services at a lower cost. Chambers and other private sector representative bodies are therefore under increasing pressure to carve out distinctive niches for themselves, and this may inadvertently further narrow their customer base and revenue streams.

Some might argue that the perceived lack of capacity within the organised business movement has prompted government to sometimes compete with, rather than outsource to, private sector service providers. This highlights the need for chambers and business associations not only to organise but to professionalise their offerings and build strong reputations in the market in line with their particular areas of expertise. If a vacuum is left, the government can hardly be blamed for wanting to fill it.

Competition sometimes creates the tendency to try to be all things to all people, which leads to a loss of focus, a thinning of resources and a dilution of expertise. This further erodes the ability of chambers and other bodies to be the true representatives of their particular constituencies. In the face of growing (and often) wasteful competition and revenue concerns, some business associations in South Africa have resorted to accepting state-owned enterprises (SOEs), such as Eskom and Transnet, as members. Although falling into the 'enterprise' category, SOEs have very different agendas from those of private sector firms, and the potential for conflict of interest is high.

To counter competitive threats, organisations in various countries have developed skills in interpreting and packaging – and thus adding value to – information. In South Africa, with government policies and regulations not always being easy to come by or to digest, chambers in particular can play a valuable role in distilling and sharing with their (frequently resource-deprived) small business clients the most salient features of company law, company registration procedures, national product and service standards, employment equity requirements, intellectual property legislation, regional and international trade agreements, and assorted municipal by-laws.

The provision of such information, likely to form part of a commercial service package, would dovetail well with chambers' advocacy role, as it would draw on some of the most common concerns of businesses in the constituency in question, while also building in-house, specialist expertise that would strengthen the policy advice given.

Why not leave it to the sectoral bodies?

Multisectoral bodies generally find it more difficult to gain traction in the market than sectoral bodies, which have a more clearly defined role. The members of the Chamber of Mines, for example, account for some 90 per cent of South Africa's annual mineral output, which makes the Chamber very influential and highly representative of its sector.

The sectoral bodies, being reservoirs of specialist knowledge and expertise, are a natural drawcard for many industry players and therefore assume a natural advocacy role on behalf of the industry. They also typically engage with relevant unions on practical matters such as working conditions and wages. However, the precise parameters of sectoral bodies' constituencies can change over time.

For example, NAAMSA (National Association of Automobile Manufacturers of South Africa) has expanded its traditional membership base of manufacturers and assemblers to include major importers and distributors of new vehicles, as part of the industry's transformation drive. In the energy sector, SAREC (South African Renewable Energy Council) was established to act as 'the voice and champion of the renewable energy sector in South Africa', representing four sectoral bodies straddling solar, wind, photovoltaic and sustainable energy.

Of course, multisectoral bodies should not try to usurp the function of the sectoral bodies, but rather play a complementary role. Multisectoral bodies are able to adopt a bird's-eye view, noting areas of concern to a relatively broad interest group and mobilising for the implementation of appropriate solutions by engaging the relevant authorities and private sector organisations. Accordingly, they are able to identify and pursue issues of common interest to business. For example, some years ago the Cape Chamber of Commerce and Industry (CCCI) launched an initiative with the South African Property Owners Association, and in cooperation with the Cape Town City Council, to clean up the city centre, reduce crime and encourage investment to flow back into the area. This was an ambitious but very successful project, highlighting the value of strong partnerships between business and government in delivering economic value to communities.

The narrower a sectoral body's interests, the more checks and balances are required to reduce the risk of rent-seeking. A multisectoral body, having a broader view of the cause and effect of policy decisions and activities across a range of economic sectors, has a particularly important role to play in demanding accountability from both its constituencies and the state.

Seeking a new economic consensus for South Africa

It has been said that business is driven largely by profit, while government is driven largely by power. Many would dismiss this view as a spurious generalisation, but it deserves some consideration. Broadly, individual businesses are motivated by the prospect of accessing (as easily as possible) high-potential markets, developing healthy market shares and profiting from their commercial endeavours. If they are unprofitable, they are unable to remain quality-driven and are unable to grow. Government, on the other hand, is interested in maintaining a fair measure of control over economic activities, primarily through regulatory means, in order to ensure a balanced economic playing field. Government therefore views markets with some circumspection.

It is from these different positions that views on capitalism often collide. The business sector would argue that capital (and capitalism) is fundamental to keeping the wheels of the economy turning. And as capital is fickle by nature, it will simply go elsewhere when it is threatened – of which South Africa has been painfully reminded in recent years. Government, on the other hand, would argue that capitalism – if not kept in check – creates winners and losers, widening the rifts in society. Are these positions compatible? And what are the implications for negotiating a new economic consensus for South Africa, which organised business will be able to draw on and promote in its interactions with the government, its members and society as a whole?

The solution is to find, if not a happy medium, at least a fair compromise between these two positions, with each side willing to yield some of their preconceived notions about markets, competition, foreign investment, job growth, old and new trade issues, governance and accountability, how policy and regulatory effectiveness should be measured, and many other issues. Ideally, this should play out in a climate in which the government and business sector enjoy the sort of engagement that encourages knowledge-sharing and accommodates a range of interests, with no one party dominating the other. As in any dynamic partnership, competing concerns and priorities are inevitable, but there must be scope for debate and a willingness to concede some ground for the common good. As far as possible, the economic debate should be evidence-driven.

At the core of the economic policy debate in South Africa is the issue of development. While there is practically universal acceptance that development is the desired end result of economic and trade policy-making and implementation, views and opinions differ sharply on what development (precisely) means and how it should be achieved. While the developmental state concept (which has seen particular success in various parts of Asia) was intended to be a central pillar of economic policy in South Africa, it has been difficult to implement.

A developmental state, while allowing for government intervention to spur on activity in certain (particularly industrial) sectors and to narrow opportunity and income gaps, also places strong emphasis on skills development, productivity improvement, technological innovation and competitiveness. Loud alarm bells have gone off in all these areas in South Africa, once regarded as the hegemon in the southern African region but in recent years having aquired a reputation for economic inertia. In fact, the system in place in South Africa is more indicative of a welfare state than a developmental state, what with the emphasis on redistribution through progressive taxation, land reform and the (ballooning) social grant system. In the process, the true drivers of economic growth have received insufficient attention.

Professor Gavin Keeton of Rhodes University has highlighted the irony of former President Thabo Mbeki's 'failed' – but essentially more business-friendly – policies being replaced by a much stronger emphasis on greater government intervention, which (it was claimed) would promote faster growth and more rapid job creation. In fact, the change in approach has unfortunately not delivered the anticipated results, given the present state of the economy.

At a global level, too, development dominates many conversations. For example, for many years the World Trade Organization (WTO) has attempted to demonstrate that development is the outcome of liberal trade policies that promote unencumbered market access and competition (with the multilateral system affording poor countries various forms of special treatment). The rationale for this approach is to stimulate global flows of goods, services, capital, technology and expertise – all vital ingredients in the creation of robust economies. Such a narrative has also been popularised in post-1994 South Africa, first under Nelson Mandela and for a while under Thabo Mbeki.

However, the liberal, market-driven and largely Western trade and development model has attracted a growing number of critics (including government authorities in South Africa), who view it as economically divisive since it tends to promote the interests of wealthier countries over those of poorer countries and the interests of big business over those of small business. The resultant inequality in many countries around the world is becoming a source of increasing tension both domestically and at the broad geo-political level. Angered by what they view as the failure of democracy, globalisation and liberal values, many marginalised communities have embraced the more radical ideologies peddled by populist leaders in their countries in the hopes of bringing about a more balanced economic playing field. Widespread weaknesses in negotiating and policy-making, evidenced in an inability to juggle and address all the prevailing issues and arguments, are adding fuel to the fire.

In order to efficiently absorb the inputs of business into these major cross-cutting issues, the private sector needs to be better organised, as this makes superior outcomes possible. Many policy studies on these complex questions tend to ignore the inputs of business, either because they are not visible or because they are not sufficiently well structured to be taken into account. Yet it is the individual business decision-makers whose activities ultimately have to give substance to the trade and investment policies that are supposed to produce desirable or expected outcomes and whose views need to be given weight.

A priority-led action agenda for the organised business sector

Assuming it is possible to infuse a new spirit of cooperation into the organised business sector, the process of tackling wide-ranging goals and priorities will nevertheless be complex and time-consuming. Chambers and business associations would therefore do well to start the process by giving special attention to a number of critical, burning issues, which would be relevant both to their advocacy work and to the business support services they direct at clients. Not only do these issues (outlined below) have inherent tipping point potential, but they could play an important role in revitalising the organised business movement in South Africa.

Developing capacity in the SMME sector
There is a school of thought that big business can look after itself when it comes to, for example, lobbying for a better policy and regulatory environment, acquiring industry and market information, unravelling legislation, building capacity, and developing new markets or sources of supply. As a result, when it comes to many of the services provided by chambers and other business associations, big business is not the typical target market. It is in the area of SMME (small, medium and micro enterprise) development that the organised business movement should and often does concentrate its efforts.

But even if it does not make too much use of their services, big business should still throw its weight behind chambers and business associations, which would help to sustain the health of the private enterprise system as a whole. For example, large corporations that have satellite offices or branches throughout the country should encourage their regional and local management teams to participate in the activities of local chambers and associations. The latter, in turn, could assist big business by being effective lobbyists at the local level in matters relating to business regulations, service delivery, municipal rates, energy costs and the quality of infrastructure.

There is a caveat, though. The cross-subsidisation of chambers and other representative bodies by big business, while welcome, does not offer a sustainable solution to the problem of financial instability. Although support from big business can provide financial security, it might even add to the precarious state of some operations if funding and other forms of support are erratic.

All over the world, SMMEs are the bedrock of countries' economies. Yet, as indicated earlier, they often receive inadequate attention and support. Start-ups, for example, may receive assistance at the outset to become operational but are then left to their own devices to grow their businesses in an ad hoc fashion. More established SMMEs, which have achieved a level of success in the local market, are often considered too experienced to warrant special attention or concessions from government or private financial institutions. Yet they, too, could find themselves in a slow-growth or no-growth trap if there are no external support measures available to them or if the regulatory environment is too constraining.

SMMEs in South Africa, while making a generous contribution to economic growth, contribute only 65 per cent to employment, compared to the global average of 95 per cent. This highlights the potential of sustainable black enterprises as an enabler of inclusive growth and development in South Africa. In this regard, SMMEs often provide the vehicle through which individuals and communities can improve their incomes and livelihoods, thus lifting them out of acute poverty. But as they are largely overlooked at the policy level (because they lack bargaining power), they often find it procedurally challenging and costly to run or diversify their operations or to expand into the global arena.

At the ANC's national elective conference in December 2017, the Minister of Small Business Development, Lindiwe Zulu, spoke about the government's target to outsource 30 per cent of government work to SMMEs as part of a local procurement drive. Unfortunately, she made no mention of how government would engage the private sector in meeting such a target or of any envisaged strategies to build SMMEs' capacity to ensure that they become reliable and quality-driven suppliers to the public sector. There have been a number of government-run or -supported financial and non-financial support programmes introduced over the years to assist the small business sector in South Africa. While these have helped to give beneficiary companies a leg-up in certain areas of their operation, they have generally not resulted in sustainable growth.

The South African government is following an industrialisation agenda underpinned by a renewed focus on manufacturing – which, it is claimed, will stimulate job creation. In terms of this agenda, it is proposed that state-owned enterprises will provide the main impetus for the manufacturing drive. Many experts believe that with SOE-driven manufacturing, the anticipated acceleration in economic growth and job creation will not materialise. The answer, they say, lies in knowledge-based and services-led growth, which is where SMMEs could play a much more meaningful role because they would face generally lower barriers to entry. The hospitality industry is a drawcard for many small businesses, with the mobile revolution and connectivity via the Internet making it easier (and cheaper) for businesses to market or deliver their services electronically.

Interestingly, the National Development Plan – which has a time horizon up to 2030 – expects that up to 90 per cent of new jobs will be generated by SMMEs in the domestically focused services sector. Although this sounds like a sensible direction and great opportunity for small business, a number of academic studies have challenged this expectation as extremely optimistic, especially in view of the limited attention given to SMMEs in the current policy environment

Although SMMEs straddle an extensive range of economic activities, they have similar needs, which can be summed up as finance for start-up or expansion purposes; practical assistance in converting business ideas into marketable products and services; assistance with the identification of customers, suppliers and service providers; and assistance with regulatory compliance. Given their broad perspectives and experience, multisectoral bodies (working with both business and government entities and sharing resources) can make a significant contribution in these areas – both from a lobbying and a service-delivery perspective. In fact, a number of chambers and business associations in South Africa have been working closely with SMMEs for many years, helping them in the areas mentioned. Often, though, their interactions are with individual companies and not associations, and so a holistic picture of the SMME sector per industry or region has not yet emerged.

At the heart of SMME development is the building of entrepreneurial talent. Entrepreneurship is a vital ingredient in a society's ability to adapt to a constantly changing environment, but it is in short supply in South Africa. There are a number of reasons for this. One is that insufficient attention is given to entrepreneurship in standard education and training curricula, while financial institutions tend to view entrepreneurial ventures as high-risk and generally not worthy of support. In addition, a culture of dependency has taken root in the country over the years which dulls people's initiative and makes them believe that little can happen without government assistance. There is even a feeling in some quarters that entrepreneurship (with its strong profit motive and natural association with the capitalist system) is somehow illegitimate and should not be vigorously pursued.

Yet as many successful entrepreneurial nations will testify, small businesses need to be profit-driven and proactive in order to get ahead. And a proactive approach stands a much better chance of bearing fruit if there is an informed and coordinated organised business movement on the sidelines, providing influence, direction and momentum. Well-organised chambers and business associations can provide a haven in which entrepreneurial principles and skills can take root; this can go a long way towards building business confidence and encouraging small businesses to grow and contribute roundly to society. The concept of entrepreneurship is not associated with start-ups only. According to the World Economic Forum (WEF), northern European countries like Sweden, Estonia and Latvia excel in the area of intrapreneurship, which involves following an entrepreneurial approach within existing firms.

For entrepreneurship to thrive in South Africa, the economy needs to grow at a more rapid pace and become a generous source of market opportunities. The low-growth trap in which South Africa currently finds itself does not create a conducive environment for entrepreneurship – even for those businesses receiving government grants or other types of assistance.

On the subject of government assistance schemes for entrepreneurs, there is always the risk that the schemes in question will be used to further the interests of a well-connected few, with little value being passed on to the wider community. The recently launched Black Industrialist Programme, a cost-sharing grant scheme managed by the Department of Trade and Industry (DTI) and aimed at a total of 100 black-owned businesses operating in the manufacturing sector, has already attracted criticism for earmarking significant amounts of money for a limited number of existing (evidently viable) businesses, while the money could have been spread among many more entrepreneurial outfits at earlier stages of development.

While a commitment to provide special assistance to entrepreneurs is in principle a good idea, schemes need to be tightly run if rent-seeking and other forms of corruption are to be discouraged. Moreover, the progress of beneficiaries should be continuously monitored to ensure that they eventually graduate (perhaps through sunset clauses) from the schemes in question to make way for new entrants.

Clearly, research into the SMME community needs much more

attention, as finding and nurturing the talents of entrepreneurs are critical elements in growing and sustaining the South African economy and tackling the serious and chronic youth unemployment problem.

There have been several earlier references to the key role of small business and the extent to which it faces regulatory and other obstacles in seeking to start up or promote different types of enterprises. We conclude that the common thread that runs through much of the small business narrative is the degree to which, in order to develop a livelihood, the entities in question often have to do battle with a formidable and obstructive bureaucracy. Despite various well-intentioned support measures, it remains a vulnerable sector.

We are reminded of the words used by Chief Justice Mogoeng in a different context when, in dealing with the Nkandla case, he referred to those 'who fight the most powerful and very well-resourced Goliath ... even at the doors of the highest chambers of raw state power'.[4] What small business needs here is to be able to mobilise the potential countervailing power of effective chambers and business associations to ensure that, when necessary, it can similarly get redress at the appropriate level.

And there is a specific target area that needs attention. It was indicated previously that organised business and the chamber movement need to forge a much closer working relationship with the Department of Small Business Development. A recent independent evaluation of that department's performance (under Minister Zulu) said:

> Internally, she has run a tight ship, and her department has received an unqualified audit and increased its overall performance from 51.6% to 71%, according to the annual report. It leads by example by paying 98% of its creditors within 30 days ... but her department, which is understaffed, underspent its budget by more than R120 million in the 2016/2017 financial year. This has caused it to under-deliver on some of its programmes.[5]

Furthermore, an acknowledged lack of skills in the department has resulted in the importance of cooperatives to SMME and community development being overlooked.

Business associations and chambers should therefore be highly geared to visibly and proactively address this ready-made agenda at the

Department of Small Business Development, in the interests of enterprise in general and small business in particular.

Encouraging competitiveness and export expansion

Policy-makers in South Africa have long acknowledged that competitiveness is one of the keys to success at both the domestic and international levels. The fact that South Africa took an unprecedented tumble in the WEF's latest (2017–2018) Global Competitiveness Index rankings is cause for serious concern as it signals an economy that has strayed far from global expectations and standards.

Among South Africa's traditional competitiveness-related shortcomings are high production and logistics costs, low levels of technological development, and weak governance in public institutions. While the quality of South Africa's private institutions used to attract high scores on the index, recent high-profile corruption scandals involving large corporate entities such as KPMG and Steinhoff have raised questions about the integrity of this sector.

Although the South African economy and the country's export performance are impressive by African standards, they are relatively insignificant in a global context, where complex value chain configurations are to an increasing extent defining trading relationships. South Africa's trade policy emphasises the need for export diversification through more intensive manufacturing activity, but the country remains heavily dependent on commodity exports. Direct services exports (largely concentrated in transportation and travel-related tourism) trail behind manufactured and mineral exports, although services contribute nearly 70 per cent of GDP. Value-added (indirect) services, as inputs in tangible exports, make a greater contribution to the export mix, but at present there are no mechanisms in place to measure this contribution accurately.

Where local companies participate in value chains, they often do so at low levels of the 'smile curve' (such as engaging in consolidation or assembly activities), whereas more high-level value chain activities might include research and design, licensing of technology, marketing and technical service. These companies also tend to be large, with considerable resources and competitiveness-enhancing economies of scale. Many of the high value-added goods and services that South Africa needs for capital expansion and consumption purposes are imported.

Relatively few SMMEs have ventured into direct exporting over the years because of the perceived risks (often stemming from a lack of knowledge) and costs involved. As a result, export-related job growth in the country has been limited. A contributing factor is that there are still relatively few providers of education and training in international trade practice and management in South Africa. This has resulted in a general lack of awareness of the types of business opportunities available at an international level and insufficient knowledge of what it takes to become competitive and to build a sustainable international operation. Knowledge and capacity limitations within government, in turn, mean that the business community is often ill informed about the various types of export assistance on offer, which have been designed to help (especially small) businesses make inroads into promising foreign markets.

Yet advances in technology, particularly the digitisation of data, are opening doors for SMMEs and giving them more affordable access to regional and global markets. E-commerce has enormous potential to bring the small business sector in South Africa into the fold of the digital economy. But it is not enough to have a buoyant ICT (information and communication technology) sector. All service sectors in the country (financial services, energy, education, transport and others) need to perform optimally if technology is to be leveraged in cost-effective ways.

The development of comprehensive services-sector and digital-policy frameworks is an urgent priority for the government, in consultation with stakeholders from the business, academic and research communities. Moreover, addressing SMMEs' concerns about the risks and costs of doing business internationally would be a significant step on the path towards economic revival in the country. In the light of this, organised business structures have a key role to play in improving the policy and regulatory environment for SMMEs.

While several chambers of commerce in South Africa are active in running international trade awareness and training programmes and assisting members (largely SMMEs) with their export endeavours, such activities typically have limited reach. Through greater collaboration with other members of the organised business sector, as well as education and training specialists, it will be possible to reach more entrepreneurs and companies and to champion the benefits of exporting more vigorously.

How to access regional and global value chains – both directly and indirectly – represents a special opportunity area for chambers of commerce and business associations. Not only could they disseminate information on market or competitive conditions and regulations to their export clients (which may lack the capacity to conduct their own research), but they could also coordinate joint activities among a number of clients aimed at strengthening these companies' position in the value chain – from realising cost savings through shared marketing to accessing cheaper inputs by buying in bulk. As an aid to their marketing advisory service, representative bodies could make use of the North-West University's TRADE-DSM® (where DSM stands for Decision Support Model), a user-friendly market selection tool that matches high-potential export markets with promising product categories, thereby removing much of the guesswork frequently associated with market identification and development.

Yet linked to all of this is the importance of preparing businesses for the future, given the speed with which accelerating urbanisation and technology are changing the nature of production and demand-and-supply patterns all over the world. Many of the jobs of today will be gone in ten years' time, replaced by a slew of new professions: bio-engineer, e-regulatory lawyer, augmented reality coach, intelligent material fashion designer, digital fintech planner, e-tech doctor, cyber ethics philosopher, 3D master chef, nano technician, climate controller, avatar manager and vertical gardener. The list goes on. The appeal of freelance work – with flexible schedules and greater discretionary powers over priority items – is also gaining momentum, and it will change corporate culture as well as collaboration and decision-making patterns.

While this view of the future may at this stage appear to be a distant speck for South Africa, given its current technology and skills deficits, global markets are changing rapidly, and the country's future product and services export potential will be dependent on the ability of producers and service providers (large and small) to adapt. The implications at both the macro- and microeconomic levels are immense. Studies have shown that already about 40 per cent of current jobs in South Africa are at risk of being at least partially automated within the next decade.

Imagination (ideas) and innovation (ideas put to good use) are the cornerstones of successful businesses today. These elements are essential for building enduring skills and capacity in South Africa and ensuring that business processes and outputs contribute to the overarching goal of growing the economy in an inclusive manner. To this end, organised business should be playing a leading role by keeping imagination alive and opportunities flowing, keeping important (and sometimes difficult) conversations going and leading by example.

The World Bank Group recently introduced a new concept of investment competitiveness, defined as the ability of countries not only to attract but also to retain and integrate private investment into their respective economies. The supporting World Bank study stresses that strengthening investment competitiveness requires establishing a favourable business environment, which includes developing more and better linkages with local, regional and global economies. Investors attach greater value to mechanisms that help them to expand their businesses than to policies used by governments simply to attract investment in the first place. As many as 68 per cent of multinational corporations now see information on the availability of local suppliers and links to these suppliers as critically important in their location decisions. This creates another opportunity for both well-organised and professionalised local business associations and bilateral national chambers to add value to this process, using their networks.

Promoting sustainability in the water and energy sectors

Of all the sectors driving an economy, water and energy are among the most critical but also among the most vulnerable. Though water and energy are national resources, much of their management devolves to the municipal level where households and businesses are located. Water and energy use (or misuse) frequently falls within the ambit of regional chambers' advocacy work.

In his prophetic book, *2052*, which was published in 2012, Jorgen Randers gives a chilling prediction of how the usual triggers of global conflict – oil and land – will pale into insignificance alongside another, increasingly scarce commodity – water. The distant reality that Randers spoke about has come sooner than expected, as evidenced in accelerating climate change and environmental degradation. South Africa is one of the casualties. In recent years, low rainfall patterns and elongated drought conditions have compromised farming activities in many parts of the country, threatened livestock and made it difficult for many businesses to operate. The Western Cape has been particularly hard hit.

Water is a critical resource in an economy – for domestic consumption and sanitation and for all manner of businesses, ranging from small farms and manufacturing outfits to massive power stations. When there are water shortages, economic activity is constrained. According to Stellenbosch University's Water Institute: 'Water can no longer be taken for granted, because resources are dwindling. It is an issue of major debate, with predictions that the next big wars will be fought over water.'[6] Is climate change really to blame?

Views on South Africa's escalating water crisis are divided. While many put the problem down to an uncharacteristically long drought and excessive water usage by consumers, others point to water mismanagement at the national and municipal levels. The fact that there is a single supplier of water (the state) has, they say, inevitably led to inefficiencies and supply shortages. Relatively low prices, in turn, have meant a lack of incentive to conserve water. Many municipalities (particularly in less developed areas where the socio-economic climate is depressed) have to carry the burden of huge unpaid water bills, making it difficult to meet their planned expenditure requirements. Communities suffer as a result.

But it is not only the quantity but also the quality of water that is causing alarm in many quarters. Critics of South Africa's water management authorities put the blame on poor planning. In the urban areas, expanding formal and informal settlements have given rise to sewerage problems, while clean water sources are at increasing risk of becoming polluted. Ageing infrastructure is also contributing to compromised water quality through leaking pipes.

Janine Myburgh, president of the Cape Chamber of Commerce and Industry, said that the Cape Town water crisis in 2017 and 2018 was the result of short-term thinking and could have been prevented. For example, a decision should have been taken years ago to build high-capacity water recycling and desalination plants. However, despite the chamber's frequent recommendations in this regard, relatively little has happened – with prohibitive costs being given as the main reason for not pursuing these options on a significant scale. Another factor is that desalination plants are electricity-intensive.

'Seventeen percent of Perth's water is desalinated sea water and the energy for the process is supplied by a wind farm,' said Myburgh. 'When the reservoirs are full and the wind is still blowing, the surplus electricity is fed into the grid. Most of the Middle East lives on desalinated sea water. Most islands, too, desalinate water and have been doing so for a long time. Malta, for instance, built its first desalination plant in 1881.'[7]

Myburgh believes that more private sector involvement could go a long way towards stabilising Cape Town's water resources by financing and building additional desalination plants and managing more water recycling projects, and that greater efficiency could ultimately drive down costs.

Hence the private sector, both individually and collectively, can still play an important role in dealing with South Africa's water challenges. Business associations and chambers should position themselves to help facilitate the process. In December 2017, the Water and Sanitation ministry called for 'a new partnership with the business and investment sector'. Private companies could step in to finance, develop and manage water infrastructure, allowing the state to redirect resources to other areas where there is a more critical need. But if the potential pitfalls in the privatisation of water distribution are to be avoided, an overall public–private sector protocol to govern any new dispensation will be needed to give consumers the best of all worlds.

The energy sector in South Africa (covering coal, gas, renewables and nuclear energy used in the production of electricity, fuel and heating or cooling for individual, commercial and industrial use) is crucial for the country's economic growth and development. But it is vulnerable to volatile costs and pricing as well as supply shortages. This has often complicated policy-making and the determination of tariffs. It has also created tensions among the different actors in the energy supply chain, including state-run Eskom (the country's largest electricity supplier) and independent power producers (IPPs) in the private sector, many of which supply renewable forms of energy (including solar and wind power). Eskom is the designated buyer of renewable energy generated by IPPs.

The situation with electricity generation and distribution in South Africa has been particularly fraught over the past decade. The growth-sapping load-shedding debacle of 2008 is still fresh in many people's minds and subsequent periodic power lapses in different regions and escalating prices point to a power sector that is far from stable. Unreliable supply of and high prices for electricity negatively impact on economic growth in the country and gnaw away at companies' chances of being competitive in local and international markets.

Renewables represent an excellent alternative (from an environmental perspective) to old-technology coal and gas, and the renewable energy sector in South Africa has grown rapidly in recent years. Renewable energy projects are often conducted on a relatively small scale, with energy sales stimulating economic growth in communities and contributing to employment and higher standards of education and health care. But Eskom and the Department of Energy have until recently been pushing back on giving too much market space to wind, solar and other producers, citing the unaffordability of adopting a bold renewable energy strategy for the country.

An expressed concern, too, is that the final draft of the Integrated Resource Plan (IRP), which forecasts South Africa's long-term electricity demand and sets out how such demand will be met in terms of a suite of measures (including generating capacity, timing and cost), has not had sufficient input from the business sector. According to Tanya Cohen, CEO of BUSA: 'Since the initial public consultation process was concluded in March 2017, business has made numerous attempts to ascertain from the Department the timing and extent of the public consultation process on the final draft IRP, to no avail.'[8]

It is worrying that the energy sector in South Africa has also been (as in the case of water) characterised by inadequate consultation among all relevant stakeholders. This makes it much more difficult to arrive at the kind of long-term solutions that are in the interests of the country as a whole.

Spreading the word about the importance of transformation
Having entered the South African lexicon a number of years ago, 'transformation' has become a common watchword in policy documents, business reports, news articles and political manifestos. However, its meaning tends to differ from one group of people to the next. For some, it suggests a gradual process of affording more economic opportunities and yielding assets – under carefully negotiated terms – to hitherto marginalised groups of people. To others, it means a more urgent and bold transfer of economic power and possessions, without the need for too many accompanying niceties.

Transformation is, rightly so, at the centre of much economic policy-making in South Africa. But the varying interpretations of the term (from moderate to radical) have slowed its implementation and complicated the business sector's interactions with government. Organised business entities like BLSA and BUSA often speak about the need for transformation and the work that they are doing in support of it. The views conveyed are by nature very broad, and the detail tends not to filter down to those working at the coalface. This paves the way for limited buy-in. By working together, BLSA, BUSA and other business associations could arrive at a common understanding of the transformation agenda from a private sector perspective, and from there derive a consistent narrative to convey to their various constituencies.

Early in 2017, BUSA embarked on a process to produce a business approach to black economic transformation, which culminated in the release in June 2017 of a wide-ranging mandated background document on the matter. This business approach identifies the guiding principles for business on black economic transformation, the current status of the phenomenon and the desired end state of a deracialised economy. The gap between the current status and the desired end state is interrogated in the document, with a view to isolating the key shifts needed in the private and public sectors to substantially broaden participation and enable inclusive growth and employment. A proactive, innovative, systemic and scalable approach to black economic transformation is needed, says BUSA.

BUSA nonetheless points out that working collaboratively as a business community is challenging, since individual BEE status is a form of competitive advantage. BEE levels can influence procurement decisions, which are driven by state procurement, licensing and private sector procurement. This can make it harder for business to collaborate in programmes. But BUSA also emphasises the size and complexity of the total transformation challenge. It is therefore clear that to promote a transformation culture in business as a whole, to develop systemic initiatives and to create a research base to reinforce the process will require business to be collectively organised in much more tangible ways. This would enable it to play a stronger role and leverage its understanding and promotion of the business environment in a less haphazard and fragmented manner.

It remains essential that business, especially organised business, should monitor and evaluate the BEE framework critically in the coming period to avoid or minimise unintended consequences, especially for the development of *new* firms. In emphasising this aspect, the international economist Ricardo Hausmann warns: 'BEE is a partial correction for past sins, but growth comes from start-ups, from new firms. Start-ups in any country typically face high death rates. By diverting attention away from creating new firms and imposing costs on existing firms, BEE is probably causing fewer of these firms to be created, and making sure that more of the firms that do get off the ground die.'[9]

And referring to the debate around 'white monopoly capital', Professor Hausmann waves another red flag: 'Besides, making the firms that exist, whoever owns them, the scapegoats for current problems is dangerous. It puts the accent on the firms that exist – when the problem for South Africa is the firms that do not yet exist – and that need to be created in order to employ the nine million people who don't work.'[10]

Whether or not we fully agree with these arguments, they nonetheless are serious enough to be weighed in any future assessment of BEE policies and their implementation, if we are to attain balanced outcomes. Apart from broader economic considerations, this is also a challenge for business associations and chambers to address, as it is new firms that must form part of their natural catchment area in the search for additional members.

What this chapter has set out to do is outline how a cooperative and rationalised organised business landscape (given the existing voluntary system of membership) could ensure that the national, provincial and local business agendas focus more on potentially relevant issues – if business could get its act together in a convincing manner. Diagnosing and changing the organised business culture remains a formidable task. The next chapter asks whether the organisational design of chambers and business associations could be reconfigured to strengthen their capacity to respond better to opportunities and challenges.

7

Is a more unified voice for business possible?

> Intelligent people, when assembled into an organisation incorrectly, will tend towards collective stupidity.
> – Albrecht's law

> When in doubt, do the courageous thing.
> – Jan Smuts

Getting the design right

Readers who are not interested in the structural aspects of organised business in South Africa and elsewhere can safely skip this chapter. It will also be necessary to recapitulate some earlier arguments in order to contextualise the options around organisational design. Provided, of course, that in passing it over readers continue to bear in mind the extent to which the design of organisations and institutions is a vital part of their success or failure, even if the detail is uninteresting to read. But a narrative about organised business in South Africa cannot avoid addressing the structural aspects of what is seen as a 'voice' in a capitalist system.

Business associations have been defined as long-term organisations with formal statutes regulating membership and internal decision-making, in which the members are individual business people, firms or other associations not necessarily linked by ownership or contractual relationship.

Studies in various countries have established that a wide range of functions and activities undertaken by business associations promote efficiency and address crucial development issues, using their institutional strength for productive ends. These studies consider associations representing business interests as potentially important instruments in guiding the path and outcome of socio-economic transformation.

Empirical studies have also confirmed the positive contributions of business associations in improving economic performance in developing countries in a variety of ways. While the studies do not reject arguments relating to the rent-seeking behaviour of business associations, they do show the positive contributions that are made despite the negative perceptions that exist. As previously noted, the contributions of business associations to economic performance may be perceived as market-supporting and market-complementing.

Market-supporting activities are particularly important in periods of consolidation for emerging economies where, as is now the case in South Africa, these economies are characterised by numerous market distortions. As the environment in which many associations operate becomes increasingly associated with widespread state and market failure, association activities are, of necessity, directed at rallying behind the proper functioning of states and markets, as opposed to using their institutional strength to distort well-functioning markets.

When we review business in general and organised business in particular in South Africa, we need to recognise that institutions of organised business are part of a highly complex set of interlocking institutions that are there to make any system work. This is particularly so in a mixed economy like South Africa. We cannot look only at their general track record but must also consider their internal operations. This applies to both the public and private sectors, and their performance clearly varies. Institutions can degenerate or malfunction over time, for both external and internal reasons, as previous chapters suggest. What tools are available in the organisational toolbox to assist as remedies?

Since businesses are not required to join a chamber (penetration levels vary widely) and because territories overlap, it can be difficult for any organisation, regardless of size, to state that it 'speaks for business', but they do. They earn that privilege by attracting numerous large and heterogeneous employers to their membership and leadership, as well as by utilising their collective voice on meaningful policy initiatives. In general, the smaller the chamber (and the community it represents), the less active the organisation will be on the policy and advocacy front. Even small organisations, however, sometimes take stands on regional issues ranging from school funding to road development.

We know that the term 'chamber of commerce' is therefore one of the oldest and most well-recognised brands in the world, but there is a significant public misunderstanding of its meaning. Chambers of commerce and business associations have attracted little interest in South Africa as a subject for study. There is an old adage in the chamber world: 'If you've seen one chamber, you've seen one.' Others who find themselves frustrated in their desire to apply universal truths to chamber of commerce models point to the Chinese parable of the seven blind men touching different parts of an elephant and coming away describing it differently ('It's a snake ... no, it's a tree ... no, it's a bush on a rope ...').

In many countries around the world, membership in the chamber of commerce movement is mandatory under law, with fees collected under some part of the business permit or taxation process. These organisations are referred to as 'public law' chambers. Many of them boast memberships in the hundreds of thousands, since literally all legitimate businesses must belong. Chambers in the UK, Canada, Australia and Eastern Europe tend to operate on a voluntary membership basis as in South Africa. In the European Union and much of Asia, public law chambers are more prevalent.

The government advocacy activities of these chambers are, of course, often substantially different from those in South Africa, but many of the issues addressed by these public law chambers would seem familiar to many chambers of commerce in South Africa – that is, workforce, infrastructure, economic development, education, community image, and so on. Indeed, the issues are very similar. But the business models are different, since they have government-sanctioned status rather than just corporate identities.

The previous chapters have highlighted the strengths and weaknesses of organised business in South Africa and the extent to which it is vested in a nation's particular historical context. In assessing the fault lines in organised business, we can identify two characteristics of the movement in South Africa: (a) at the national level it probably represents a minority of businesses in the economy, and (b) it is based on voluntarism, with the attendant free-rider phenomenon contributing significantly to the problem. The free-rider problem is a classic dilemma of group behaviour. The usual solution is for the group to impose some form of coercion or to seek to have it imposed externally to limit or eliminate the free-riders. Free-riders exist because they are willing and able to put their individual interests ahead of those of the group.

This is less of a problem for business associations at sectoral level, where there is minimal scope for fragmentation or wasteful competition. For example, there is really room for only one Chamber of Mines or AgriSA. But at other levels, and especially among multisectoral bodies, there is considerable duplication and confusion about the roles that they should play. This may also explain why the lack of structural discipline within organised business leaves many businesses outside the fold and therefore outside the sphere of influence of business leadership.

This could partly explain why such negative perceptions of business under apartheid have emerged, despite the claimed track record of organisations like ASSOCOM, the FCI, NAFCOC and later SACOB in earlier policy processes. This was emphasised in the supplementary submission made to the TRC (at its request) by SACOB in May 1998 on how the violation of human rights under apartheid could be avoided in future. The submission again stressed the 'structural limitations' from which the organised business sector suffered, preventing it from influencing public affairs to the maximum extent.

All these efforts leave business open to the constant and recurring charge that it is 'not doing enough' to promote change and transformation, despite laudable diverse initiatives and commitments to the contrary. There is no one central point at which the integrity pacts and similar business programmes permanently stay on message and report progress. They get lost in the tyranny of the here and now, and transformational processes are frequently simply neutralised by endless recriminations.

The global landscape

Globally we find that there are basically *two* organised business or chamber models in existence. The one is the Continental model, which developed from the medieval guilds in Europe. This kind of institution is also known as the public law prototype because it is created by natural legislation. The other is the Anglo-Saxon model, which emerged in the UK and was exported to its overseas possessions. This is not subject to public law statute but operates under loose private or tax law.

While most organised business structures can be grouped under one of these two models, some countries have blended attributes of both systems within the context of their own economic and political developments. Hence there are several economies that house a mixed or hybrid system of organised business. (See Annexure 1 for an international classification.)

The different combinations are outlined in Tables 7.1 and 7.2.

Table 7.1: Features of the Anglo-Saxon model		
Features	Strengths	Weaknesses
1. No chamber legislation (private law status)	• Independence • Freedom of individual business to join or establish a chamber	• Overlapping chambers in certain geographical locations • Wasteful competition • Considerable duplication
2. Voluntary membership	• Strong incentive to work efficiently and remain demand-orientated	• 'Free-rider' behaviour • Limited influence because of low membership • Lack of financial income from membership dues or unstable income
3. No delegation of public tasks	• Freedom of chamber to decide on a range of activities	• Lack of financial income from fees for delegated services • Big business usually has to contribute to financial sustainability • Unable to sanction unethical behaviour

Source: Adapted from Robert J Bennett (ed.), *Trade Associations in Britain and Germany* (London and Bonn: Anglo-German Foundation, 1997)

Table 7.2: Features of the Continental model

Features	Strengths	Weaknesses
1. Special chamber law (public law status)	• The designation 'chamber' is legally protected	• Often limited range of activities
2. Mandatory membership	• Fully representative • No 'free-rider' behaviour • Broad and stable income	• Incentive challenges to always work efficiently and be demand-orientated
3. Formal consultative status vis-à-vis government	• Formal access to public administration • Public sector more likely to outsource to organised business	• Difficulty in sometimes presenting clear-cut position due to an obligation to represent balanced view
4. Regulated regional coverage	• Only one chamber per location	• Incentive problems due to monopoly
5. Delegation of public tasks	• Chambers are closer to private sector	• Risks of alienation from private sector
6. Special public supervision	• Protection • Provides leadership for bulk of business • Being fully representative enhances clout • Penalises unethical behaviour	• Possible government interference

Source: Adapted from Robert J Bennett (ed.), *Trade Associations in Britain and Germany* (London and Bonn: Anglo-German Foundation, 1997)

Strengthening organised business?

Against this background, the overall impression remains that, while business organisations vary in depth and breadth, excessive duplication and fragmentation strongly define the organised business landscape in South Africa. As things look now, organised business, especially at national level, is very much a house divided against itself, despite token efforts from time to time to collaborate. Are the conditions really in place to make the Anglo-Saxon model work more successfully in South Africa? Or is it a case of what economists would call 'wasteful competition' and 'spurious product differentiation', which will not self-correct of its own volition?

Where business associations are poor, unrepresentative and understaffed, they are not well placed to redress state and market failure. Institutional strength and capacity are needed to perform value-added economic functions adequately. The definition of strength lies in a business association's capacity to induce members to commit resources and comply with rules and decisions aimed at furthering collective goals. The problem with many business associations in South Africa is not that they are too strong, but rather that they are often perceived as too weak.

To recapitulate, if South Africa were to opt for a mandatory system of business association membership, it would ideally:

- strengthen membership density;
- ensure an adequate and stable source of income;
- improve service delivery to members;
- ensure fair and broad representation;
- eliminate the free-rider problem;
- enlarge spheres of influence; and
- penalise unethical behaviour.

It is evident that chambers with mandatory membership – and with the financial strength that accompanies it – offer a strong competitive edge. But is this a Faustian bargain? What are the risks of public regulation? These aspects need to be distilled out of a realistic assessment of how effective organised business is in South Africa under present arrangements and what can be done to strengthen it. It is, of course, one thing to recognise the importance of institutional quality, but quite another to specify what makes for quality and how it might be improved.

All over the world business associations, like their members, have been facing a changing and more complex environment. When individual enterprises change their strategies in order to become or remain competitive, their expectations of their business associations or employer organisations also undergo change. What this all means is that organised business in South Africa has to constantly renew its relevance and reassess its structures.

National business associations often underestimate the importance of interaction with provincial and local government. Despite its long traditions, the organised business network is very uneven in its coverage across the country as a whole and there are large gaps. Although South Africa does not operate a federal system, there are significant points of access for business at other levels of government in this country. There are 283 local authorities and nine provincial governments with which to engage. This is where much delivery takes place and where extended cooperative action would help not only to improve delivery, but also to enhance business opportunities. Business associations need to strengthen collaboration with structures such as the South African Local Government Association and the relevant state departments to mobilise business more effectively at the local level.

Many of the current changes play into the hands of business associations. After all, they are by their very nature information brokers. The information age presents a great opportunity for association growth, by providing sifted information on a value-added basis. What members really need from business associations is not so much information, but ideas, knowledge and analysis, underpinned by good research. Organised business should be both a consumer and a contributor of ideas on policy.

But does South Africa need a chamber of commerce with a public law status?

It is useful to look at the experience of the UK chamber of commerce network, which has gone through several years of continuing and radical reform. Historically, South Africa shares many institutional approaches and values with the UK in respect of organised business. In the search for new ways to improve its competitiveness in the global economy, the UK reorganised the chamber movement there in recent years to provide a national network of approved chambers, which was assigned the role of raising the quality of its service to the business community.

The umbrella body, British Chambers of Commerce, wants to enjoy strong government support to improve its functioning, while stopping short of acquiring public law status. However, this approach has been criticised by some academic commentators and business people who believe that public law UK chambers would optimise the quality of business support and representations.

For South Africa, the similarities and differences between the chamber systems are captured in Table 7.3.

Table 7.3: Similarities and differences between chamber systems

Structural aspects	South Africa	France and Germany
Legal status	Private law	Public law
Membership	Voluntary	Compulsory
Business coverage	Incomplete	Complete
Funding	Non-statutory	Largely statutory
Organisational size	Often small	Often large
Quality control	Possible voluntary accreditation	Public control
Status and recognition	Typically low	High
National network	Incomplete	All areas
Local overlaps	Likely	No
Statutory mission	No	Yes
Delegated and autonomous tasks performed	Maybe	Yes
Business advice and information	Yes	Yes
Representational role	Limited in scope	Major
Local economic development role	Minor role	Major role

Source: Adapted from Robert J Bennett (ed.), *Trade Associations in Britain and Germany* (London and Bonn: Anglo-German Foundation, 1997)

When we draw on experiences abroad and an analysis of the organised business landscape in South Africa, it appears as if the strengths of the voluntary system are increasingly being outweighed by its weaknesses. There is widespread evidence that chambers of commerce in South Africa, for example, are experiencing cumulative disadvantages because of their lack of membership numbers and business coverage, lack of adequate funding and financial instability, uneven geographical coverage and the intense competition experienced from both the private and public sectors through duplicating business support structures.

While it is just as well that the CEO Initiative was formed to assist in addressing socio-economic challenges and for a period fending off investment downgrades, this development was also symptomatic of the extent to which organised business as such has lost ground. It also tends to reinforce the stereotype that South Africa is run by 'monopoly capital'. But there is a more important requirement: the need to restore a degree of unity in business. We must not necessarily see the proliferation of business associations and groupings as a healthy sign of business pluralism or democracy. It may instead be a sign of a malady – a weakening of the business voice.

An analysis of the rates of membership trends in organised business in South Africa on the whole shows evidence of reluctance to join and high lapse rates. The overwhelming motive for business membership of chambers and business associations is to access services with specific, rather than collective, benefits. The downside risk in the voluntary system is that few businesses are willing to pay for general collective goods, as they see advocacy and lobbying as advantages that others can enjoy at no cost (the free-rider problem).

Voluntarism is, of course, a valuable thing – but, like most valuable things, limited in supply and efficacy. It needs to be assessed anew whether there is a better organisational dispensation that will prevent these useful qualities of cooperation from being wastefully squandered through being set tasks that are increasingly outside their compass to perform effectively in South Africa's mixed economy.

If we want to reverse and improve the situation, there needs to be at the outset a general recognition that the current organised business landscape is not serving the interests of business or the country effectively. A more streamlined and disciplined organised business set-up would create a much more powerful mechanism to formulate a truly national business agenda. The difficulty with recent highly proactive and constructive policy initiatives from organisations like BUSA, BLSA and the BBC is the limited traction that they appear to generate among the mainstream of business. There are just too many weak links in the organised business chain – too many gatekeepers and gateways.

Although organised business leaders often seem confident about the way things are structured, various commentators have been questioning whether organised business in South Africa might have something to learn from elsewhere. Even business leaders who say all the right things and show good intentions tend to reflect the systems through which they have emerged. At the time of writing, the same business person, for example, was heroically serving as president of both BUSA and BLSA. If these systems are flawed, we might blame the leaders for their failure, but it is unrealistic to expect a different outcome. There is a need to support strong institutions, not strong individuals.

Yet although there may often be rumblings around the fragmented nature of organised business in South Africa, there is indeed likely to be substantial disagreement as to whether the South African system should move in, say, the French-German direction. It may be argued that there is a perceived lack of transportability to South Africa of another system, or just outright opposition from many business people to the adoption of mandatory membership and statutory levies. But it is also clear that the existing organised business set-up is sub-optimal and not serving either the business community or the national economy very well.

Change may need to come from the bottom up, even if this is harder, messier and takes longer. Commendable as the foundation of BUSA was in 2003 to promote a 'peak' organisation for business, we need to revisit why, despite the existence of BUSA, the organised business world remains so divided. The BBC was re-established in 2011 when it was thought that BLSA had 'hijacked' BUSA and was furthering the interests of large corporates at the expense of black business. 'Power struggle between the BMF and BUSA gave rise to radical policy,' claimed a headline.[1] The argument about who represents business in NEDLAC is another example of the lack of cohesion in business that needs to be addressed. 'The general observation is this: There is no organisational structure in the world that will work without a shared sense of purpose or a commitment to collaboration from key personalities. Oversized egos and destructive factionalism can undermine even the most perfect structures.'[2]

The way ahead

Although the government may also like to see a more rationalised and streamlined organised business arrangement (a former President once appealed to business for 'one telephone number to call'), the initiative needs to be seen to come in the first instance from the private sector itself. If organised business wishes to enlarge its sphere of influence, it should seriously introspect. Given the inevitable conflict of interest and turf

'There are no great men, my boy – only great committees.' (©1975 Charles Addams Foundation, Renewed 2002; with permission Tee and Charles Addams Foundation)

problems that exist, there must be political will in the first instance to look at the need to restructure organised business, at least at the national multisectoral level.

A more disciplined organised business framework that empowers self-regulation could also help to purge business of negative behaviour, which often stigmatises the sector and brings business generally into disrepute. Organised business would then have the machinery and power to impose sanctions to enforce business-promulgated standards of business conduct, or to discipline those who would damage the canons of sound business practices. Recent examples in South Africa of companies that have been accused of breaching good corporate governance standards could then have been dealt with by organised business itself.

Where prominent companies fail to live up to ethical standards, said economist Iraj Abedian, 'it is hurtful to the economy, and even though they portray themselves as captains of industry, they don't seem to realise that their seemingly unethical conduct hurts job creation and stifles growth. South Africans rightly "go to town" when politicians and bureaucrats are accused of ethical shortcomings. The same should go for captains of industry.'[3]

Leaving aside other compliance requirements and criminal sanctions, companies may more likely behave ethically and act against corruption if they are confident that their competitors also conform to the same ethical standards. Business associations and chambers of commerce can potentially offer a good platform for business to engage collectively against corruption and level the playing field. They also create an umbrella under which from time to time the question 'Is it right?' can be asked when business policy is being shaped. In other words, they need to encourage a value-based approach.

Most institutions are not lightly changed, even when clearly imperfect or outdated. What may also torpedo any renewed efforts to build a more effective business coalition are the low levels of trust that permeate so much of South Africa. The trust deficit cuts across many sectors. But such a dystopian view of the future of organised business will inevitably mean that the collective voice of business will be much weaker than it ought to be in South Africa.

There have been several earlier references to 'trust' and 'trust deficit' in South Africa, especially between government and business. Again we must emphasise the extent to which we rely on the mechanism of trust to play a defining role in bringing about economic success. A lack of trust inevitably leads to economic inefficiency and less-than-optimal impact. 'It isn't only rulers and governments who prize and need trust. Each of us and every profession and every institution needs trust. We need trust because we have to rely on others acting as they say that they will, and because we need others to accept that we will act as we say we will.'[4]

Then, if the spirit is willing, as was the case when ASSOCOM and the FCI contemplated merging to form SACOB, an independent person or group of persons should be appointed to act as a kind of commission of inquiry on agreed terms of reference to study the current profile of organised business as it presently operates. To succeed, as a first step we must bring together those who belong together, and it will require rising above narrow sectoral views and seeing the bigger picture.

On the basis of the necessary research and consultation, such an investigative process can then make recommendations for current structures to consider and decide on the way ahead. Several options might be explored. 'Structure follows strategy' is the appropriate adage. It will probably be necessary to follow a path of gradualness – to mould and rationalise, not to violently uproot. But 'gradualism' must not be a polite word for standing still.

Such an investigation would unpack the organised business landscape to assess, among other things:
- organisational structure;
- governance and accountability;
- capacity to engage in dialogue and provide business development services;
- constraints and problems (legal, policy and others);
- mechanisms of consultation and dialogue;
- support areas; and
- intervention strategies that need to be followed.

If a more disciplined and streamlined system is contemplated, the institutions concerned will then need to negotiate with government on what legislative framework or other incentives may be needed to give effect to any new structure or structures for organised business in South Africa. A useful analogy is the extent to which trade unions have a regulatory framework which governs their existence but which does not limit their policy agenda or ability to act.

To navigate and manage this process will require business leadership of the highest order and a shared vision of the role that a better organised business community can play in a future South Africa. 'Organisations and institutions must be grounded in their national context if they are to flourish. By the same token, there is more at stake here than a sterile debate about organisational structure. The type of business organisation a country ultimately elects will leave a lasting imprint on its political and economic direction.'[5]

8

Business in South Africa: The answer or the enemy?

> Businessmen have a different set of delusions from politicians; and need, therefore, different handling. They are, however, much milder than politicians, at the same time allured and terrified by the glare of publicity, easily persuaded to be 'patriots', perplexed, bemused, indeed terrified, yet only too anxious to take a cheerful view ... You could do anything you like with them, if you would treat them (even big ones), not as wolves and tigers, but as domestic animals by nature ... If you work them into a surly, obstinate, terrified mood, of which domestic animals, wrongly handled, are so capable, the nation's burdens will not be carried to market.
> – JOHN MAYNARD KEYNES TO US PRESIDENT FRANKLIN ROOSEVELT (1938)

> The most distinctive characteristic of the businessman – the thing that most sharply distinguishes him from the lawyer, the college professor or, generally speaking, the civil servant – is his capacity for decision.
> – JOHN KENNETH GALBRAITH

PREVIOUS QUESTIONS AROUND HOW LONG South Africa will survive might rather be answered by saying, 'Yes, it will survive, but is *survival* good enough?' And to what extent would a more effective role and voice for business as a whole help to make for more positive outcomes? These are the broad issues that this book has thus far sought to address in looking at the past and present role of business around the theme of 'good capitalism, bad capitalism'. This must be set within the context of South Africa's economic decline in recent years and of the prospects of doing better in future.

With Cyril Ramaphosa now President of South Africa, together with Cabinet changes and other developments on the policy front, the tide seems to be turning for South Africa economically and politically. '2017 was a year of eruptions in both political and business leadership,' said economist Iraj Abedian, 'and much evidence emerged showing deep ethical rot in business and government.'[1] In South Africa, almost more than in other countries, public perceptions around these developments became increasingly fraught over the years.

Against this background, we need to acknowledge that strong anti-business sentiment has emerged in South Africa. Yet 'business is the answer, not the enemy,' said BLSA CEO Bonang Mohale in November 2017. Business will nevertheless need to forge a new relationship with the broad public to rebuild trust in 'good capitalism'. This approach at least creates an opportunity for the business community to consolidate the role of enterprise and entrepreneurship in a mixed economy and to recapture the intellectual and moral high ground from its critics. 'Now that Zuma is gone, real work begins for big business ... it cannot be business as usual,' said BASA (Banking Association South Africa) MD, Cas Coovadia.[2]

Economic perceptions depend, more than many analysts realise, on what people *believe* about the system and its benefits. Yet we need to remind ourselves of our original definition in Chapter 2 that capitalism is intended to be an adaptive economic process potentially able to offer inclusive economic outcomes, provided the policy environment and framework are right. The big economic challenges for South Africa lie in mobilising the system to get inclusive growth up and unemployment down. Fixing the root causes of inequality also means fixing the root causes of low growth.

As we assess South Africa's economic performance, we also need to recall that sustained growth empirically reduces poverty and that the private sector is supposed to drive growth. Indeed, as former UN Secretary-General Kofi Annan has said: 'It is the absence of broad-based business activity, not its presence, which condemns much of humanity to suffering.' Without sustainable enterprises, there can be no job-rich growth.

Yet society and enterprises remain interdependent. Sustainability is not about excusing what business might have done wrong or even about corporate philanthropy. 'It is about recognising that business should be good for society and society good for business,' says *The Economist Intelligence Unit*.[3] But these considerations cannot just be left at a conceptual level. Business is in reality still vulnerable to populist pressure, especially when things are thought to have veered badly off course.

Here, too, business needs to do a much better job of explaining its role, what progress it has made to date, how expectations must be managed and what the boundary conditions are for success. For example, the wider public is more familiar with the wrongdoings of several businesses than they are with the major commitments by the CEO Initiative to promote small business and youth employment projects. The challenge is to meet multiple economic and social goals contemporaneously in an informed and evidence-based manner, in the face of rapidly shifting perceptions in some quarters towards radical populism.

Nor must business take the support of the private enterprise system and property rights for granted, nor allow its fundamentals to be undermined by blatant anti-competitive behaviour. Markets and business thus need political support, yet their very functioning often erodes that support. If the system is not seen to be competitive and rule-based, and if crony capitalism is thought to be the reality, the risk of a backlash against business inevitably rises. 'A truly free and competitive market occupies a very delicate middle ground between the absence of rules and the presence of suffocating rules,' say economists Raghuram Rajan and Luigi Zingales. They think that 'it is because this middle ground is so narrow that capitalism in its best form is very unstable. It easily degenerates into a system of the incumbents, by the incumbents, for the incumbents.'[4]

Hence, of course, the important role played by competition policy and law in South Africa as well as in many other jurisdictions. It nonetheless becomes necessary to find a sensible level of policy intervention to identify the middle ground on which South African business must stand and from which it must still be allowed to operate effectively.

While business must be seen to condemn predatory or collusive behaviour which harms the public interest as well as the image of private enterprise, bad policies and state capture have also clearly distorted the proper functioning of markets in South Africa. It is often difficult to separate cause and effect, which frequently then degenerates into a deeply polarising ideological debate about capitalism and socialism. Both markets and state intervention must be regarded as policy tools, *not* presented as dogmas.

And this is also where the 2017 ANC elective conference decision to interrogate the issue of expropriating property without compensation is relevant. In fact, the highly praised South African Constitution itself provides for a 'mixed' system of property, partly private and partly common. Provision is also made for a number of adjustments to the proportions of the two categories, mainly in Section 25 of the Constitution.

As at least one authoritative legal expert among several others has explained:

> Section 25 is not well understood and has not been put to optimal use in the striving for a better life for all in the new South Africa. A misconception that it envisages the 'willing buyer, willing seller' policy of the ANC has wide currency ... This interpretation is simply not correct ... It can be seen from any fair reading of the text [of the Constitution] that a delicate balance was devised ... Tinkering with Section 25 could upset the felicitous state of affairs, to the detriment of the poor more so than those whose property is expropriated.[5]

The reality is that the state has thus far not possessed the capacity or ability to settle new farmers successfully on transferred or acquired land. This was confirmed by the 2017 'Report of the High Level Panel on the Assessment of Key Legislation and the Acceleration of Fundamental Change', chaired by Kgalema Motlanthe. The land reform challenge needs more practical solutions based on the commitment to widespread consultation with interested parties.

Yet seriously problematic questions currently circulating about the land reform challenge must not be underestimated. The motion on expropriation of land without compensation passed by Parliament on 27 February 2018 was an indication of how divided political parties are in this matter. For example, the Economic Freedom Fighters (EFF) are pushing a strong restitution agenda, advocating the nationalisation of all land in the country. In contrast, the Democratic Alliance (DA), while supporting land reform, opposes the idea of expropriation of land without fair compensation packages being negotiated. Although robust political debate within the parliamentary system should be welcomed, structured inputs from other stakeholders (including the banks) are also essential to arrive at well-informed and balanced decisions.

With things coming to a head, South Africa ignores the land issue – whether in rural or urban areas – at its peril. The University of Cape Town's Professor Anthony Butler sums it up well as follows:

> The redistribution strategy has lacked urgency, and most of the 8% of land transferred back has not resulted in viable black-owned farms ... Two-thirds or more of productive farmland cannot continue to be owned by whites, while major historic grievances remain unaddressed, and poverty and unemployment are at such extreme levels. Hasty policy changes pose major systemic risks ... Generalised expropriation without compensation would have catastrophic consequences for the banks, and for future investment and employment.[6]

Both internationally and locally there has been valuable research conducted on the role of property rights and land reform in economic development. In a recent wide-ranging study on this subject from a South African perspective, Professor Stefan Schirmer from the University of the Witwatersrand concludes: 'What has to be avoided ... are populist practices in which the State gives in to demands for quick solutions irrespective of the broader, long-term consequences ... In other words, the property system needs to expand and transform without undermining the integrity of property as an abstract right ... but it will not be tomorrow and it will not be easy.'[7]

Noting the potentially serious economic consequences of these developments, the business community and its representative bodies must participate fully in the consultative process that is accompanying the debate around property rights in South Africa, failing which the matter will continue to be dogged by uncertainty and the final outcome is likely to be ill-informed. A wrong decision on a matter as fundamental as this carries huge downside risks for the economy, which is why the ANC resolution and even the parliamentary motion on the subject are hedged with certain economic conditions. How the land issue is tackled – both inside and outside Parliament – will be an important test of South Africa's ability to forge consensus on one of the most critical and emotive issues on the country's economic agenda.

Business must nonetheless be able to set its engagement on the land reform issue in a wider context over and above the inevitable economic and legal aspects involved. There is scope for it to broaden its horizons on the matter. The challenge and inherent dilemma are well summed up in the following comment:

> So what can business do to be part of the solution? The temptation will be that it heaves a big sigh of relief as Ramaphosa holds the barbarians from the door. But what it really needs to do to survive in the long term is to commit to changing the patterns of wealth and poverty in South Africa. Black economic empowerment, equity stakes, employment equity and the appointment of black CEOs has been just a small start. A bigger development effort is needed. The catch is that capitalists like to (and must) pursue the project of individual endeavour and wealth creation. Nation-building tends to be beyond the scope of profit making and taking in a capitalist society.[8]

Business must accept that it is in it for the long haul. It therefore needs to take a long-term view of its decisions about the South African economy since the country's socio-economic challenges, as we have seen in earlier chapters, will remain an ongoing process. Just when we think we have solved one of the problems, others emerge, often from the previously attempted solutions themselves. We understandably seek solutions, but the reality is often different. Even the best solutions will often be only a temporary achievement, though not to be despised for that reason.

Thus we need to safeguard the institutions and mechanisms with which, whether in the public or private sectors, we tackle the flow of challenges that, like the waves on the beach, will continue to come. South Africa must therefore protect and strengthen the institutions that make solutions possible, as well as mobilise them within an overall socio-economic framework like the National Development Plan (NDP). Public and private sector institutions should ideally be the steel framework of

South Africa's economy, its formal rules and informal constraints, which help to enhance the predictability and certainty that the business sector frequently seeks.

An important lesson of the past few years in South Africa is that good institutions work badly if the wrong procedures are followed (e.g. cadre deployment and state capture) or accountability is not enforced or implementation simply fails. Good institutions sag under the weight of corruption, racism, careerism and patronage. And as experience with certain key state-owned enterprises has also sadly demonstrated, development without efficiency tests can ultimately lead to collapse, as such structures are intrinsically brittle.

Yet it is only through effective institutions that the debate and decision-making around policy dilemmas can take place and the tough trade-offs that are often needed can be made. South Africa has been praised for the resilience of those institutions that still constitute centres of excellence in society. And the country also requires an indispensable contribution from business, which is, after all, the main driver of the economic factors – ostensibly responsible for both the convergent and divergent forces in the South African economy.

We nonetheless need to reiterate that different countries have different approaches to a mixed economy. 'No single blueprint fits all,' says economist Professor Dani Rodrik, and he emphasises 'the diversity of capitalist arrangements that still prevail in advanced economies, despite the considerable homogenisation of our policy discourse'.[9] Once a certain minimum number of market conditions have been met to encourage enterprise and entrepreneurship, several additional institutional options exist. There is no one model of capitalism that is best at all times and in all places.

But even though there remains a wide range of structures and cultures that can produce similar results, there are obviously bad policies that can seriously damage economic prospects. It comes down to the policy choices that a country makes within the institutional framework at its disposal. The lesson for South Africa is clear – it has seen how in recent years bad choices have led to bad outcomes and ultimately to poor economic performance. So what can be done?

'Any real world economy is riddled with market failure,' says Professor Daron Acemoglu, 'so a benevolent and omnipotent government could sensibly intervene quite often. But who has ever met a benevolent or omnipotent government? ... Modern economic growth, even under inclusive institutions, often creates deep inequalities and tilted playing fields ... The modern regulatory and redistributive state can, within certain bounds, help to address the problems. But the success of such a project crucially depends on society having control over the state – not the other way around.'[10]

No responsible business person or commentator would see the prevalence of state capture and corruption in South Africa as consistent with any legitimate model of private enterprise or compatible with a system that must hold the state and other stakeholders accountable. Crony capitalism is therefore not perceived as a system that gives many more people in South Africa a broad stake in the economy to uphold and defend, but rather as one that favours only a few. This lopsided outcome then becomes a source of alienation and protest.

And there are also choices for business to make. It is evident that the expectations of business are changing as rapidly as the society around it. 'Corporations must find a way to lead' is the repeated message from countless media statements and think tanks in South Africa. There is growing acceptance that a business can take specific actions that improve both profit and the socio-economic conditions in the community where it operates. These new realities need to take centre stage in evolving appropriate business strategies.

Hence, an increasing number of businesses now believe that the era of focusing only on corporate social responsibility is passing and that the mantra of 'doing well by doing good' is gaining ground. 'Doing well by doing good' is, however, not alien to some businesses and is a natural course for others: it is a matter of choice. It is a question of deciding what constitutes responsible leadership in business. And as the business community, individually and collectively, gradually works to rebuild trust, proactive steps must be taken to develop a narrative and engage with stakeholders to balance the profit motive with the creation of societal value. To this end the concept of 'wealth creation' needs a more holistic definition.

Socio-economic issues in South Africa are therefore not so much tangential to 'the business of business' as fundamental to it. Things need to be better steered and managed in order to get the right balance in a society that needs to reconcile economic efficiency, social justice and individual liberty. From a defensive point of view, those businesses that ignore public sentiment make themselves vulnerable to attack from various stakeholders.

South African business is not immune from the global trend identified in a World Economic Forum publication:

> Businesses are now more conscious than ever that the people they serve have the power to mortally hurt them, often via social media, if they fail to live up to their side of the social contract ... It is becoming more evident that the long-term sustainability of a business of any level is directly tied up to its understanding of how its supply chain and all its facets impact on the lives of those they touch.[11]

Social pressures and expectations in a changing environment can also operate as early indicators of trends that are key to the profitability and transformation of businesses. Business must remain most sensitive to the conditions of the next moment – like a Geiger counter of future trends. To monitor and manage these trends, companies need to introduce specific processes to ensure that social issues and emerging social forces are discussed at the highest level. Mistakes in business management of these issues now carry heavier risks and need to be foreseen and averted through responsible business decision-making. Good corporate citizenship needs to be taken to the next level.

This also means establishing ever-higher standards of integrity and transparency, whether through King IV on corporate governance or other relevant codes of conduct, and avoiding the calamities that befell corporates like KPMG, McKinsey and Steinhoff. The apparent weakening in previous self-regulation by the auditing profession seems to be an important contributing factor to the business sagas that have developed. Accountants and auditors have received a serious wake-up call. President Ramaphosa has also urged professional and regulatory bodies to take action against members who are found to have acted improperly and unethically.[12]

Individual companies should also use their annual reports and other platforms more proactively to profile what they have achieved in terms of broader socio-economic goals. Business has good cards to play but must do so skilfully. There are still important arguments to be won.

A perceptive observer summed up the challenge as follows:

When most people feel they have virtually no chance of economic success playing by the rules, they will be tempted by populism and corruption. By extension, if business wants a better investment environment, it should add some success indicators that support more inclusive growth. It could give job creation, support for small business and equitable access to education and promotions the same weight as fiscal rectitude and property rights. That approach would help counter populist rhetoric and, by shaping a more dynamic and inclusive society, enable increased investment and growth.[13]

The turn of the ANC political wheel

In his original 2007 biography and frank appraisal of Cyril Ramaphosa, Professor Anthony Butler described him as a 'visionary pragmatist'. 'Many South Africans', said Butler at the time, 'see problem-solving and institution-building Ramaphosa as a future State President of South Africa.' He concluded that 'Ramaphosa is a natural politician who gravitates towards and embraces power. It would not be a surprise to find that his time, at last, has come.'[14] And now it has happened. As someone who has successfully climbed to the top of Disraeli's 'greasy pole' of politics, there are high expectations about the type of leadership he brings to South Africa.

We have seen that the explanations for why and how South Africa got into its present situation are invariably plural and interrelated. In retrospect, the past twenty-four years in South Africa were a mixture of experiences and processes which promised that, in the name of liberation and freedom, the country was democratising and was replacing apartheid with non-racialism, and that shared prosperity would gradually emerge. But this was hijacked to a large extent by state capture and other forms of corruption, which saw the governance clock turned back by several degrees. Serious reforms are now patently needed at several levels of South African society.

As a range of political scientists have stressed, a successful reformer is a leader who is able to steer and bring policy change to fruition in a consistent way, despite opposition from economic actors, interest groups and political forces whose interests or worldviews may be threatened. 'Political economy is the battleground of reform,' said Dr Greg Mills.[15]

Yet a set of policies that may seem inept or incoherent to the outside world may nonetheless serve the political economy purpose of holding together a governing coalition that is facing a general election in 2019. President Ramaphosa has committed himself to 'unity'. But if anyone could navigate all this successfully, it would be Ramaphosa, to whom we will return again in the final chapter. What are some of the other mechanisms or processes in the meantime that might assist South Africa in its formidable task?

Revitalising and updating the NDP: Does South Africa need an 'economic CODESA' or a 'delivery state'?

As the South African economy has been increasingly besieged by its problems – and by the credit rating agencies – calls have gone up in some circles for an 'economic CODESA' to sort matters out. It is a seductive proposal. The great danger is that once again 'the can is kicked down the road' in the face of another series of fruitless meetings and summits, which will not only waste time that South Africa can ill afford to lose but will not resolve inner contradictions. Of course, there is always a strong case for dialogue and negotiation. The track record, however, suggests that South Africa needs now to move beyond the staging of endless conferences, while pressure for delivery mounts.

And we need to be clear about one thing: South Africa has so far certainly not lacked for public debate about its economic performance. Countless diagnostics and analyses have confirmed this over the years. The past couple of decades have abounded with summits, seminars, country studies, plans, policies, projects and disappointments.

So *why* are we here yet again? Each time South Africa preaches the 'high road' but is perceived to deliver only the 'low road', the challenges become more formidable and frustration builds. Endless debate is not a substitute for the good governance and leadership now needed to face up to the tough decisions and difficult trade-offs required in both the public and private sectors.

Indeed, for South Africa there is a choice between interminable debate and effective implementation. Deep frustration occurs when these processes become part of the problem, instead of the solution. Top-level summits should now have a *strategic* purpose in arriving at decisions and in changing stakeholder behaviour. Participation and effectiveness need to be balanced. If a CODESA-like gathering nonetheless becomes inevitable, it should rather be focused on how to create a *delivery state* in South Africa. This is a goal to which most South Africans of whatever political persuasion are likely to aspire.

In the meantime, there is the NDP. It *exists*. As the overarching vision for South Africa's socio-economic development by 2030, the NDP was liberally cited in ANC policy documents in 2017, as well as by Ramaphosa in his campaign to become ANC President. Subsequently he referred to a 'New Deal' for the economy, which obviously drew heavily on the NDP for its inspiration.

The NDP must be viewed as a focus, not a substitute, for decision-making. As previously stressed, it could have provided – but regrettably did not – a systematic way of coordinating policy approaches in recent years. Judged by the key tests of consistency and policy certainty, the NDP has failed to provide the necessary grip on the policy machinery required for successful implementation. Except for the National Treasury, visible commitments by various government departments to the NDP have been minimal. At the national level, the links between what was planned in the NDP and its offshoots like Operation Phakisa and the Medium-Term Strategic Plan (MTSP) have become increasingly tenuous and detached from reality.

Despite the official commitment to the NDP, contradictory policy decisions – whether on land reform, nuclear power or building state capacity – have in the past been bad for business confidence as well as costly in terms of economic performance. Predictable government conduct is at least as important to investors as South Africa's laws and regulations. And the decisions by the 2017 ANC elective conference on the expropriation of land and the nationalisation of the Reserve Bank appear to have no resonance with the original NDP. It is obviously one thing to advocate an active national plan, but it is quite another thing to take the right measures to carry it out.

In the words of the Planner's song in Lewis Carroll's *Through the Looking Glass*:

> But I was thinking of a plan,
> To dye one's whiskers green,
> And always use so large a fan,
> That they could not be seen.

Instead of talking about an economic CODESA and similar gatherings, we should therefore rather be seeking an 'implementation summit' on how best to give effect to what has been agreed and decided. This would be a tangible step. What South Africa needs is a focused effort on effective implementation and delivery. As Ramaphosa himself said in his maiden speech after being elected ANC President: 'The people of South Africa want action. They do not want words.'

But it would be unwise to think that the solution lies only in implementation of what has been promised and agreed to date. There are still other fundamental issues at stake. Well-designed summit agendas will take us only so far, and South Africa has indeed been there many times before. The deep polarisation in South African society cannot be overlooked or treated lightly. Professor Steven Friedman reminds us of this: 'Deep divisions are bridged by hard, lengthy bargaining, not by three-day meetings ... Since tough bargaining is needed, the government would do more to start the process if it said how it wanted the economy to change and invited other interests to respond. This seems more likely to focus minds than another event that stresses dubious common ground.'[16]

So, what of the NDP? South Africa is now already one-third of the way towards 2030, the NDP having been launched in 2012. An overall plan like the NDP can continue to be a major guide to policy coherence and consistency. But it also needs to be brought up to date. Although the NDP still offers a clear-sighted vision of where South Africa should go and how it proposes we get there, it can only be kept alive if it is seen to adapt to changing circumstances. What matters is not the plan as such but the effort and foresight that go into its revision. The NDP cannot be treated like a Phoenix, rising every few years from its own ashes. South Africa has lost a great deal of economic ground since 2012, and the drivers of higher growth now need to be revitalised.

An additional advantage of having an overarching plan is that, if properly managed, it facilitates what might be called 'anticipatory government'. It is unfortunately too often the case in South Africa that action only comes when the country has reached the proverbial cliff edge and options have narrowed. And a practical plan also lessens the risks of unexpected, 'raw' policy proposals constantly undermining business confidence and delivering shocks to the investment community. Of course, it will be argued that draft proposals can be modified later, after discussion. But having a sensible, long-term plan available heightens the chances of getting more things right the first time around and helps to build trust.

In particular it discourages erratic, unilateral policy changes or proposals. For example, the existence and enforcement of a disciplined planning framework would have avoided the debacle around the unilateral free higher education announcement in December 2017. The issue of expropriation of land without compensation might also then have been better handled. What South Africa does not need are brittle policy achievements that are too dependent on the political status quo. Future outcomes should rather be rooted in a plan that offers a degree of predictability about the road ahead.

Does South Africa need a social compact?

The idea of a social compact for South Africa has been on and off the national agenda for many years – indeed, ever since the early 1990s. The NDP in 2012 also proposed a social compact marked by equity and inclusion, for which it said a number of conditions needed to be in place. It considered that a successful social compact tailored to South Africa's circumstances would require a much greater degree of convergence around aims and means than had hitherto been possible.

The NDP rightly concluded that this said a great deal about the history of the country and the lack of trust. In his campaigning for the ANC Presidency and since becoming President of South Africa, Ramaphosa has also referred to the importance of closer collaboration between government and key stakeholders like business, labour and civil society, through a social compact that he has long espoused.

In an earlier, thoughtful address to MISTRA (the Mapungubwe Institute for Strategic Reflection) in October 2013 on 'The South African Journey to a Social Compact', Ramaphosa said:

> We need a different kind of compact ... a compact that will work for South Africa today is one that has win-win features and clearly defined objectives and trade-offs that all partners will have to make to set our country on a winning path ... These challenges are real, present and not insubstantial ... As a society, we have in the past confronted far greater difficulties, and we have prevailed.[17]

But Ramaphosa added that, to overcome the impediments to a possible agreement, a number of conscious and deliberate steps needed to be taken to:
- establish trust, through greater engagement between the social partners;
- shift the paradigm of engagement by indicating what social partners are each willing and able to contribute to the national effort;
- address fragmentation within constituencies, especially business and labour;
- ensure bold and courageous leadership willing to make difficult decisions;
- forge consensus on South Africa's priorities, where the NDP could assist; and
- start the process.

And, we might add, there should be *timelines* set for the process. Readers will need to gauge for themselves whether by now South Africa is converging towards – or diverging from – the above conditions outlined by Ramaphosa for a successful social compact. There are factors at work both ways. But that does not mean that exploratory talks should not take place on a possible social compact, perhaps under the auspices of NEDLAC, to begin the journey referred to by Ramaphosa in 2013.

The NEDLAC process at least provides a recognised framework for a disciplined preliminary engagement. It would then be necessary to test the waters as to the possible shape and size of a social compact for South Africa, who the participants might be, and indeed whether there is even consensus on the need for such a compact.

> We need to act together, consciously and deliberately, to ensure that the differences and discord of the present do not define our future. We have a duty not to see our country through a prism

that emphasises difference, disunity and destruction ... We have a historical responsibility to seize this moment. We need to agree that our differences cannot be allowed to overshadow the aspirations that we together share.[18]

Thus, Ramaphosa. These concluding comments that he made several years ago are even more relevant today. It will require hard thinking by key players in the economy to address a situation in which there are no soft options and in which the margin for error has shrunk considerably. Social cohesion is fragile. Put less prosaically, an agreement has ultimately to be reached on how the 'pain' of getting the South African economy right is to be distributed among the various stakeholders.

A few years ago, *The Economist* said that although President Obama had done much to improve government in the United States, patronage and corruption still needed to be replaced with a measure of meritocracy. It was suggested that government 'needs to become a "platform" for services rather than a machine. It needs to engage citizens rather than treat them as subjects. But citizens need to change, too: becoming problem solvers, not whingers; and volunteers, not supplicants.'[19] These comments could just as easily be applied to South Africa today.

Are there any other related avenues to be explored, such as growth or reform 'coalitions'?

More narrowly, there has been wide experience in several parts of the world, around which considerable literature has developed, of growth coalitions or reform coalitions between business and government. These are coalitions between policy-makers and members of the business community, who work together for the intended purpose of achieving economic reforms. It might be argued that the recent interaction between the CEO Initiative and government to some degree falls into this category.

Yet it is helpful to see to what extent the conditions for a successful business–state coalition might overlap with those required in broader arrangements or agreements involving other actors, especially the important labour constituency. A growth coalition arises when state and business 'relations take the form of active cooperation towards a goal of policies that both parties expect will foster investment and increases in productivity,' says one group of experts.[20]

Based on available research, the following selective success factors on the business side have been identified as being important to business–state growth reform coalitions. But they clearly have wider application, and reinforce as well as amplify the above-mentioned points made by Ramaphosa. They include:[21]

- Reform coalitions generally require that actors have a common understanding of the challenges they are addressing and the incentives needed to work together in a productive manner.
- The leaders of well-organised business associations are able to effectively represent a wide range of interests and, once in a coalition with government, are more likely to pursue reforms that impact on the broader economy. Put differently, all-encompassing business associations are more likely to press for policies that bring about economic growth throughout the economy, rather than favour particular sectors at the expense of others.
- Reform coalitions are more likely to succeed when a business association has a certain degree of political and technical capacity, which can match or complement that of the state.
- Reform coalitions need to recognise the extent to which long-term, shared prosperity depends on productivity gains at various levels. Even those who are hostile to the capitalist system are pro-productivity. 'The notion of productivity', says French economist Jean Fourastié, 'has no fatherland or any political colour; it is the only notion accepted by both Marxist and liberal economic theories.'[22]
- Reform coalitions need winners – that is, success – in order to be sustainable.

In searching for a better collaborative mechanism in South Africa, we need to decide on a collective response that would work best for the country as a whole.

What else might business consider?

There are a couple of other mechanisms that may be helpful to business and the policy-making process. First, as originally advocated in *Zumanomics: Which Way to Shared Prosperity in South Africa?* but even more pertinent now, South Africa needs to better monitor the extent and quality of state activity.[23] For those who remain concerned, after reading these pages, about the dangers of excessive state intervention or 'creeping collectivism', it would be helpful for an independent think tank to construct a 'collectivism index', as suggested by social scientist and historian Professor Robert Skidelsky some years ago.[24]

This would provide an empirical basis for the monitoring of state involvement in the South African economy and would also allow the debate about the role of the state to be more evidence-led. The index could be distilled out of various elements, such as the proportion of output that the state spends, the ratio of public–private investment, the share of output produced by the state where it has direct control over production, the extent to which the tax system is an instrument of redistribution, and the degree of regulation and the extent of the regulatory burden. It is technically feasible to capture this data in ways that would be helpful.

The division of labour between the state and the private sector in South Africa is not something that falls like manna from heaven; it is the outcome of interaction between key political, economic and social forces, which business itself should have a critical role in shaping. The new political dynamics make this an even more important trend for business to watch. Whatever the future framework of stakeholder collaboration in South Africa, business needs to ensure that it is sufficiently well informed and equipped to address these aspects.

Secondly, there are perceptions around the decision-making methods of organised business that, although at first glance may seem mundane, nonetheless can make a difference to the efficacy of their advocacy and lobbying. At its best, organised business must address policy problems in three stages: analysis, administrative technique and persuasion. It becomes necessary to think about these processes both bureaucratically and strategically and, where necessary, to mobilise the necessary alliances.

Yet there now seems to be something else missing. It will have been noted, especially in Chapter 2, that the ability to reliably reconstruct the views of organisations like ASSOCOM, the FCI and SACOB hinged largely on resolutions and motions passed, which mandated the views of these organisations. Participative business debate was also encouraged through such instruments of decision-making. Moreover, these decisions were disseminated by the media and proved to be a reliable record of where these associations stood on a variety of issues of importance to business and government (see Annexure 2).

This practice seems to have fallen into disuse in recent years and it may have left a vacuum in terms of profiling tangible policy positions held by key components in organised business. While, for example, BUSA documents on economic transformation and integrity in business are valuable statements about wider business commitments, they need the additional support of specific decisions to enhance credibility. These excellent policy documents appear irregularly – often enjoying their fifteen minutes of fame – and then do not appear to develop traction. It also leaves the impression that the annual conferences of these associations (which also appear to have dwindled) are often dominated by panel discussions which do not yield any concrete outcomes or decisions.

The strategic but selective use of resolutions or motions also builds up a stable and disciplined framework of policy decisions (rather like that of most political parties), reinforces institutional memory in organisations prone to high office-bearer and staff turnover, and generally provides a fixed point of reference for decision-makers in these associations. While research documents, background memoranda and panel discussions must obviously play an increasingly important role in modern policy-making, it may be that in completely abandoning the mechanism of specific resolutions the pendulum has swung too far the other way.

There is another area that might be explored in managing the perceived 'them' and 'us' gap between the general public and business. Economic behaviour does not consist solely in responding to price incentives, in exchanging this for that, through market-driven activity. In reality it overlaps with much that occurs *within* firms that produce and *within* households that consume. There are types of economic decisions that are in fact universal to both – and the activities of a firm have much in common with the activities of the household. If the conventional antithesis between business and households could be bridged, we could achieve not only a better understanding of our economy but also a less abstruse view of economic processes.

For as long as firms are regarded as creatures of mysterious forces that ordinary citizens cannot always understand, they will tend to be regarded with suspicion and even antagonism. But the more they are perceived as analogous to the household in which everyone lives, the more comprehensible they will seem and the less hostility they may generate.

Certainly there is scope for a fuller analysis of spill-over of converging changes in either direction in business and household activities. In this manner it becomes possible to look at the multifarious phenomena of business life and analyse them in a different way.

All this eventually brings us back in this chapter to the significant role of business associations, especially the peak organisations, in shaping overall outcomes for better or worse. Organisations tend to be regarded, especially by those in charge, as ends in themselves. No organisation is ever that. Collective business groupings are a means, at least, to the freedom of their members.

But no collective organisation is absolutely justified – even if it promotes the economic freedom of all its members – in promoting *their* freedom only. It may well do that successfully and yet be inimical to broader economic interests. That is why each partial organisation needs the criticism and balance of some higher entity. This remains one of the strongest arguments for building a more unified and credible overall voice for business in South Africa.

9
Lessons and choices for South Africa

> The best way to predict the future is to create it.
> – Peter Drucker

> May your choices reflect your hopes, not your fears.
> – Nelson Mandela

IN THE MYTHOLOGICAL TALE AT the end of Plato's *Republic*, an Interpreter addressed the souls who were standing on the brink, about to plunge into a new cycle of existence. Mounted on a high platform, he said: 'Souls of a day, here shall begin a new round of earthly life … No guardian spirit will cast lots for you, but you shall choose your own destiny … The blame is his who chooses; Heaven is blameless.'

South Africa faces a new incarnation – which, depending on the choices made, could either put the country onto a steadier economic path or perpetuate deeply rooted tensions and uncertainties. In fact, not since the early 1990s has South Africa reached such an important juncture in its political and economic history. Decision-makers need to seriously reflect on what has gone wrong (and right) and why, and to make informed and responsible choices to shape the country's destiny. As the National Development Plan (NDP) indicates, 'We need to fix the future, starting now.'

The previous chapters have illustrated how a complex blend of economic, social and political factors has brought South Africa to where it is today. The strengths and weaknesses of business's role in the past up to the present have also been under the spotlight. 'The People's Tribunal on Economic Crimes' (past and present) held in Johannesburg in early 2018 was a reminder of the lingering debate on these matters. What is more important, though, is that although some significant changes have occurred since 1994, a glaring deficiency is that the economic gains have not been evenly spread throughout society. This has weakened social cohesion and left even the most resilient segments of the economy vulnerable. The need for serious change – often spoken about but generally attracting insufficient commitment – has never been so great, with business and a *new* generation of business leaders having a crucial role to play in the much-needed turnaround.

'Cracks in the crystal ball' (Author's personal collection)

As most countries have a poor track record in learning from history, we should not be naive in thinking that South Africans (particularly those in the political sphere) will now proactively look for the lessons from the past and use these to shape future plans and strategies. In this regard, Professor Robert Skidelsky, cautioned:

> In political life we can easily unlearn what we have already learnt – indeed we have done so many times – because we are never sure of what we know. We can never be sure why any political or social project failed – whether the flaw lay in the project itself, or in the conditions or methods of its application. Since large-scale social experiments cannot be decisively refuted by events, there is no guarantee that they will not be tried again. Perhaps there is a learning curve in these matters, but it is very gradual and liable to huge memory loss.[1]

Of course, South Africans must not throw up their hands in despair or abandon their desire for change just because there is a risk of intended policies and plans going awry. After all, things go wrong in many other parts of the world, not just in South Africa. The countries that succeed, though, make the least mistakes. Poor judgement and mistakes can be minimised if at least some of the lessons of history are acknowledged and used to inform decisions about how institutions should operate and cooperate with one another, and where checks and balances are needed the most.

Key lessons

From the many views expressed and the events outlined in this book, a number of important lessons can be discerned, which should be useful reference points for decision-makers going forward.

1. The painful memories of the apartheid era have not receded, with the pervasive poverty and inequality in evidence in South Africa today being constant reminders of how millions of people were, and continue to be, deprived of economic opportunities and an acceptable quality of life. Post-apartheid South Africa is clearly still a project-in-the-making, representing a resounding success so far for some and a dismal failure for others. Poverty and inequality (exacerbated by high levels of unemployment) represent the dark side of South Africa's economic journey out of the past. Indeed, institutional shortcomings and weak governance in several quarters have sharpened the sting of deprivation for many. The dangers of not tackling problems head-on and simply allowing memories of the country's torrid past to ferment

are all too apparent. Therefore, decisive action is required on the part of government, business and civil society, working from their positions of strength, to turn the country around.

2. The business sector's timidity in the face of a deteriorating political and economic climate in recent years has led to the sector's growing marginalisation in policy-making and planning circles in South Africa and, by default, enabled poor governance and corruption to escalate, particularly within state-owned enterprises. Several organisations have refused to be intimidated, but these have been relatively few in number. For example, the banking sector, through its sectoral body, BASA (Banking Association South Africa), has often taken a strong public line on policy matters, but this has tended to be the exception. 'Business', said Dr Greg Mills, 'was unlikely to complain given the reality that some would profit where others feared to tread.'[2]

As we have seen, a lack of trust between important role-players in society is extremely debilitating. It robs the country of a clear vision of the future and the motivation to get there, and plays out messily in declining business confidence and faltering economic performance. The importance of trust to economic growth is now generally accepted and cannot be over-emphasised in South Africa's case.

3. The slowness of transformation over the years has been evidenced in rising frustration levels and the introduction of increasingly onerous (and costly) legislation to force businesses to comply. Indeed, fair, efficient and inclusive transformation needs to be embraced, not resisted. South Africa's future well-being depends on a process of cooperative and collaborative transformation and active citizenry. No interest group can continue to function as they have been doing in the past and expect improved results. For example, to thrive in South Africa today, private enterprise needs to adopt a different approach – one that perhaps attaches just as much importance to inclusiveness as profitability.

4. South Africa's recent history has highlighted the dangers of too much power in too few hands. Where there is excessive power, there is little incentive to engage seriously with different stakeholders or to find ways to disperse economic benefits throughout society. Temptation abounds and inevitably morphs into phenomena like state capture and other forms of institutionalised corruption. State capture can be likened to a 'weapon of mass corruption'. In such a climate, problems

simply multiply and proposed remedies lag hopelessly behind.

A key lesson from the Zuma era is the importance of vigilance by key institutions such as Parliament and the courts as well as civil society to hold decision-makers accountable for their actions. The resolve to strengthen surveillance should not now weaken. The relevant institutions must diligently perform their oversight functions no matter who is in power. And it goes without saying that businesses need to take the issue of accountability more seriously and to self-regulate to the highest standard, failing which the government may decide to adopt this role. Fortunately, it seems as if South Africa now also has a more aware and critical citizenry who will continue to be the voice of constructive dissent in the background. According to historian Andrew Duminy: 'A war is being waged against state capture, once again suggesting that ... there is widespread popular commitment to honesty, fair play and the principles of good government. Our condition may well be improving, even now, in ways that are not obvious to us but will be discerned by historians.'[3]

5. An important lesson from the recent, but also more distant, past is that liberal media and brave journalists (and editors behind the scenes) are a powerful force in getting the truth out into society despite attempts (often by government) to suppress it or subvert it. The media also play a key role in stimulating awareness and debates about important local and global issues, and exposing various forms of impropriety in both the public and private sectors. The late George Palmer, editor of the *Financial Mail* for many years, was an example of a fearless media man who resisted many attempts by the apartheid government to muzzle his journal. In more recent times, the media have played a vital role in reporting on the deterioration in South Africa's political and economic environment, revealing the main culprits in many unfolding sagas and the reactions from different interest groups.

In their book, *Why Nations Fail: The Origin of Power, Prosperity, and Poverty*, Professors Daron Acemoglu and James Robinson refer to the media as a set of actors who can play a transformative role in the empowerment of citizens.[4] Empowerment of society at large is difficult to coordinate and maintain, they say, without widespread information about whether there are economic, financial or political abuses by those in power, either in the public or private sectors. A reliable flow

of information and analysis through the different levels of the media therefore helps a country to make good public choices about the future, including finding ways to ensure that markets function properly.
6. Countries differ considerably in the quality of their policy structures, and the cost to their economies of policy mistakes and economic mismanagement. Referring to the departure of former President Jacob Zuma, *The Economist* spoke about 'South Africa's lost decade'.[5] Various assessments suggest that by most measures South Africa is worse off than a decade ago. 'One economist estimates that former President Jacob Zuma's rule cost South Africa's economy in the region of R1 trillion, but that's just the tip of the iceberg. The economy could have been 25% bigger if positive trends had continued.'[6] (See Annexure 4.)
7. South Africa needs competent and effective leaders (both in the public and private sectors) to turn broad aspirations and goals into tangible and sustainable outputs. South Africa has a strong Constitution and justice system, which have often acted as buttresses against poor governance and a lack of accountability, and have enabled many organisations and individuals to cope and carry on in the face of uncertainty.
8. A policy environment that is able to clear the path for sustainable enterprises and induce job-rich economic growth is inevitably the outcome of national political processes that require national actors. Among these actors are national business organisations which enjoy credibility in their constituencies and which have clearly defined values and goals linked to promoting the collective interests of business. Importantly, too, national actors from the business world must be able to speak for business as a whole, not just parts of it.
9. Business must accept that day-to-day questions surrounding economic policy inevitably kindle discussions on the economic order in South Africa. Many seem intent on proposing solutions in accordance with their own views about economic policy imperatives. A steady and predictable approach to clarifying and implementing economic policy is possible – but only if a practical meeting of minds can be achieved among different interest groups on the fundamental problems in the economic order. The resolution of such problems must be pursued within an agreed framework, including labour market reform and property rights.

Clearly, the more ambitious a country's socio-economic programme (from providing more decent work and fairer wages and driving stronger growth, to improving health, education and other social services), the bigger the productivity gains that need to underpin it. Unless the future policy framework allows for substantial efficiency gains, the economy will not break out of its low-growth trap. If South Africa goes down the road of seeking a social compact, a productivity accord should form part of the package.

Unfortunately, the World Economic Forum's Global Competitiveness Index surveys over the years have regularly reported that South Africa's labour market is hobbled by inefficient hiring and firing practices, minimal cooperation between employers and employees, and a poor relationship between pay and productivity. In fact, South Africa is near the bottom of the class in these critical areas. Management has a crucial role to play here. And business needs to engage more strenuously with trade unions like COSATU, FEDUSA and their affiliates as well as other labour groupings in a bid to remedy these chronic weaknesses in the economy.

10. Business in South Africa has attracted – and will probably continue to attract – mixed reactions from government and labour. On the one hand, it is often associated with 'bad capitalism', that is, the perceived erosion of social values, market failure and growing inequality. On the other hand, it plays a critical role in stimulating economic growth, providing jobs and implementing government policies. Businesses therefore need to find new ways to successfully navigate the contradictory landscape in which they find themselves.

In her book *The Case for Business in Developing Economies*, Ann Bernstein emphasises that profits should not be confused with greed.[7] If businesses were not profitable, they would not survive and consumers would be deprived of the goods and services that they need. Also, jobs would disappear, as would the businesses' contribution to the tax base. In many people's haste to associate business with monopoly capital, the opposite is often true. Private enterprises (unlike state-owned enterprises) generally face competition and need to look constantly for new and cost-efficient ways to retain or expand their market share.

11. Many people have a love–hate relationship with the concept of competition and its natural links with capitalism. In George Orwell's book *Animal Farm*, four legs are presented as good, whereas two legs

are regarded as bad.[8] Borrowing this analogy to reinforce the theme of this book, we can now say that 'competitive capitalism' must be generally viewed as good and 'monopoly capitalism' (of whatever hue) should broadly be seen as bad. Competition and the large number of choices that are unleashed then become the justifying and distinguishing factors. Yet in the real world, even this often remains a chimera for economists and competition authorities across the globe, as they seek to understand anti-competitive behaviour in several shades of grey. Competition policy remains a highly complex area; it cannot be a case of 'one size fits all'.

What of South Africa? The most plausible first approximation would be that South Africans, in general, favour more competition than they have at present, in those parts of the economy where it works weakly or is interfered with or threatened. Yet they seem to want to dilute it where it comes in full strength, such as from foreigners. One remedy is that if the spirit of enterprise and market forces fail to produce the necessary outcomes, the competition authorities can initiate the restoration of competitive forces where these are lacking. Consistent action from such authorities, particularly if accompanied by adequate publicity and penalties, influences not only the conduct of those subject to particular investigations by the Competition Commission and other regulatory bodies, but also the conduct of those engaged in similar restrictive practices in other spheres.

Some observers are inclined to give small businesses the benefit of the doubt where there may be discrimination or where larger competitors enjoy advantages that are unfair or do not represent actual productive efficiency. Other analysts go further, in that they simply dislike 'bigness' of the kind that seems to overwhelm those who have to deal with it or find their niche alongside it somehow. Adam Smith had the same feeling in his era, but he did not have the complex task of adjusting it to the exigencies of the mass-production economies of the twenty-first century. We cannot ignore the realities of economies of scale and technological innovation in most economies in the world of today. We want the best possible balance to ensure that 'workable competition' will serve the South African economy well through a pragmatic approach to competition policy and law.

12. To the many who favour competition, apart from the benefits it brings

to consumers, there is the opportunity to become an entrepreneur. This is important for South Africa's economic transformation. Clearly, more people need to embrace the independence and responsibilities associated with entrepreneurship. After all, economies will only thrive if entrepreneurship is able to flourish, evidenced in the growth of new enterprises and people becoming increasingly 'enterprising'.

Out-of-touch education and training curricula and a lack of attention given to small businesses in South Africa have been strong contributing factors to the entrepreneurship deficit in the country. Entrepreneurship is not about creating survivalist businesses – it is about creating viable businesses that have growth potential and a culture in which productivity and innovation are promoted and rewarded. True entrepreneurs (like Herman Mashaba, Raymond Ackerman and many others) see opportunities that no one else does (or do not see the obstacles that others see) and are able to create profitable, sustainable businesses – often from nothing.

In his comprehensive study of entrepreneurship and growth, Professor Ben Vosloo said:

> People make things happen. Enterprises begin with people. Enterprising people give rise to production, which in turn gives rise to employment. Without the spirit of enterprise as expressed in entrepreneurial activity, there can be no employment-creating economic growth. The entrepreneur is the prime mover in economic development. Hence we need to think of our entrepreneurial stock as precious human capital that requires to be nurtured and mobilised.[9] (See Annexure 3.)

Research scholar, Nassim Taleb, puts it even stronger: 'We need people to take (bounded) risks ... Courage (risk-taking) is the highest virtue. We need entrepreneurs. You *must* start a business. Put yourself on the line, start a business.[10]

13. It is time to stop talking and planning, and start doing. As emphasised in Chapter 8, South Africa has had many economic plans and blueprints, but their implementation has been hampered for a variety of reasons – ranging from capacity shortcomings in government to differences

of opinion across many interest groups on the merits of such plans and blueprints – and this has led to inertia and procrastination. In fact, procrastination has been elevated to a high art form. The NDP should be championed as the core guide to economic policy implementation in the public and private sectors. Given the magnitude of the task of rehabilitating the South African economy, all role-players need to be persuaded to take a long-term view.

President Ramaphosa is known for being a long-term strategist who is able to visualise the end game – which is expansively described in the NDP (of which he is a strong proponent). If he can get others to adopt this way of thinking, it could be one of the crucial ingredients in South Africa's slow but deliberate economic recovery.

14. Assuming there will be better times ahead, it would nevertheless be unrealistic to expect social dialogue to be consistently smooth in the face of so many conflicting worldviews and opinions. However, what is important is that social partners are willing to engage, rebuild trust and, where necessary, yield ground. To resolve the deep conflicts that persist in South Africa, we need to acknowledge that a culture of hard bargaining and compromise is still necessary. Much of the progress that South Africa made in the early 1990s was attributable to pragmatism on the part of key stakeholders participating in CODESA.

'Pragmatism ... [which] Tocqueville first identified as a distinctive quality of American democracy, facilitates bargaining and compromise by rendering goals flexible and opinions and beliefs open to engagement and new information ... Thus pragmatism restrains the role of ideology in politics and hence the danger of conflict polarisation.'[11] In the same way, South Africa needs to find a common narrative. 'The question of whether there is sufficient consensus and incentive ... to agree and pursue a social compact must be resolved,' said the National Planning Commission (NPC).[12]

15. For a process of national reconciliation to take root, there needs to be a shared national vision – even if thoughts on the finer details of what is needed to get there differ from one group to the next. The bedrock of such a process is strong and accountable institutions. Wiseman Nkuhlu was recently quoted as saying:

> All leaders have the responsibility of making sure the right environment is created so that future generations can thrive

in our country. Sure, this will take much-improved political leadership, but having the right environment extends beyond the government into almost all areas of society, especially in the institutions and organisations on whose probity, expertise and independence we all depend.[13]

Political personalities will come and go; and besides, it is dangerous to put too much faith in individuals. However, achieving the right environment, as envisaged by Nkuhlu, and upholding the values of Mandela involve getting the fundamentals right, which will endure well into the future.

Getting South Africa's public finances in order

Fundamental to South Africa's economic recovery and future growth is getting its public finances in order. Public finances constitute one of the major sinews in an economy as, if managed properly, they promote stability, growth and redistribution. As successive budgets have come and gone, so concerns about deficits, government spending, taxes and investment downgrades by the major credit rating agencies have crowded in. Both the Medium-Term Budget Policy Statement (MTBPS) and the main budget are important events in South Africa's economic calendar, which have sought to capture and manage these concerns over a period of some years.

Elaborate and sophisticated machinery for the rational implementation of fiscal policy has been built up in the National Treasury over the decades, helping to project a high level of professionalism. However imprecise its results might have been from time to time, no one can reasonably doubt that South Africa would have been much worse off without the strenuous efforts of the National Treasury to control access to the government's chequebook. Fiscal probity remains an essential requirement for good governance.

In very general terms, success in the public finances arena hinges on a prudent balance between stability and flexibility. 'Great swerving runs are permissible and even necessary – but they ought to be in the same direction,' said Roy Jenkins, former British Chancellor of the Exchequer.[14] Stability is required because unnecessary shifts cause uncertainty and weaken the established threads of control, while flexibility is needed because in a developing economy public finances need to be responsive to the socio-economic situation. The positive side ('what is') of public finances cannot be kept separate from the normative side ('what should be'). Analysing the workings of taxes or expenditures is therefore not an end in itself, but a step in the bigger process of crafting the best policy mix. Tough choices usually have to be made and trade-offs contemplated. This has, to a greater or lesser extent, been the challenge facing South Africa's succession of Finance Ministers since 1994, although it has become more acute as the country's economic performance has deteriorated.

In formulating the budget in recent years, the government has been faced with a seven-fold challenge:
- controlling government spending;
- avoiding a debt trap;
- maintaining the right balance between consumption and investment spending by government;
- financing the losses of state-owned enterprises like Eskom and South African Airways;
- tackling the growing difficulty of raising taxes, either because of a small tax base or weakened 'tax buoyancy';
- dealing with the growing public demand for value for money from government; and
- enhancing public service delivery.

The difficulty of juggling all these priorities was starkly revealed in the 2018–19 Budget Review:

> Although the outlook has improved, the complexity of the economic and fiscal environment should not be underestimated. Economic growth is tepid, unemployment remains very high, and the finances of major state-owned companies have become more precarious. The extent of corruption and wasteful expenditure in the public sector, together with governance and efficiency challenges in tax administration, have adversely affected tax morality. The medium-term costs of free higher education and training, and public service compensation are uncertain.[15]

These concerns will continue to shape future fiscal imperatives. There are still long-term risks in the fiscal outlook. But in knitting them all together under the general heading of *affordability*, we must not forget that public sector spending and taxation directly and indirectly influence the rate of national productivity growth. If we want to raise productivity growth in the economy, there must be regular and critical interrogation of the large share of national output that constitutes goods and services supplied by the public sector at all levels. If a productivity accord ever materialises in South Africa, the public sector would need to be an integral part of it.

Changes in government spending and taxation policies have a key role to play in directly bringing about necessary structural changes and facilitating supportive adjustments in the private sector. Public spending and taxation influence the allocation of scarce community resources in ways that can both facilitate and detract from the efficiency of the private sector. Constant vigilance and oversight are therefore necessary, particularly as South Africa's public sector is widely regarded as being bloated and weighed down by inefficiencies.

It is worth revisiting the advice given by BLSA in 2012 that greater policy certainty would be achieved if a body entirely independent of government was created to provide independent economic forecasts and assessments of whether the government is likely to meet its targets. BLSA had in mind structures like the Office for Budget Responsibility in the UK and the Congressional Budget Office in the US, both of which help to boost confidence in the targets set by the government. But the proposed Presidential Economic Advisory Council (discussed later in this chapter) may be able to fulfil this purpose.[16]

In 2017 the Davis Committee on tax reform released a draft 'bill of rights' for taxpayers, which is worthy of serious attention. In the wake of widespread concern over government spending, there should be a mechanism whereby people can influence the extent and direction of government expenditure. One suggestion is that South African taxpayers should receive a questionnaire with their tax returns on which to record their views and preferences. While not intended to be binding, these inputs would allow taxpayers to be part of the debate surrounding state spending and would provide valuable insights for the National Treasury. Already members of the public are invited each year by the Minister of Finance to give suggestions that will help inform the national budget.

The conventional use of GDP as a measure of growth expectations and outcomes, and as a major denominator, must obviously continue to prevail in budget reviews and estimates of tax revenue. But it could be usefully supplemented by references to a broader metric of national economic success, which was released by the World Economic Forum at its annual meeting in Davos in early 2018. Called the Inclusive Development Index (IDI), it is similar to the UN's Human Development Index and is based on a wide definition that combines factors like growth and development, inclusivity, and intergenerational equity and sustainability. It could usefully enrich the budget presentation and, indeed, the broad economic debate in South Africa.[17]

What seems to be lacking is a general authoritative and credible scorecard that demonstrates what socio-economic targets have been achieved and where South Africa is falling short of the goals it has set itself. This would allow more accurate, evidence-led assessments of progress made and what still needs to be done as reforms get under way. Otherwise, one is left with a series of ad hoc, snapshot impressions of the socio-economic situation at given times, which do not do justice to the underlying realities. Good things can happen in an economy in an incremental and diffused way, which is not necessarily captured in GDP statistics. Ultimately, though, what clearly shines through the fiscal gloom of recent years is the overwhelming need for a dramatic and sustainable boost in South Africa's flagging growth rate on the basis of structural reforms.

In the interim, the welcome decision by Moody's in March 2018 to leave South Africa's credit rating unchanged and to raise the outlook from negative to stable means that the country has for the time being avoided universal junk status. This gives South Africa extra time to get its house in order and to implement the necessary reforms, although the agencies remain cautious. There is no room for complacency. South Africa must use the breathing space wisely. A striking example of failure to use time well is Brazil. In early 2018, two years after the impeachment of President Dilma Rousseff and the accession to power of Michel Temer, Brazil was again downgraded by S&P Global Ratings because of the country's perceived failure to give adequate effect to the desired economic and fiscal reforms. 'It's now all about what South Africa can prove we can do better than Brazil in the next three to five years,' said Konrad Reuss, head of S&P's South African office.[18]

There is always the prospect of better outcomes. Some other economies have eventually been able to regain positive investment status, as the following comment shows:

> The ratings agencies data show at least that it can be done, even if the walk back to investment grade is a long one. Over the past year there have been 24 'fallen angels' that have been downgraded by S&P, 16 of them in emerging markets and Africa (including South Africa). But there have also been 26 'rising stars' that have been returned to investment grade status.[19]

The following story amusingly illustrates the importance of taking the gap in terms of time when the opportunity presents itself:

> A peasant, accused of some misdeed, is brought before the King who happens to be passionate about horses. The King shouts, 'I will cut off your head.' The peasant pleads, 'Please, oh mighty King, spare me.' 'Why should I spare you?' asks the King. 'Give me one year and I will teach your favourite horse to sing.' The King shrugs, 'What have I got to lose? If in a year's time you have not taught my favourite horse to sing, then I will cut off your head.' As the peasant leaves the King's presence, a friend who has overheard the conversation remonstrates, 'Are you crazy? You will never teach the King's horse to sing.' 'You never know,' replies the peasant. 'I have twelve months. During that time the King might die. I might die. The horse might die. Or I might just teach the horse to sing.'[20]

A new President, a new start

The election of Cyril Ramaphosa as ANC President and subsequently as President of South Africa early in 2018 and his plans for renewal and change have set the country in a new direction. South Africa could well regain its moral compass. There is a new sense of hope as to what may now be achieved under a Ramaphosa presidency. Whereas under former President Jacob Zuma the glass was seen as half empty, with Ramaphosa now in the driver's seat it is more readily perceived as half full.

It is early days, though – there remain many hills to climb and sceptics to convince along the way. Despite Ramaphosa's appointment of a number of heavyweights to key positions in Cabinet, it is too soon to arrive at a proper assessment of the potential success or failure of plans and actions that are still unfolding or await implementation. And there is a lingering propensity in government to subject certain decisions to the inevitable summits, investigations and task teams, from which outcomes may be delayed. But there is no missing the political will that lies behind several of the changes and a clear determination by many to move South Africa on a different trajectory.

In assessing the impact of Ramaphosa's appointment of his first Cabinet in February 2018, the new incumbents in the three portfolios of particular importance to the economy – finance, public enterprises and mining – elicited a positive response from business and the markets. Although there were strong reform elements in the Cabinet appointments, two factors suggest that the reconstituted Cabinet is inevitably an interim one. Firstly, there is an election pending in 2019, which is bound to be followed by a further Cabinet reshuffle. Secondly, the promised and welcome in-depth review of the size and functions of the Cabinet will in due course see the likely rearrangement or elimination of certain ministries and ministers. But we hope that after this transitional period, stability – both within the Cabinet and at director-general level – will prevail over the long term in order to reduce policy uncertainty.

Hypothetically speaking and on the basis of certain political assumptions, Ramaphosa could be in office for eleven years – until 2029 – with the next election looming in 2019. However, it would be safer at this juncture to take only a five-year view. 'Politics', said nineteenth-century UK Prime Minister Benjamin Disraeli, 'is the science of the unexpected.'[21] Political legacies are hard to judge until long after a President has left office; hence any definitive assessment so early in the incumbent's first few months in office is highly risky. The fact remains, though, that many commentators are already beginning to evaluate possible outcomes. The way to make the Ramaphosa presidency memorable, the way to secure or at any rate retain the confidence of the people of South Africa, would be to let each year be marked by some large, solid achievements and to avoid their becoming buried under the weight of too many investigations and summits.

But it needs to be reiterated that changing economic and political circumstances call for a clear and urgent choice if South Africa wants a bigger, stronger and better economy in the years ahead. Either promote growth, expedite transformation, keep government affordable and the tax burden reasonable, or face persistent delivery failures, which will lead to rising costs, the breakdown of services and greater financing demands.

In other words, the choice is between real economic growth with all its advantages or the yoke of low growth with its creeping socio-economic costs and welfare dependency. We want to turn many more South Africans into victors over adversity and deprivation, rather than victims trapped in the welfare vice, particularly as the number of people receiving social grants now exceeds the number of employed people. The challenge for President Ramaphosa now is to ensure effective government and the use of power and collaboration to achieve the best results.

President Ramaphosa has two overarching priorities: recovery and reform. With the political landscape changing for the better, the previous tentative economic recovery is gradually strengthening and broadening such that a growth rate of about 2 per cent could be reached in the short term. But to get beyond that growth rate will need serious structural reforms that require 'buy-in' from key stakeholders.

Apart from the lessons for South Africa which might be apparent from earlier chapters, and which have been outlined above, Michael Barber – in his authoritative book *Instruction to Deliver* – outlines ten universal principles for governments to turn well-intended plans into reality:

- A week may be a long time in politics but five years is unbelievably short to deliver.
- Sustained focus on a small number of priorities is essential.
- Flogging a system can no longer achieve these goals: reform is the key.
- Nothing is inevitable: 'rising tides' can be turned.
- The numbers are important but not enough: citizens have to see and feel the difference, and expectations need to be managed.
- The quality of leadership at all levels is decisive.
- Good system design and management underpin progress.
- Getting the second step change is difficult and requires precision in tackling variations and promoting best practices.
- Extraordinary discipline and persistence are required to defeat the cynics.

- Grinding out increments is a noble cause, but where progress is slow, it is even more important for people to understand the strategy.[22]

What might be termed the Ten Commandments for the effective implementation of policy, these create a valuable framework for the complex and arduous task of reform facing the Ramaphosa government over the long haul. Even if not all the promised changes can be effected, they nonetheless present the possibility that by the time he decides to give up office (once again, on certain political assumptions), Ramaphosa will be able to leave the South African economy in a better state than he found it when he became President.

In this regard, his useful decision to establish a new Presidential Economic Advisory Council resonates with a similar proposal made in *Zumanomics Revisited*.[23] The intention to improve South Africa's policy-making by creating extra economic advisory machinery for the President could fill a real gap in our present institutional arrangements (also see Chapter 3). But the council's role needs to be carefully defined to avoid it overlapping with existing structures like the National Planning Commission and NEDLAC.

There are also some important wheels that do not need to be reinvented. The better and more vigorous use of mechanisms like regulatory impact assessments and public–private sector partnerships will save the Ramaphosa government much grief and avoid recriminations. It will help to expedite matters if these existing and quite acceptable instruments are broadened and deepened for the purpose of improving decision-making and results.

'South Africa's best shot at raising the growth rate is to give the private sector a bigger role in the government's traditional terrain, including providing infrastructure for power generation and helping to run SOEs,' said the *Financial Mail's* Claire Bisseker. 'This means the ANC has to fundamentally change the way it thinks about the economy.'[24]

The matter of the nationalisation of the Reserve Bank is just one of those contentious issues on the ANC agenda. It is difficult to understand the preoccupation with this matter when South Africa has much more important challenges to address. We have had in the Reserve Bank a semi-independent institution within the state – with prestige, historical tradition and international credibility, and at arm's length from the wayward influence of politics. The private shareholding in the Reserve Bank is harmless enough and might even be useful for corporate governance and oversight purposes. But it has no relevance for monetary policy decisions. Shareholders' participation is largely symbolic. The government gets ninety per cent of the Reserve Bank's profits while private shareholders receive only a nominal dividend.

Yet the persistence with which this matter is being pursued suggests that there may be an intention in the longer term to tamper with the constitutional mandate of the Reserve Bank and perhaps to gain greater influence over the commercial banking system in this way. It is important that the central bank is seen as a major institution with enough autonomy and credibility to maintain a stable financial environment within which the economy can achieve maximum growth.

Whatever the real agenda surrounding the Reserve Bank, if aggressively pursued it could eventually trigger a negative reaction from the markets and upset confidence. Perceptions are important, both domestically and abroad, even over and above the application of monetary policy in South Africa. The last thing South Africa now needs is unnecessary interference with a respected institution like the Reserve Bank when the country has to build investor confidence.

President Ramaphosa has opted for a collaborative and inclusive approach to decision-making and implementation by involving key stakeholders. Yet to lead, Ramaphosa must balance populism and pragmatism. Some observers have described him as a 'pragmatic populist'. He is nevertheless bound by certain strong and far-reaching ANC conference decisions which he did not necessarily espouse when he was campaigning for the ANC presidency, but which he now has to implement in a pragmatic way.

Developing an inclusive economic agenda, said Professor Adam Habib, 'will require Ramaphosa's administration to think through the kind of economic reforms that are feasible in the contemporary moment, yet sufficiently transformative that they have a cumulative effect ... even if it requires some short-term economic, political and social compromises.'[25] We saw the initial broad strategy along these lines embodied in the 2018 State of the Nation Address (SONA). President Ramaphosa's track record in labour, business and political negotiations suggests that he genuinely believes that consensus-based solutions are always possible.

Compromise has to be distinguished, of course, from the genuine accord that might emerge from discussion and negotiation. Agreement may represent the general consensus of opinion after that process, or it may be reached through concessions, but as a rule it embodies a combination of elements. Compromise, therefore, far from being the exception, is from a democratic standpoint one of the cardinal political virtues.

On the other hand, *Business Day* editor Tim Cohen strikes a salient cautionary note: 'It's important to remember that South Africa's root problems lie essentially in fiscal dynamics and labour productivity, and there is nothing in Ramaphosa's policies or public stance that comes close to dealing with these problems. They precede him, they are evident in all wings of the ANC, and they are thoroughly part of its socialist DNA.'[26]

The shift in policy dynamics will require all stakeholders to redefine their relationship with government in South Africa as the basis for cooperation and collaboration on the way ahead. Government is opening its door to business again. Business must therefore boldly step through it and help to strengthen the partnerships that can bring about the sustained revival of the economy. As recent bad experiences have clearly demonstrated, government–business relationships should rather be based on the healthy principle that 'neither should be suspicious of the other, but let each be watchful'!

And for the business community's voice to be effectively projected and heard, it needs strong and more unified representation from organised business. 'When you want to meet business people', emphasised Pravin Gordhan recently, 'you have to either meet "black business" or "white business". We need to create a new solidarity …'[27]

John Stuart Mill famously pointed out that a good cause seldom triumphs unless someone's interest is bound up in it. In the modern context, one could say that having 'skin in the game' strongly influences the outcome. Luckily enough, the people of South Africa are sufficiently concerned about the county's future to have responded positively to President Ramaphosa's vision of a 'new dawn' and how it may create a better life for all. With the help of new leadership there is a much greater awareness in the population at large that ultimately we are all in the same boat and that it is in the interests of both plutocrats and plebeians in this country to row together.

And our efforts must be judged by our performance, not by our promises. We must therefore not promise to create a paradise, much less a fool's paradise. There is a jocular saying that 'to improve is to change; to be perfect is to have changed often'. We must not lose patience or abandon hope that a corner in South Africa's economic fortunes is now being turned for the better.

As the author said some years ago:

> There *is* a virtuous circle of high growth, democratic governance and social development. The transition to a high-skill, high-productivity and rising wage economy is both economically necessary and politically desirable. The forces of globalisation abroad, and the dynamics of transformation within, must meet in faster 'catch up' growth for South Africa, of the kind experienced by many other emerging economies.[28]

In summary, therefore, South Africa now needs to break out of the virtual stagnation (characterised by a persistent low-growth trap and high unemployment) into which the economy has been drifting. Stagnation may be a rather strong term considering the complex external and internal phenomena that, over time, have produced negative socio-economic consequences. But as we have seen, major contributing factors in the past have included a growing failure to grasp the proper role of government, to retain the confidence of major stakeholders like business and labour, and to stay on message regarding policy.

To suggest that significant remedies lie within the remit of government does not, though, imply that all these phenomena were equally tractable to government policy or that there are no limits to what government can do. Indeed, it is the capacity of government and not its scope that is important for long-term growth. That government overreach in South Africa has been a serious problem has already been reflected in widespread delivery failures, corruption and policy uncertainty. The streamlining of government and the attack on state capture and other forms of corruption are therefore welcome developments.

Nor does it mean that the negative phenomena appeared suddenly when Jacob Zuma took office in 2009; economic history does not work that way. Nevertheless, there is a sharp enough difference between the economic conditions of South Africa over the past decade and the preceding period to justify using the term 'stagnation'. There were far more clouds than sunshine in the Zuma era of governance in South Africa. Highly negative economic and governance factors came into play during that period, which then precipitated the major challenges now faced by the Ramaphosa government. A formidable agenda now confronts South Africa.

What are the chances of success? Much of the answer depends on the flexibility and resilience of the private enterprise system itself in South Africa, in which – despite the many difficulties outlined – we may still entertain a fair degree of confidence. Business must help to set the national agenda and propose creative solutions. But much now also depends on the wisdom and coherence of government policy, and especially the extent to which future government reform policy facilitates or hinders the restoration of long-term investor confidence, which is sorely needed to drive growth and employment. In particular, we need to get growth rates above 3 per cent sooner rather than later if we are to successfully combat unemployment, poverty and inequality.

President Ramaphosa has committed himself to improving the investment climate in South Africa. If an economy is reasonably flexible and sensibly managed, it is possible to steadily improve economic performance. In such an economy – and the South African economy is reasonably flexible and *could* be sensibly managed – better outcomes are possible, even at the cost of some disturbance to a few cherished ideological shibboleths. Ideological flexibility will be critical for success. As suggested earlier, Ramaphosa has the leadership credibility and negotiation skills to help blend growth and transformation policies in a pragmatic and collaborative way. Yet several tough decisions may have to wait until after the 2019 elections.

In a study of policy-making and economic policy in smaller developing countries, Professor Arnold Harberger defined the challenge as follows:

> The art of good policymaking consists of perceiving at any given moment the forces and pressures working to change the policy structure; in sensing at what points the existing structure is more plastic, more amenable to change; and finally in channelling the pressures (enlisting their aid, as it were) so as not just to modify the structure but also to improve it (among other things, by reducing

the aggregate price that is paid by the economy, day in and day out, for its policy weaknesses).[29]

While effective and stable leadership will remain important, the real tests will now increasingly revolve around the content of policy and its successful implementation. There is no reason why the goal of well-planned, inclusive growth in South Africa should not provide win-win outcomes over time. Economic growth thus emerges as the conceptual hero in this book. Growth is not 'a cure for all diseases, an end to all distress'. But it makes all the other aims easier to attain and eases potential conflict. (See Annexure 5.)

But prudent statesmanship must recognise a significant lesson of history – that in the long run a nation does not become prosperous through policies alone but rather through the unlocking of capacity, energy and versatility of its people, and that misdirected or damaging policies can thwart rather than promote these fundamental attributes. South Africa must have faith in what can be initiated and administered by a multiplicity of fertile minds and adventurous wills. This must constantly inform our decision-making in the public and private sectors.

South Africa still has basic strengths in technology, human and financial capital, entrepreneurship, natural resources and many of its institutions, which it must mobilise to address its weaknesses. If South Africa successfully capitalises on the latest political changes, there is every chance of renewed prosperity and growth, provided its leaders have the courage and wisdom to manage its economic and business affairs intelligently from now on.

In the words of TS Eliot: 'For last year's words belong to last year's language. And this year's words await another voice. And to make an end is to make a beginning.'

Annexures

Annexure 1: Classifications of selected chamber systems

Classification of selected chamber systems		
Continental model	Anglo-Saxon model	Mixed system
Africa: Algeria Benin Burkina Faso Cape Verde Cameroon Central African Republic Chad Comoros Congo Côte d'Ivoire Djibouti Egypt Eritrea Ethiopia Madagascar Mali Morocco Niger Senegal Sudan Togo Tunisia	*Africa:* Botswana Burundi Equatorial Guinea Gabon Gambia Ghana Guinea Guinea-Bissau Lesotho Liberia Mauritius Malawi Mozambique Namibia Nigeria Rwanda São Tomé and Principe Seychelles Sierra Leone Somalia South Africa Swaziland Tanzania Zambia Zimbabwe	

Classification of selected chamber systems		
Continental model	Anglo-Saxon model	Mixed system
Europe: Andorra Austria Bosnia and Herzegovina France Germany Greece Hungary Italy Luxembourg Netherlands Portugal Serbia and Montenegro Slovak Republic Slovenia Spain	*Europe:* Belgium Bulgaria Czech Republic Denmark Estonia Ireland Iceland Latvia Liechtenstein Lithuania Malta Monaco Norway Poland Sweden Switzerland UK	
	North America: Canada USA	*Latin America:* Brazil Mexico
Latin America: Bolivia Ecuador Guadaloupe Peru Suriname	*Latin America:* Argentina Antigua and Barbuda Bahamas Barbados Belize Chile Dominica Grenada Guyana Jamaica St Kitts and Nevis St Vincent and the Grenadines Trinidad and Tobago Venezuela	

Classification of selected chamber systems		
Continental model	Anglo-Saxon model	Mixed system
Asia and Australia: Bahrain Jordan Oman Palestinian Territories Qatar South Korea Turkey UAE Vanuatu Yemen	*Asia and Australia:* Australia Azerbaijan Brunei Fiji Guam Israel India Kazakhstan Kiribati Malaysia Maldives Marshall Islands Micronesia Nepal New Zealand Palau Papua New Guinea Philippines Singapore Sri Lanka Solomon Islands Tonga Tuvalu Uzbekistan Western Samoa	*Asia:* Japan Thailand

Source: Presentation to BUSA by Deputy CEO Raymond Parsons on 20 February 2012: 'International Experience on Business Associations: Lessons for BUSA?'

Annexure 2: Consolidated list of SACOB policy positions

Affirmative Action
Aids in the Workplace
Autonomy of the South African Revenue Service
Basic Conditions of Service
Cash Basis of Taxation
Charter of Economic, Social and Political Rights
Collective Bargaining
Company Tax Rate
Competition Policy

Corporate Governance
Daylight Saving
Decentralisation of the South African Police Service
Devolution of Provincial and Local Powers
Electricity Distribution
Employment Equity
Environmental Management Strategy
Exchange Control
Excise Duties
Export Promotion
Fiscal Policy
Free Trade Agreement with the European Union
Free Trade Agreement with the Southern African Development Community
Funding of Training
Growth, Employment and Redistribution Strategy
Health Care Reform
Industrial Policy
Inflation Targeting
Intellectual Property Protection
Judicial Reform
Labour Market Reform
Liquid Fuels
Local Government Structures and Financing
Minerals and Mining Policy
Minimum Wages
National Economic Development and Labour Council
Outdoor Advertising
Postal Policy
Pricing of Basic Municipal Services
Privatisation
Public Holidays
Public Sector Procurement
Public Sector Restructuring
Reconstruction and Development Programme
Regional Service Council Levies
Reserve Bank Independence

Road Management and Funding
Road Traffic Offences
Science and Technology Policy
Secondary Tax on Companies
Sexual Harassment
Small and Medium Enterprise Development
Supply-Side Measures
Tariff Policy
Tax Burden
Telecommunications Policy
Trade Policy
Truth and Reconciliation Commission
User Charges
Value-Added Tax
Water Policy

Source: SACOB publication, 1998

Annexure 3: Importance of entrepreneurship in economic development

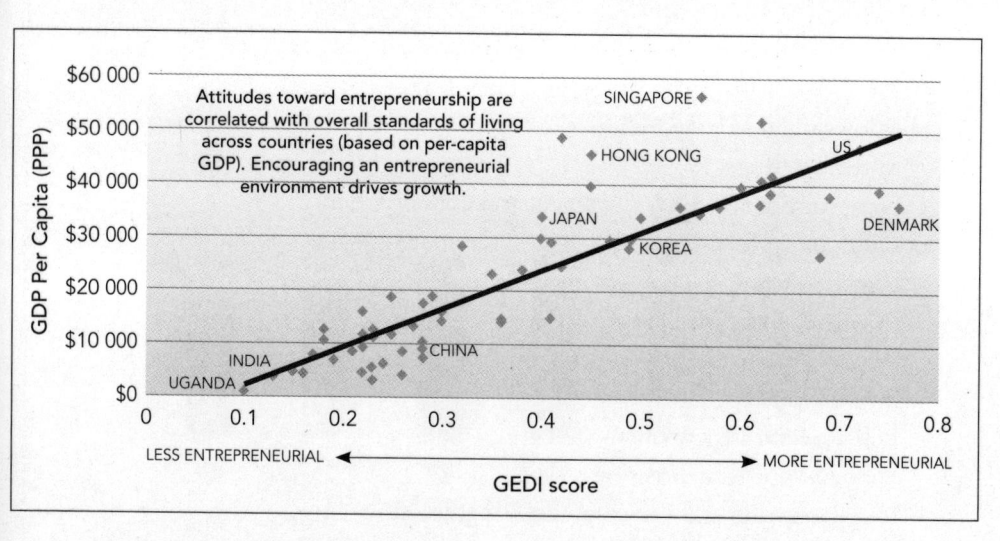

Source: Payden & Rygel, 'The Importance of Businesses in Developing Economies', *Point of View*, 2nd quarter (2011), 14

Annexure 4: Perceptions of South Africa in a global context

Ranking indicator	Ranking 2008	Ranking 2017	Trend
Global Competitiveness Index	45	61	↓
Corruption Perceptions Index	54	64	↓
Ease of doing business	32	82	↓
Quality of primary education	104	116	↓
Transparency in government policy-making	29	74	↓
Favouritism in decisions made by government officials	50	127	↓
Quality of overall infrastructure	46	72	↓
Time involved in starting a business	70	125	↓
Country's capacity to retain talent	72	78	↓
Domestic market size	22	30	↓

Source: Keith Lockwood, Johannesburg, 2018

Annexure 5: Measure of progress: Impact of different economic growth scenarios

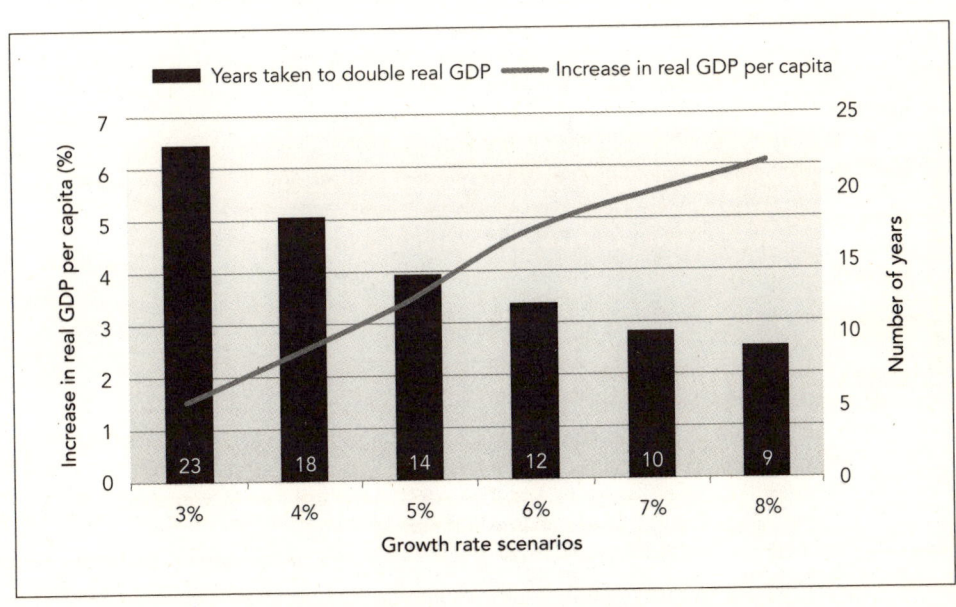

Growth rate scenario	Years taken to double real GDP
3%	23
4%	18
5%	14
6%	12
7%	10
8%	9

Source: Jacob van Rensburg, North-West University Business School, 2018

Endnotes

Chapter 1
1. Alexis de Tocqueville, *Democracy in America*, vol. 2 (New York: J & HG Langley, 1841), p. 324.

Chapter 2
1. Cicely Veronica Wedgwood, quoted in Raymond Parsons, 'Social Dialogue: New Light on an Old Story', in Busani Ngcaweni (ed.), *Liberation Diaries: Reflections on 20 Years of Democracy* (Johannesburg: Jacana Media, 2014).
2. *Macmillan Dictionary of Modern Economics*, 3rd edn (London: Macmillan, 1986), p. 54.
3. Recorded at the TRC hearings, 1997.
4. Nicoli Nattrass, 'The Truth and Reconciliation Commission on Business and Apartheid: A Critical Evaluation', *African Affairs*, 98, 392 (1999), 373–91.
5. Allister Sparks, *The Sword and the Pen* (Johannesburg: Jonathan Ball, 2006), p. 500.
6. TRC Business Sector hearings, <http://www.justice.gov.za/trc/special%5Cbusiness/busin1.htm> (accessed 20 May 2017).
7. In 1960, Verwoerd created an Economic Advisory Council (EAC), a truncated 'tripartite' structure of government, business and labour as then constituted, chaired by his economic advisor. The EAC existed until early 1994 and was replaced by NEDLAC in early 1995 (see Chapter 3).
8. BJ Vorster, quoted in the *Digest of Proceedings*, ASSOCOM Congress, 1978.
9. Merle Lipton, *Capitalism and Apartheid: South Africa 1910–1984* (Cape Town: David Philip, 1985).
10. Quoted in *Commercial Opinion*, November 1958.
11. *Die Afrikaner* was the newspaper of the Herstigde Nasionale Party (HNP) – started up in the 1970s.
12. Peter Harris, quoted in *The Sunday Star*, 14 November 1993.
13. *Financial Mail*, 16 May 1994.

Chapter 3
1. Merle Lipton, *Liberals, Marxists, and Nationalists* (New York: Palgrave Macmillan, 2008).
2. Hermann Giliomee, 'Adapt or Die, 1978–1984', in Fransjohan Pretorius (ed.), *A History of South Africa* (Pretoria: Protea Books, 2014).
3. Frederik van Zyl Slabbert, *The Last White Parliament* (New York: St Martin's, 1987), p. 64.

4   Helen Suzman, *In No Uncertain Terms: A South African Memoir* (Johannesburg: Jonathan Ball, 1993), p. 101.
5   *Financial Mail*, 14 June 1991.
6   Philip Mohr, Krige Siebrits and Estian Calitz, 'Economic Policy in South Africa', Unisa study guide (Pretoria: University of South Africa, 2002).

Chapter 4
1   This chapter draws extensively on the author's previous academic and other wide-ranging publications on social dialogue in South Africa.
2   ILO, *Annual Report 1996* (Geneva: International Labour Organization, 1996).
3   Republic of South Africa, *Report of the Commission of Inquiry into Labour Legislation* (Wiehahn Commission Report) (1979).
4   J Botha, 'Wiehahn, NE (1929–2006), Obituary', *South African Journal of Economics* (June 2006), pp. 359–61.
5   Opening address by Nelson Mandela at the NEDLAC launch, 18 February 1995.
6   Just as we must recognise that there are successful national economies that do not depend on 'institutionalised social dialogue' in the form we are currently discussing – in itself a valuable source of comparative analysis.
7   'It can be plausibly argued that much of the economic backwardness in the world can be explained by a lack of mutual confidence', Kenneth J Arrow, 'Gifts and Exchanges', *Philosophy and Public Affairs* (Summer 1972), p. 357.
8   The 'community' constituency widened participation in social dialogue and to a large extent reflected the constituency with the biggest stake in the new government's Reconstruction and Development Programme (RDP). It broadly included women, rural, youth, civic and similar organisations. For some years it was a difficult group from which to derive mandates.
9   The developments and trends in the work of NEDLAC from 1995 to 2016 are mainly captured in the detailed annual reports that the organisation is required by law to submit to Parliament each year. Although they tend to put a favourable gloss on NEDLAC's activities, they are nonetheless a reliable overview of the institution's yearly work programme.
10 Quoted in William Gumede, *Thabo Mbeki and the Battle for the Soul of the ANC* (Cape Town: Zebra Books, 2005).
11 Organised labour had thrown its weight behind the Reconstruction and Development Programme (1994) but that document did not embody an *economic* strategy.
12 This was part of the address given by Thabo Mbeki at the launch of the Millennium Labour Council in July 2000. It can be accessed online at: <http://www.sahistory.org.za/archive/address-launch-millenium-labour-council-7-july-2000>.
13 Quoted in Claire Bisseker, *On the Brink* (Cape Town: Tafelberg, 2017).
14 Ibid.
15 NEDLAC, 'Report on Repositioning of Peak-Level Social Dialogue in South Africa: NEDLAC in the Future' (2013).
16 *Fin24*, 13 June 2017.
17 Charles Curtis, 'A Commonplace Book', in WW Rostow, *The Stages of Economic Growth* (Cambridge: Cambridge University Press, 1960).
18 Quoted in William Davis, *The Lucky Generation: A Positive View of the 21st Century* (London: Headline, 1995).

Chapter 5
1. Personal interview, 21 August 2017.
2. Address by Nelson Mandela at HJ Heinz Company Foundation Distinguished Lecture, Pennsylvania, USA (1991).
3. Ann Bernstein, quoted in Chris Landsberg and Lesley Masters (eds.), *From the Outside In: Domestic Actors and South Africa's Foreign Policy* (Johannesburg: Jacana Media, 2017), pp. 156–7.
4. *Business Report*, 2 December 2017.
5. *Rand Daily Mail*, 15 November 2016.
6. Personal interview, 1 November 2017.
7. Ibid.
8. Pre-budget speech by Pravin Gordhan to Parliament, February 2017.
9. *Business Day*, 7 November 2017.

Chapter 6
1. Nicoli Nattrass, 'From Fragmentation to Fragile Unity: Organizational Fault-Lines in South African Business', *South African Journal of Business Management*, 29, 1 (1998), 21–9.
2. CNBC Africa, 'This Is How Much Business Contributes to South Africa', 20 November 2017, <https://www.cnbcafrica.com/news/financial/2017/11/20/much-business-contributes-south-africa/> (accessed 1 December 2017).
3. Personal interview, 29 September 2017.
4. *News24*, Constitutional Court judgment on Nkandla, 31 March 2017.
5. *Mail & Guardian*, 30 November 2017.
6. *Sunday Times*, 17 December 2017.
7. Janine Myburgh, 'Answer to #CapeWaterCrisis Is Not Rocket Science', 17 December 2017, <https://www.iol.co.za/news/opinion/answer-to-capewatercrisis-is-not-rocket-science-12450761> (accessed 18 December 2017).
8. *Engineering News*, 15 December 2017.
9. Presentation to the Centre for Development and Enterprise, 'Is South Africa About to Make an Historic Mistake?' (Johannesburg, February 2017).
10. Ibid.

Chapter 7
1. *GetBiz*, 18 April 2017.
2. Michael Barber, *Instruction to Deliver* (London: Methuen, 2007), p. 317.
3. Iraj Abedian, 'SA's Capitalist Class in Crisis: Steinhoff, Naspers Battered', *Huffington Post*, 6 December 2017, <http://www.huffingtonpost.co.za/2017/12/06/sas-capitalist-class-in-crisis-steinhoff-naspers-battered_a_23298523/> (accessed 30 December 2017).
4. Onora O'Neill, The BBC Reith Lectures, No. 1 (2002).
5. Maria Helena Price, *Economic Reform Today*, 2, 1995.

Chapter 8
1. Quoted in social media, 28 December 2017.
2. Address by Cas Coovadia to the Cape Town Press Club, 26 February 2018.
3. 'Doing Good: Business and the Sustainability Challenge'. *The Economist Intelligence Unit*, February 2008.
4. Raghuram Rajan and Luigi Zingales, *Saving Capitalism from the Capitalists* (New

York: Crown Business, 2003), p. 312.
5 Paul Hoffman, *Fin24*, 3 January 2018.
6 Anthony Butler, *Business Day*, 12 January 2018.
7 Stefan Schirmer, 'Property Rights, Institutional Change and Development in South Africa', *Acta Commercia*, 17 (2017)
8 Carol Paton, *Business Day*, 6 March 2018.
9 *The Guardian*, 14 November 2017.
10 Quoted in Raymond Parsons, *Zumanomics Revisited: The Road from Mangaung to 2030* (Johannesburg: Jacana Media, 2013), p. 138.
11 Tonye Cole, 'Leadership Lessons for a Fractured World', World Economic Forum, 14 December 2017.
12 State of the Nation Address, 16 February 2018.
13 Neva Makgetla, *Business Day*, 21 November 2017.
14 Anthony Butler, *Cyril Ramaphosa* (Johannesburg: Jacana Media, 2007).
15 Greg Mills, *Why Africa Is Poor and What Africans Can Do About It* (Cape Town: Penguin Books, 2010), p. 17.
16 *Business Day*, 21 February 2018.
17 Address by Cyril Ramaphosa to MISTRA (Mapungubwe Institute for Strategic Reflection), October 2013.
18 Ibid.
19 *The Economist*, April 2013.
20 Deborah Brautigan, Lise Rakner and Scott Taylor, 'Business Associations and Growth Coalitions in Sub-Saharan Africa', *Journal of Modern African Studies*, 40, 4 (2002).
21 Based largely on Caryn Peiffer, '"Reform" Coalitions: Patterns and Hypotheses from a Survey of the Literature', Concept Paper 03, Development Leadership Program, 2011.
22 Quoted in Raymond Parsons, *Zumanomics Revisited: The Road from Mangaung to 2030* (Johannesburg: Jacana Media, 2013), p. 27.
23 Raymond Parsons (ed.), *Zumanomics: Which Way to Shared Prosperity in South Africa?* (Johannesburg: Jacana Media, 2009), p. 204.
24 Robert Skidelsky, *The World After Communism: A Polemic for Our Times* (London: Macmillan, 1995).

Chapter 9

1 Robert Skidelsky, *The World After Communism: A Polemic for Our Times* (London: Macmillan, 1995).
2 Greg Mills, *Why Africa is Poor and What Africans Can Do About It* (Cape Town: Penguin Books, 2010), p. 288.
3 Andrew Duminy, *The Past is Present: Looking Back on South Africa's Troubled History* (Pinetown: Pinetown Printers, 2017), p. 208.
4 Daron Acemoglu and James Robinson, *Why Nations Fail: The Origin of Power, Prosperity, and Poverty* (New York: Crown Business, 2012), p. 461.
5 *The Economist*, 17 February 2018.
6 Lisa Steyn, *Mail & Guardian*, 23 February 2018.
7 Ann Bernstein, *The Case for Business in Developing Economies* (Johannesburg: Penguin Books, 2010).
8 George Orwell, *Animal Farm* (New York: Harcourt, Brace, 1946).
9 WB Vosloo, *Entrepreneurship and Economic Growth* (Pretoria: HSRC Press, 1994), p. 251.

10 Nassim Taleb, *Skin in the Game* (New York: Allen Lane, 2018), p. 189.
11 Larry Diamond, 'Civil Society and Democratic Consolidation: Building a Culture of Democracy in a New South Africa', in Hermann Giliomee and Lawrence Schlemmer with Sarah Hauptfleish (eds.), *The Bold Experiment: South Africa's New Democracy* (Johannesburg: Southern Book Publishers, 1994).
12 National Planning Commission, 'Towards a Social Compact for South Africa', Discussion Document 1/2015, p. 23.
13 *Business Day*, 17 January 2018.
14 Roy Jenkins, *The Chancellors* (London: Macmillan, 1998), p. 187.
15 2018–19 Budget Review, p. 14.
16 BLSA, 'Building Competitiveness: Business Leadership South Africa's Response to the National Development Plan' (2012).
17 South Africa was ranked 69th out of 103 countries on the WEF's 2018 Inclusive Development Index.
18 *Business Day*, 22 February 2018.
19 Hilary Joffe, *Business Day*, 22 February 2018.
20 Graham Williams and Dorian Haarhoff, *The Halo and the Noose: The Power of Story Telling and Story Listening in Business Life* (Johannesburg: Graysonian Press, 2009), p. 44.
21 Quoted in Raymond Parsons, *Zumanomics Revisited: The Road from Mangaung to 2030* (Johannesburg: Jacana Media, 2013), p. 157.
22 Michael Barber, *Instruction to Deliver: Fighting to Transform Britain's Public Services* (London: Methuen Publishing, 2007), pp. 193–4.
23 Raymond Parsons, *Zumanomics Revisited: The Road from Mangaung to 2030* (Johannesburg: Jacana Media, 2013), p. 164.
24 *Business Day*, 23 January 2018
25 *Daily Maverick*, 12 February 2018.
26 *Business Day*, 23 January 2018.
27 Address to the SA Ubuntu Foundation, reported in *Fin24*, 26 February 2018.
28 Raymond Parsons (ed.), *Manuel, Markets and Money: Essays in Appraisal* (Cape Town: Double Storey Books, 2004), p. 221.
29 Arnold Harberger, 'Policymaking and Economic Policy', in Rudiger Dornbusch and Leslie Helmers, *The Open Economy: Tools for Policy Makers in Developing Countries* (New York: Oxford University Press, 1995), p. 255

Bibliography

Acemoglu, Daron and James A Robinson, *Why Nations Fail: The Origin of Power, Prosperity, and Poverty*, Crown Business, New York, 2012

Acemoglu, Daron and James A Robinson, *Is State Capitalism Winning?* Project Syndicate, 31 December 2012, <https://www.project-syndicate.org/commentary/why-china-s-growth-model-will-fail-by-daron-acemoglu-and-james-a--robinson?barrier=accessreg>

AHI (Afrikaanse Handelsinstituut), Various policy documents and statements

ANC (African National Congress), Various policy documents

Arrow, Kenneth J, 'Gifts and Exchanges', *Philosophy and Public Affairs*, 1972, 343–62

ASSOCOM (Association of Chambers of Commerce of South Africa), Various policy documents and statements, 1960–1990

Atkinson, Anthony B, *Inequality: What Can Be Done?*, Harvard University Press, Cambridge, 2015

Barber, Michael, *Instruction to Deliver: Fighting to Transform Britain's Public Services*, Methuen Publishing, London, 2007

Barber, Michael, *How to Run a Government*, Allen Lane, London, 2015

Basson, Adriaan and Pieter du Toit, *Enemy of the People*, Jonathan Ball Publishers, Johannesburg, 2017

BBC (Black Business Council), Various policy documents and statements

Bell, Daniel, *The Cultural Contradictions of Capitalism*, Basic Books, New York, 1976

Bennett, Robert J, 'The Logic of Local Business Associations: An Analysis of Voluntary Chambers of Commerce', *Journal of Public Policy*, 15, 1996, 251–79

Bennett, Robert J (ed.), *Trade Associations in Britain and Germany: Responding to Internationalization and the EU*, Anglo-German Foundation, London and Bonn, 1997

Bennett, Robert J, *The Voice of Liverpool Business: The First Liverpool Chamber of Commerce and the Atlantic Economy, 1774–c.1796*, Liverpool Chamber of Commerce, Liverpool, 2010

Bennett, Robert J, *Local Business Voice: The History of Chambers of Commerce in Britain, Ireland, and Revolutionary America, 1760–2011*, Oxford University Press, Oxford, 2011

Bernstein, Ann, *The Case for Business in Developing Economics*, Penguin Books, Johannesburg, 2010

Bethlehem, Ronald, *Economics in a Revolutionary Society: Sanctions and the Transformation of South Africa*, Ad Donker, Johannesburg, 1988

Bisseker, Claire, *On the Brink*, Tafelberg, Cape Town, 2017

BLSA (Business Leadership South Africa), Various policy documents and statements

BLSA, *Building Competitiveness: Business Leadership South Africa's Response to the National Development Plan*, 2012

Botha, Joubert, 'Down Memory Lane: Past Presidents of the Economic Society of Africa 1925–1963', *South African Journal of Economics*, September 2002

Botha, Joubert, 'Wiehahn, NE (1929–2006), Obituary', *South African Journal of Economics*, June 2006

Brautigan, Deborah, Lise Rakner and Scott Taylor, 'Business Associations and Growth Coalitions in Sub-Saharan Africa', *Journal of Modern African Studies*, 40, 4, 2002

BUSA (Business Unity South Africa), Various policy documents and statements

Butler, Anthony, *Cyril Ramaphosa*, Jacana Media, Johannesburg, 2007

CDE (Centre for Development and Enterprise), Various research reports

Center for International Private Enterprise, *How to Advocate Effectively: A Guidebook for Business Associations*, 2003

CNBC Africa, *This Is How Much Business Contributes to South Africa*, 20 November 2017, <https://www.cnbcafrica.com/news/financial/2017/11/20/much-business-contributes-south-africa/>

COSATU (Congress of South African Trade Unions), Various policy documents

Curtis, Charles, 'A Commonplace Book', in Walt Whitman Rostow, *The Stages of Economic Growth: A Non-Communist Manifesto*, Cambridge University Press, Cambridge, 1960

Davis, William, *The Lucky Generation: A Positive View of the 21st Century*, Headline Book Publishing, London, 1995

Diamond, Larry, 'Civil Society and Democratic Consolidation: Building a Culture of Democracy in a New South Africa', in Hermann Giliomee and Lawrence Schlemmer with Sarah Hauptfleisch (eds.), *The Bold Experiment: South Africa's New Democracy*, Southern Book Publishers, Johannesburg, 1994

Dinokeng, Scenario, *Sponsorship and Support*, Old Mutual and Nedbank, 2010

Doner, Richard F and Ben R Schneider, 'Business Associations and Economic Development: Why Some Associations Contribute More than Others', *Business and Politics*, 2, 3, 2000, 261–88

Dror, Yehezkel, *Avant-Garde Politician: Leaders for a New Epoch*, Westphalia Press, Washington DC, 2014

Duminy, Andrew, *The Past is Present: Looking Back on South Africa's Troubled History*, Pinetown Printers, Pinetown, 2017

Du Preez, Max, *A Rumour of Spring: South Africa after 20 Years of Democracy*, Penguin Random House, Cape Town, 2013

Duvanova, Dinissa, *Defending Common Business: Business Associations vs Predatory Bureaucrats in Eastern Europe and Eurasia*, Cambridge University Press, New York, 2005

FCI (Federated Chamber of Industries), Various policy documents and statements 1960–1990

Fedotov, Victor, *Organizational and Legal Models of Chambers* (Business Associations Study), Washington DC, 2007

FEDUSA (Federation of Unions of South Africa), Various documents and statements

Feinstein, Charles H, *An Economic History of South Africa: Conquest, Discrimination and Development*, Cambridge University Press, Cambridge, 2005

Ferguson, Niall, *The Great Degeneration: How Institutions Decay and Economies Die*, Allan Lane, London, 2012

Fukuyama, Francis, *Trust: The Social Virtues and the Creation of Prosperity*, Hamish

Hamilton, London, 1995
Giliomee, Hermann, 'Adapt or Die, 1978–1984', in Fransjohan Pretorius (ed.), *A History of South Africa: From the Distant Past to the Present Day*, Protea Book House, Pretoria, 2014
Goldsmith, Arthur A, 'Business Associations and Better Governance in Africa', *Public Administration and Development*, 22, 1, 2002, 39–49
Goodwin, Bob, *Presidents of the Association of Chambers of Commerce of South Africa 1892–1980*, internal ASSOCOM publication
Gumede, William, *Thabo Mbeki and the Battle for the Soul of the ANC*, Zebra Press, Cape Town, 2005
Habib, Adam, *South Africa's Suspended Revolution: Hopes and Prospects*, Wits University Press, Johannesburg, 2013
Harberger, Arnold C, 'Policymaking and Economic Policy', in Rudiger Dornbusch and Leslie Helmers (eds.), *The Open Economy: Tools for Policy Makers in Developing Countries*, Oxford University Press, New York, 1995
Harrison, Lawrence E and Samuel P Huntington, *Culture Matters: How Values Shape Human Progress*, Basic Books, New York, 2000
Hartley, Ray, *Ramaphosa: The Man Who Would Be King*, Jonathan Ball Publishers, Johannesburg, 2018
Hayek, Friedrich A (ed.), *Capitalism and the Historians*, University of Chicago Press, Chicago, 1954
Helpman, Elhanan (ed.), *Institutions and Economic Performance*, Harvard University Press, Cambridge, 2008
Herring, E Pendleton, 'Chambres de Commerce: Their Legal Status and Political Significance', *American Political Science Review*, 25, 3, 1928, 689–99
Hoogenraad-Vermaak, Salomon and Grietjie Verhoef, 'The Role of the South African Business Community Regarding Political Mobilisation in the Run-up to a New South Africa, 1980–1992', *Historia*, 55, 2, 2010, 204–25
ICC (International Chamber of Commerce), Various documents and statements
ILO (International Labour Organization), Various documents and statements
IOE (International Organisation of Employers), Various documents and statements
Jenkins, Roy, *The Chancellors*, Macmillan, London, 1998
Johnson, RW and David Welsh (eds.), *Ironic Victory: Liberalism in Post-Liberation South Africa*, Oxford University Press, Cape Town, 1998
Johnson, RW, *How Long Will South Africa Survive? The Crisis Continues*, Jonathan Ball Publishers, Johannesburg, 2015
Kielstra, Paul, 'Doing Good: Business and the Sustainability Challenge', *The Economist Intelligence Unit*, 2008
Landsberg, Chris and Lesley Masters (eds.), *From the Outside In: Domestic Actors and South Africa's Foreign Policy*, Jacana Media, Johannesburg, 2017
Lang, John, *Bullion Johannesburg*, Jonathan Ball Publishers, Johannesburg, 1986
Lipton, Merle, *Capitalism and Apartheid: South Africa 1910–1984*, David Philip Publishers, Cape Town, 1985
Lipton, Merle, *Liberals, Marxists, and Nationalists: Competing Interpretations of South African History*, Palgrave Macmillan, New York, 2008
Lipton, Michael, *Land Reform in Developing Countries: Property Rights and Property Wrongs*, Routledge, London, 2009
Luxemburg, Rosa, *The Accumulation of Capital*, Routledge, London, 1913
Macmillan Dictionary of Modern Economics, 3rd edn, Macmillan, Basingstoke, 1986

Mbeki, Moeletsi (ed.), *Advocates for Change: How to Overcome Africa's Challenges*, Picador Africa, Johannesburg, 2011

Miller, Peter, *Smart Swarm*, HarperCollins Publishers, London, 2010

Mills, Greg, *Why Africa Is Poor and What Africans Can Do About It*, Penguin Books, Cape Town, 2010

Mills, Greg, *Why States Recover: Changing Walking Societies into Winning Nations, from Afghanistan to Zimbabwe*, Hurst & Company, London, 2014

Mohr, Philip, Krige Siebrits and Estian Calitz, *Economic Policy in South Africa*, Study Guide, Unisa, 2002

Mortimer, Thomas, *The Elements of Commerce, Politics and Finances, in Three Treatises on Those Important Subjects*, R Baldwin, London, 1772

NAFCOC (National African Federated Chamber of Commerce), Various policy documents and statements

National Planning Commission, *National Development Plan – 2030*, 2012, and various other documents

Nattrass, Nicoli, 'The Truth and Reconciliation Commission on Business and Apartheid: A Critical Evaluation', *African Affairs*, 98, 392, 1991, 373–91

Nattrass, Nicoli, 'From Fragmentation to Fragile Unity: Organizational Fault-Lines in South African Business', *South African Journal of Business Management*, 29, 1, 1998, 21–9

NEDLAC (National Economic Development and Labour Council), Annual reports and other publications

Ngcukaitobi, Tembeka, *The Land Is Ours*, Penguin Random House, Cape Town, 2018

North, Douglass C, 'The New Institutional Economics and Development', in John Harris, Janet Hunter and Colin M Lewis (eds.), *The New Institutional Economics and Third World Development*, Routledge, London and New York, 1993

Olson, Mancur, *The Rise and Decline of Nations: Economic Growth, Stagflation, and Social Rigidities*, Yale University Press, New Haven, 1982

Orwell, George, *Animal Farm*, Harcourt, Brace and Company, New York, 1946

Parsons, Raymond, *The Mbeki Inheritance: South Africa's Economy, 1990–2004*, Ravan Press, Johannesburg, 2000

Parsons, Raymond, *Parsons' Perspective: Focus on the Economy*, Jonathan Ball Publishers, Johannesburg, 2002

Parsons, Raymond (ed.), *Manuel, Markets and Money: Essays in Appraisal*, Double Storey Books, Cape Town, 2004

Parsons, Raymond, 'Monetary Policy, Corporate Governance and the SA Reserve Bank: Should the Bank Be Nationalised?' Paper presented at the Economic History Society of Southern Africa Biennial Conference, 8 September 2005

Parsons, Raymond, 'Investing in Social Capital in South Africa', *International Labour and Social Policy Review*, International Organisation of Employers, Geneva, 2007

Parsons, Raymond, 'The Emergence of Institutionalised Social Dialogue in South Africa', *South African Journal of Economics*, March 2007

Parsons, Raymond (ed.), *Zumanomics: Which Way to Shared Prosperity in South Africa? Challenges for a New Government*, Jacana Media, Johannesburg, 2009

Parsons, Raymond, *Zumanomics Revisited: The Road from Mangaung to 2030*, Jacana Media, Johannesburg, 2013

Parsons, Raymond, 'Economic Policy-Making: Narrowing the Gap between the Worlds of Ideas and Action', *Journal for Development and Leadership*, 3, 2, 2014

Parsons, Raymond, 'Social Dialogue: New Light on an Old Story', in Busani Ngcaweni (ed.), *Liberation Diaries: Reflections on 20 Years of Democracy*, Jacana Media, Johannesburg, 2014

Pauw, Jacques, *The President's Keepers*, Tafelberg, Cape Town, 2017

Payden & Rigel, 'The Importance of Businesses in Developing Economies', *Point of View*, 2nd quarter 2011

Peiffer, Caryn, *'Reform' Coalitions: Patterns and Hypotheses from a Survey of the Literature*, Concept Paper 03, Development Leadership Program, 2012

Piketty, Thomas, *Capital in the Twenty-First Century*, Harvard University Press, Cambridge, 2014

Poolman, Joe, *Report on a Possible Merger between ASSOCOM and FCI*, unpublished report, 1982

Pretorius, Fransjohan (ed.), *A History of South Africa: From the Distant Past to the Present Day*, Protea Book House, Pretoria, 2014

Pretorius, Louwrens, 'The Heads of Government and Organised Business', in Robert Schrire (ed.), *Leadership in the Apartheid State: From Malan to De Klerk*, Oxford University Press, Cape Town, 1994

Pretorius, Louwrens, 'From Conflict to Order? Corporatism in South Africa', in Stuart Nagel (ed.), *Handbook of Global Economic Policy*, Marcel Dekker, New York, 2000

Pretorius, Louwrens, 'Giving and Governing Policy Advice: The South African Economic Advisory Council, 1960–1985', *Politikon*, 38, 3, 2011, 367–87

Price, Maria Helena, *Economic Reform Today*, 2, 1995

Prichard, Denise, *Hearing Grasshoppers Jump: The Story of Raymond Ackerman*, David Philip Publishers, Cape Town, 2001

Rajan, Raghuram G and Luigi Zingales, *Saving Capitalism from the Capitalists*, Crown Business, New York, 2003

Ramphele, Mamphela, *Laying Ghosts to Rest: Dilemmas of the Transformation in South Africa*, Tafelberg, Cape Town, 2008

Randers, Jorgen, *2052: A Global Forecast for the Next Forty Years*, Chelsea Green Publishing, Hartford, 2012

Republic of South Africa, *Report of the Commission of Inquiry into Labour Legislation* (Wiehahn Commission Report), Government Printer, Pretoria

Richter, Rudolf, 'The New Institutional Economics: Its Start, Its Meaning, Its Prospects', *European Business Organization Law Review*, 6, 2, 2002, 161–200

SACCI (South African Chamber of Commerce and Industry), Various documents and statements

SACOB (South African Chamber of Business), Various policy documents and statements, including submissions to the TRC, 1990–2000

SAIRR (South African Institute of Race Relations), *South African Survey 2010/2011*, various tables, charts and research documents

Schirmer, Stefan, 'Property Rights, Institutional Change and Development in South Africa', *Acta Commercia*, 17, 2017

Schneider, Ben R, 'The New Institutional Economics, Business Associations and Development', *Brazilian Journal of Political Economy*, 20, 3, 2000, 39–62

Schumpeter, Joseph A, *Capitalism, Socialism and Democracy*, Harper & Brothers, New York, 1942

Skidelsky, Robert, *The World After Communism: A Polemic for Our Times*, Macmillan, London, 1995

Slabbert, Frederik van Zyl, *The Last White Parliament: The Struggle for South Africa by the Leader of the White Opposition*, St Martin's Press, New York, 1987

South African Government, Economic Development Department, 2010, *New Growth Path* and other publications

South African Government, Parliament of the Republic of South Africa, *Report of High Level Panel on Assessment of Key Legislation and Acceleration of Fundamental Change*, 2017

South African Reserve Bank, Various publications and media releases

Sparks, Allister, *The Sword and the Pen*, Jonathan Ball Publishers, Johannesburg, 2016

Stiglitz, Joseph, *Making Globalization Work*, WW Norton & Company, New York, 2006

Sullivan, John D, 'Corporate Governance: Transparency between Government and Business', *Mediterranean Development Forum*, 3, 2000

Suzman, Helen, *In No Uncertain Terms: A South African Memoir*, Jonathan Ball Publishers, Johannesburg, 1993

Taleb, Nassim, *Skin in the Game*, Allen Lane, New York, 2018

Tocqueville, Alexis de, *Democracy in America* (vol. 2), J & HG Langley, New York, 1841

TRC (Truth and Reconciliation Commission) documentation, 1998, <http:/www.justice.za/trc>

TRC Business Sector hearings, <http://www.justice.gov.za/trc/special%5Cbusiness/busin1.htm>

Turner, Adair, *Just Capital: The Liberal Economy*, Macmillan, London, 2001

Turok, Ben, *From the Freedom Charter to Polokwane: The Evolution of ANC Economic Policy*, New Agenda, Cape Town, 2008

Van Onselen, Charles, *The Cowboy Capitalist: John Hays Hammond, the American West, and the Jameson Raid in South Africa*, Jonathan Ball Publishers, Johannesburg, 2018

Van Vuuren, Hennie, *Apartheid, Guns and Money: A Tale of Profit*, Jacana Media, Johannesburg, 2017

Vosloo, WB, *Entrepreneurship and Economic Growth*, HSRC Press, Pretoria, 1994

Webster, Edward, Katherine Joynt and Anthea Metcalfe, *Repositioning Peak Level Social Dialogue in South Africa: Nedlac into the Future*, NEDLAC publication, 2013

Williams, Graham and Dorian Haarhoff, *The Halo and the Noose: The Power of Story Telling and Story Listening in Business Life*, Graysonian Press, Johannesburg, 2009

Wilson, Lindy, *Steve Biko*, Jacana Media, Johannesburg, 2001

Woll, Cornelia, 'The Difficult Organization of Business Interests: Lessons from the French Case', *West European Politics*, 29, 3, 2006, 489–512

World Economic Forum, *Global Competitiveness Index 2017–2018*, 2017

Index

A

Abedian, Iraj 152, 156
Accelerated and Shared Growth Initiative for South Africa (AsgiSA) 99–100, 101
Acemoglu, Daron 161–2
  Why Nations Fail 18, 179
Ackerman, Raymond 183
active citizenry 17, 84, 178
African National Congress (ANC) 38, 40, 63, 64, 70, 81, 87, 97, 101, 107, 127, 158, 159, 166, 168, 189, 192–4
  ANC–SACP–COSATU alliance 64, 71, 75, 81, 98, 107
Afrikaans 4, 12
Afrikaanse Handelsinstituut (AHI) xvii, 10, 12, 22, 23, 37, 91, 96
Aggett, Neil 35
Agri South Africa (AgriSA) 143
Anglo American 21, 49, 76, 96, 146
Anglo-Saxon chamber model 26, 144, 198
Angus, Brian xvii
Annan, Kofi 156
apartheid xvi, 1, 2, 4, 6, 7, 13, 14, 16, 18, 19, 20, 21–2, 23, 24, 25, 26, 29, 31, 32, 33, 34, 38–9, 42–3, 46, 47, 60, 62, 63, 96–7, 113, 114, 143, 164, 177
Association of Chambers of Commerce of South Africa (ASSOCOM) xvii, 5, 10, 12, 25, 26, 27, 28, 29, 30, 31, 32, 33, 34, 35, 36, 37, 38, 39, 46, 52, 53, 143, 153, 172
Australia 142

B

Bacon, Francis xv

Banking Association South Africa (BASA) 156, 178
Bantu Education 30
Bantu Education Act (1953) 29–30
Bantu Investment Corporation (BIC) 44
Bantu Laws Amendment Act (1970) 31, 33
Barber, Michael
  Instruction to Deliver 191–2
Barlow Rand 21, 49
Basic Conditions of Employment Act (BCEA) 73–4
Baxter, Roger 79, 119
Belgium 38
Bernstein, Ann
  The Case for Business in Developing Economies 181
Bezuidenhout, Koos 76
big business 23, 54, 79, 92, 110, 118, 126, 156
Big Business Working Group 98
Biko, Steve 29
Bill of Rights 40
Bisseker, Claire 192
  On the Brink 79
Black Business Council (BBC) xvi, 5, 10, 102, 104, 120, 150
Black Business Working Group 98
Black Economic Empowerment (BEE) 1, 100, 102, 104, 138–9
black entrepreneurship 31–2
Black Industrialist Programme 129
Black Management Forum (BMF) 102
Botha, PW 20, 29, 37, 45, 48, 49–50, 51, 53, 115
Boyd, Leslie 76
Brand, Dr Simon 45

Brazil 188
Budget Review (2018–2019) 186
Business Against Crime 14
business associations 10, 12, 13, 40, 41, 42, 52, 88, 90, 91, 92, 93, 100, 102, 103, 104, 106, 111, 113, 115, 117, 120, 121, 126, 128, 129, 130, 134, 136, 139, 140, 141, 142, 143, 146–7, 149, 152, 171, 174
Business Day 194
Business Leadership South Africa (BLSA) xvi, 79, 102, 105, 116, 117, 118, 120, 138, 150, 156, 187
Business South Africa (BSA) 102
Business Unity South Africa (BUSA) xiii, xvi, 5, 10, 90, 101–2, 103, 105, 137, 138, 150, 173, 200
Buthelezi, Dr Mangosuthu 41
Butler, Prof Anthony 159, 164

C
Canada 142
Council of Economic Advisers 45
Cape Chamber of Commerce and Industry (CCCI) xvi, 105, 122, 135
Cape Town 10, 48, 52, 135–6
Cape Town City Council 122
capitalism xv, 3, 7, 13, 16–7, 18, 19, 22, 24, 26, 101, 123, 140, 156, 158, 160, 161, 181, 182
Carlton Hotel Conference (1979) 29, 48–9, 53
Carroll, Lewis
Through the Looking Glass 166–7
Centre for Development and Enterprise (CDE) 26, 96
CEO Initiative 116, 149, 157, 170
chamber of commerce 4, 6, 7, 8, 9, 10, 12, 13, 14, 27, 29, 34, 36, 38, 40–1, 42, 88, 90, 91, 92, 93, 103, 104, 106, 111, 112, 113, 115, 117, 120, 121, 125, 126, 128, 130, 132, 136, 139, 141, 142, 147, 148, 149, 152
chamber of industry 4, 27
Chamber of Mines xvi, 119, 122, 143
Churchill, Winston 114
Cohen, Tanya 137
Cohen, Tim 194
Cold War 57
collective bargaining 33, 62

colonialism 1
Commercial Agriculture Working Group 98
Commonwealth of Nations 46
communism xv
Companies Act 90
Competition Commission 182
competition policy 96, 157, 182
Congress of South African Trade Unions (COSATU) 64, 71, 75, 76, 81, 87, 98, 101, 181
ANC–SACP–COSATU alliance 64, 71, 75, 81, 87, 98, 107
Constitution of the Republic of South Africa 35, 41, 158, 180
Section 25 158
Consultative Business Movement (CBM) xvii, 14, 40, 41, 42, 63
Continental chamber model 45, 143, 198
Convention for a Democratic South Africa (CODESA) 41, 165, 167, 184
Coovadia, Cas 156
corporatism 57, 59, 83
corruption 22, 87, 100, 105, 107, 116, 119, 129, 131, 152, 161, 162, 164, 170, 178, 195
Council for Scientific and Industrial Research (CSIR) 44
Crick, Bernard
In Defence of Politics 58–9

D
Dakar Conference (1987) 38
Davis Committee on tax reform 187
Democratic Alliance (DA) 158
Department of Energy 137
Department of Labour 73
Department of Small Business Development 130–1
Department of Trade and Industry (DTI) 129
developmental state 99, 100, 103, 124
Die Afrikaner 39
Disraeli, Benjamin 164, 190
Duminy, Andrew 179

E
e-commerce 132
Economic Advisory Council (EAC) xvii,

6, 33, 37, 44, 45, 46–51, 53–6
Economic Development Programme (EDP) 54, 103
Economic Freedom Fighters (EFF) 158
Economic Society of South Africa xiii
Economist, The 170, 180
Economist Intelligence Unit, The 157
Eliot, TS 197
Employment Act (1946) 45
entrepreneurship xvi, 17, 31, 32, 128–9, 156, 161, 183, 197, 202
Erwin, Alec 64
Eskom 121, 136–7, 186
Estonia 129
European Union (EU) 71, 142
Expropriation Bill 102

F
Factories Act 30
Federated Chamber of Industries (FCI) xvii, 4, 5, 10, 12, 25, 26, 28, 30, 31, 32, 33, 34, 35, 36, 37, 38, 39, 40, 52, 53, 143, 153, 172
Federation of Unions of South Africa (FEDUSA) 76, 181
Financial Mail 5, 43, 53, 179, 192
First World War (1914–1918) 1
Fitch 78
Foreign Funding Bill 38
Foundation for African Business and Consumer Services (FABCOS) 5–6, 14, 23, 102
France 38
Freedom Charter 101
'free-rider' problem 92, 142–3, 144, 146, 149
Friedman, Prof Steven 167

G
Gauteng e-toll system 116–7
Germany 38
    German Council of Economic Experts 45
Ghana
    National Development Plan (2018–2057) 45
Giliomee, Hermann 52
globalisation 60, 66, 125, 195
Godsell, Bobby 76

'golden triangle' 63, 64, 65, 70, 79
Good Hope Conference (1981) 48, 53
Gordhan, Pravin 79, 106, 194
Government of National Unity (GNU) 65
Great Recession (2008) 18
Group Areas Act (1950) 27, 28, 29
Growth, Employment and Redistribution (GEAR) strategy 74, 75, 98, 101

H
Habib, Prof Adam 193
Hall, John 40
Harberger, Prof Arnold 196–7
Hausmann, Ricardo 139
Holland 69, 76

I
independent power producers (IPPs) 136
India 45
    Indian Economic Advisory Council 45
Industrial Conciliation Act (1956) 31
Industrial Policy Action Plan (IPAP) 102
Inkatha Freedom Party 41
Integrated Resources Plan (IRP) 137
International Chamber of Commerce (ICC) 9
International Investment Council 98, 102
International Labour Organization (ILO) 58, 61, 88
International Trade Institute of Southern Africa (ITRISA) xiv
Ireland 69, 76

J
Jenkins, Roy 185–6
Johannesburg Chamber of Commerce and Industry (JCCI) xvi, 86, 91, 105

K
Keeton, Gavin xvii, 124
Keys, Derek 63, 64
Khoza, Humphrey 25
King IV 163
King, Judge Mervyn 9
de Klerk, FW 39, 45, 56
de Kock, Dr Gerhard 48, 49, 54
KPMG 131, 163

L

Laboria Minute 35, 62, 67
labour relations 33, 48, 60, 61
Labour Relations Act (LRA) (1995) 35, 62, 73–4
land expropriation without compensation 158, 159, 168
Latvia 129
Leutweiler, Dr Fritz 50
Lipton, Merle 32, 47
Lockwood, Keith xvii, 203
Lombard, Prof Jan 37
Lombard Report 37
low-growth trap 129, 181, 195

M

Mandela, Nelson (Madiba) 38, 41, 60, 64, 67, 68, 70, 74–5, 85, 86, 88, 97, 125, 185
Manifesto for Reform (1985) 37
Mapungubwe Institute for Strategic Reflection (MISTRA) 168–9
Marseilles 8
Marseilles Town Council 8
Marx, Karl 17, 18
Marxism
Mashaba, Herman 183
Mauritius 94–5
Mbeki, Thabo 64, 76, 97–8, 99, 101, 102, 115, 124, 125
Mboweni, Tito 73
McKinsey 163
Medium-Term Budget Policy Statement (MTBPS) 185
Medium-Term Strategic Plan (MTSP) 166
Mill, John Stuart 194
Millennium Labour Council (MLC) 76, 77
Miller, Peter
  Smart Swarm 110
Mills, Dr Greg 164, 178
Mining Charter 100
Ministry of Finance 4
Ministry of Labour 74, 79
Ministry of Small Business Development 94, 127
mixed economy 83
Mogoeng, Chief Justice Mogoeng 108–9, 130
Mohale, Bonang 118, 156
Moody's 78, 99, 188
Motlanthe, Kgalema 158
Motsuenyane, Sam 9
multisectoral bodies 10, 86, 122, 128, 143
Myburgh, Janine 105, 106, 135–6

N

National African Federated Chamber of Commerce (NAFCOC) xvi, 5, 9, 10, 14, 23, 37, 47, 102, 104, 143
National Association of Automobile Manufacturers of South Africa (NAAMSA) 122
National Business Initiative 42
National Council Bill 38
National Development Plan (NDP) 17, 45, 76, 82, 83, 84, 87, 99, 102, 103, 108, 120, 128, 160, 166, 167, 168, 175, 184
National Economic Development and Labour Council (NEDLAC) xiii, xvii, 6, 42, 57, 59, 60, 65, 66, 67, 68–9, 70, 71, 73, 74, 76, 77, 78–9, 80, 81–2, 84, 92, 102, 116, 150, 169, 192
  Development Chamber 71
  Labour Market Chamber 71
  NEDLAC Act 59, 67
  Public Finance and Monetary Policy Chamber 71, 75
  Trade and Industry Chamber 71, 73
National Economic Forum (NEF) 6, 42, 60, 63–4, 67, 69
National Manpower Commission (NMC) 35, 48, 56, 60, 61, 65, 67, 69
National Party 52, 61, 96
National Peace Accord 40, 65
National Planning Commission (NPC) 102, 103, 184, 192
National Regional Development Council (NRDC) 44
National Roads Agency 116
National Skills Fund 88
National Treasury 44, 166, 185, 187
Nattrass, Nicoli 21, 22, 115
Nelson Mandela University xiii
Nene, Nhlanhla 115
New Deal 166
New Growth Path (NGP) 102, 103
New Partnership for Africa's

Development (NEPAD) 99
Nkuhlu, Wiseman 184–5
North-West University 6
   Faculty of Economic and Management Sciences xvi
   Business School xiii, xvi
   Policy Uncertainty Index 120
   TRADE-DSM® 133
   TRADE research entity xiii
Nupen, Charles 76

O
Oil crisis (1973) 32
van Onselen, Gareth xv
Operation Phakisa 103, 166
Oppenheimer, Harry 49
Oppenheimer, Nicky 76
Organisation for Economic Co-operation and Development (OECD) 100
organised business xvi, 2, 4, 5, 6, 7, 8, 12–4, 24, 26, 27, 32, 36, 37, 38, 39, 43, 46, 47, 61, 62, 63, 79, 86, 88, 90, 92, 97, 101, 103, 105, 107, 108, 111–3, 114–6, 117, 119, 123, 126, 129, 132, 134, 138, 140, 141 142, 143–7 , 149, 152, 172
organised commerce 5, 8, 33
Orwell, George
   Animal Farm 181–2

P
Palmer, George 5, 179
Parry, Ali xiii, xvii
Parsons, Raymond xiii, xvii, 195
People's Tribunal on Economic Crimes, The (2018) 175
Physical Planning and Utilisation of Resources Act (1967) 31
Piketty, Thomas 19
   Capital in the Twenty-First Century 18
du Pisanie, Prof Andre 37
Plato
   Republic, The 175
du Plessis, Barend 63
du Plessis, Dr Fred 49, 53, 54
policy uncertainty 119, 120, 195
Policy Uncertainty Index 120
Popper, Karl 19
Population Registration Act 27

du Preez, Max 21
Presidential Commission into the labour market 73, 74
Presidential Economic Advisory Council 187, 192
privatisation 51, 101
public law chamber 142, 147–8

Q
Qobo, Mzukisi 82

R
radical economic transformation 2, 7
Rajan, Raghuram 157
   Saving Capitalism from the Capitalists 18
Ramaphosa, Cyril xv–xvi, 108, 156, 160, 163, 164, 165, 166, 167, 168–70, 171, 184, 189–94, 196
Randers, Jorgen
   2052 134
Reconstruction and Development Programme (RDP) 98
reform coalition 170–1
Relly, Gavin 49
Rembrandt 49, 76, 96
renewable energy 137
van Rensburg, Ben xvii
van Rensburg, Jacob xvii, 89, 203
rent-seeking 10, 129, 141
Report of the High Level Panel on the Assessment of Key Legislation and the Acceleration of Fundamental Change 158
Reservation of Separate Amenities Act (1953) 30
Reuss, Konrad 188
Rhodes University 124
Riekert, Dr Piet 45, 46, 48, 54
Robinson, James
   Why Nations Fail 18, 179
Rodrik, Prof Dani 161
Rosholt, Mike 49
Rousseff, Dilma 188
Rubicon Speech (1986) 37, 50, 51
Rugby World Cup 85
Rupert, Anton 49
Rupert, Johan 76
Rwanda 94–5

S

Sanlam 49, 53, 54
Santayana, George 2
Schirmer, Prof Stefan 159
Schumpeter, Joseph
  Capitalism, Socialism and Democracy 18
Sector Education and Training Authorities (SETAs) 108
sectoral bodies 91, 122
Selematsela, Godfrey 76
Separate Amenities Act 30
Sharpeville massacre (1960) 46
Sharpeville Six 38
Shops and Offices Act 30
Skidelsky, Prof Robert 172, 176
Slabbert, Dr Van Zyl 36, 52
Small Business Institute (SBI) 91, 93, 96
small, medium and micro enterprises (SMMEs) 93–4, 95, 118, 120, 126–31, 132
Soccer (FIFA) World Cup 85
social capital 9, 57, 69
social compact 76, 82, 168
social dialogue xvii, 26, 60, 57–8, 66, 67, 69, 70, 74, 75, 76, 77, 78, 79, 80, 81, 82, 84
social media 92, 163
socialism xv, 3, 158
South Africa xvii, xv, 1, 2–5, 7, 8, 9, 10, 12–14, 16, 18, 19, 20, 21, 22, 27, 28, 29, 30, 32, 36–7, 38, 43, 45, 46, 50, 51, 54–5, 57–62, 65, 66, 69, 70, 73, 75, 77, 78–9, 80, 82–8, 90, 91, 93, 94, 95–100, 102–8, 111, 113–25, 127, 128, 130–4, 135–7, 138–42, 146, 147, 149, 150, 152, 153–4, 155–63, 164–70, 171–2, 175–6, 177–88, 189–97
South Africa Foundation xvii, 49, 102
South African Airways 186
South African Bureau of Standards (SABS) 44
South African Chamber of Business (SACOB) xiii, xvii, 5, 10, 14–5, 22, 23, 24, 25, 26, 38, 39, 40, 41, 42, 43, 46, 47, 76, 91, 143, 153, 172, 200
South African Chamber of Commerce and Industry (SACCI) 5, 10, 91, 120
South African Communist Party (SACP) 64, 71, 75, 81, 87, 101
  ANC–SACP–COSATU alliance 64, 71, 75, 81, 87, 98, 107
South African Employers' Consultative Committee on Labour Affairs (SACCOLA) 34, 35
South African Local Government Association 147
South African Property Owners Association 122
South African Renewable Energy Council (SAREC) 122
South African Reserve Bank (SARB) 4, 41, 44, 48, 49, 54, 166, 192–3
Sparks, Allister 23
Spicer, Michael 79, 100–1
Standard & Poor's (S&P) 78
  Global Ratings 188, 189
state capture 87, 105, 107, 161, 162, 164, 178
State of the Nation Address (SONA) 193
state-owned enterprises (SOEs) 87, 106, 121, 127, 178, 186, 192
Steel and Engineering Industries Federation of Southern Africa (SEIFSA) xvi
Steinhoff 131, 163
Stellenbosch University's Water Institute 135
Steyn, Dr Hennie 45
Suzman, Helen 5, 52
Swanepoel, Bernard 93, 94
Sweden 129

T

Taleb, Nassim 183
taxation 18, 98, 106, 118, 172, 191
  general sales 63
  progressive 124
  value-added 63
Temer, Michel 188
Thatcher, Margaret 111
de Tocqueville, Alexis
  Democracy in America 8–9, 184
'total onslaught' 35
Trade Matters (Pty) Ltd xiii
Trade Union Working Group 98
trade unions 10, 33, 35, 46, 48, 61, 62, 63,

98, 116, 153, 181
transformation 41, 100, 101, 104, 106, 137, 178, 183
Transnet 121
Tricameral Parliament 36
tripartism 42, 46, 57, 59, 60, 65, 71
Tripartite Alliance 98, 103, 107
Truth and Reconciliation Commission (TRC) 14–5, 20, 21, 23–5, 26, 32, 143

U
United Kingdom (UK) 1, 38, 58, 112, 142, 144
   British Chambers of Commerce 148
   Office for Budget Responsibility 187
United Nations (UN) 37
   Human Development Index 188
United States of America (USA) 38, 50, 112, 170
   Congressional Budget Office 187
   Council of Economic Advisers 44–5
University of Cape Town 3, 159
University of Johannesburg 82
University of Pretoria xiii, 6
University of the Witwatersrand xiii, 5, 6, 79, 159
Urban Foundation 14, 37, 42

V
value chain 131, 132–3
Vavi, Zwelinzima 76, 101
Verwoerd, Hendrik 21, 28, 45, 46, 114
voluntarism 142, 149
Vorster, John 29, 45, 115
Vosloo, Prof Ben 183
van Vuuren, Hennie
   Apartheid, Guns and Money 22, 50–1

W
Warburton-McBride, Joan 86
Water and Sanitation ministry 136
Webster, Prof Eddie 79, 80, 81
Wedgwood, CV 16
Western Cape 3, 135
white monopoly capital 7, 13, 83, 104, 118, 139
Wiehahn Commission 33, 34, 42, 48, 61, 62, 67
Wiehahn Report (1979) 34, 60, 61, 62, 67
World Bank Group 134
World Chambers Network 9
World Economic Forum (WEF) 94, 129, 163, 188
   Davos 188
   Global Competitiveness Index (2017–2018) 94–5, 131, 181
   Inclusive Development Index (IDI) 188
World Trade Organization (WTO) 124

Z
Zambia
   Lusaka 38
Zimbabwe 98–9
Zingales, Luigi 157
   Saving Capitalism from the Capitalists 18
Zulu, Lindiwe 127, 130
Zuma, Jacob xv–xvi, 101, 102, 103, 105, 106, 107, 114, 115, 156, 179, 180, 189, 195–6
Zumanomics: Which Way to Shared Prosperity in South Africa? 171–2, 192
Zumanomics Revisited: The Road from Mangaung to 2030 192